Introductory
dBASE® 5
for Windows™

Introductory
dBASE® 5
for Windows™

Charles Hommel
University of Puget Sound

Roy Ageloff
University of Rhode Island

Course Technology, Inc. One Main Street, Cambridge, MA 02142

An International Thomson Publishing Company

Albany • Bonn • Boston • Cincinnati • London • Madrid • Melbourne • Mexico City
New York • Paris • San Francisco • Singapore • Tokyo • Toronto • Washington

Introductory dBASE 5 for Windows is published by Course Technology, Inc.

Managing Editor:	Mac Mendelsohn
Product Manager:	Barbara Clemens
Production Editor:	Catherine Griffin
Text Designer:	Sally Steele
Cover Designer:	John Gamache

© 1995 Course Technology, Inc.
A Division of International Thomson Publishing, Inc.

For more information contact:
Course Technology, Inc.
One Main Street
Cambridge, MA 02142

International Thomson Publishing Europe
Berkshire House 168-173
High Holborn
London WCIV 7AA
England

Thomas Nelson Australia
102 Dodds Street
South Melbourne, 3205
Victoria, Australia

Nelson Canada
1120 Birchmount Road
Scarborough, Ontario
Canada M1K 5G4

International Thomson Editores
Campos Eliseos 385, Piso 7
Col. Polanco
11560 Mexico D.F. Mexico

International Thomson Publishing GmbH
Königswinterer Strasse 418
53227 Bonn
Germany

International Thomson Publishing Asia
211 Henderson Road
#05-10 Henderson Building
Singapore 0315

International Thomson Publishing Japan
Hirakawacho Kyowa Building, 3F
2-2-1 Hirakawacho
Chiyoda-ku, Tokyo 102
Japan

Trademarks

Course Technology and the open book logo are registered trademarks of Course Technology, Inc.

I(T)P The ITP logo is a trademark under license.

dBASE is a registered trademark of Borland International, Inc. and Windows is a trademark of Microsoft Corporation.

Some of the product names and company names used in this book have been used for identification purposes only and may be trademarks or registered trademarks of their respective manufacturers and sellers.

Disclaimer

Course Technology, Inc. reserves the right to revise this publication and make changes from time to time in its content without notice.

ISBN 1-56527-285-4

Printed in the United States of America

10 9 8 7 6 5 4 3 2

From the Publisher

At Course Technology, Inc., we believe that technology will transform the way that people teach and learn. We are very excited about bringing you, college professors and students, the most practical and affordable technology-related products available.

The Course Technology Development Process

Our development process is unparalleled in the higher education publishing industry. Every product we create goes through an exacting process of design, development, review, and testing.

Reviewers give us direction and insight that shape our manuscripts and bring them up to the latest standards. Every manuscript is quality tested. Students whose backgrounds match the intended audience work through every keystroke, carefully checking for clarity, and pointing out errors in logic and sequence. Together with our own technical reviewers, these testers help us ensure that everything that carries our name is error-free and easy to use.

Course Technology Products

We show both *how* and *why* technology is critical to solving problems in college and in whatever field you choose to teach or pursue. Our time-tested, step-by-step instructions provide unparalleled clarity. Examples and applications are chosen and crafted to motivate students.

The Course Technology Team

This book will suit your needs because it was delivered quickly, efficiently, and affordably. In every aspect of our business, we rely on a commitment to quality and the use of technology. Every employee contributes to this process. The names of all of our employees are listed below:

Diana Armington, Tim Ashe, David Backer, Stephen M. Bayle, Ann Marie Buconjic, Jody Buttafoco, Kerry Cannell, Jim Chrysikos, Barbara Clemens, Susan Collins, John M. Connolly, Myrna D'Addario, Lisa D'Alessandro, Jodi Davis, Howard S. Diamond, Kathryn Dinovo, Joseph B. Dougherty, Laurie Duncan, Karen Dwyer, MaryJane Dwyer, Kristin Dyer, Chris Elkhill, Don Fabricant, Viktor Frengut, Jeff Goding, Laurie Gomes, Eileen Gorham, Catherine Griffin, Jamie Harper, Roslyn Hooley, Marjorie Hunt, Matt Kenslea, Marybeth LaFauci, Susannah Lean, Kim Mai, Margaret Makowski, Tammy Marciano, Elizabeth Martinez, Debbie Masi, Don Maynard, Kathleen McCann, Sarah McLean, Jay McNamara, Mac Mendelsohn, Karla Mitchell, Kim Munsell, Michael Ormsby, Debbie Parlee, Kristin Patrick, Charlie Patsios, Darren Perl, Kevin Phaneuf, George J. Pilla, Nicole Jones Pinard, Nancy Ray, Brian Romer, Laura Sacks, Carla Sharpe, Deborah Shute, Roger Skilling, Jennifer Slivinski, Christine Spillett, Audrey Tortolani, Michelle Tucker, David Upton, Mark Valentine, Karen Wadsworth, Renee Walkup, Tracy Wells, Donna Whiting, Janet Wilson, Lisa Yameen.

Preface

Course Technology, Inc. is proud to present this new book in its Windows Series. *Introductory dBASE 5 for Windows* is designed for a first course on dBASE 5 for Windows. This book capitalizes on the energy and enthusiasm students have for Windows-based applications and clearly teaches students how to take full advantage of the power of dBASE. It assumes students have learned basic Windows skills and file management from *An Introduction to Microsoft Windows 3.1* by June Jamrich Parsons or from an *equivalent* book.

Organization and Coverage

Introductory dBASE 5 for Windows contains six tutorials that provide hands-on instruction. In these tutorials students learn to create and maintain a database. They learn to retrieve information by issuing queries and developing professional-looking reports. Students also learn to create customized forms to access and enter data in a table.

The text emphasizes the ease-of-use features included in the dBASE software: SpeedBar buttons, Object Inspector, graphical design tools, and graphical Query By Example (QBE). Using this book, students will learn how to do more advanced tasks sooner than they would using other introductory texts; a perusal of the table of contents affirms this. By the end of the book, students will have learned "advanced" tasks such as creating check boxes and drop-down edit fields to facilitate data entry in a form, defining and using a lookup table for data entry, and generating reports based on queries.

Approach

Introductory dBASE 5 for Windows distinguishes itself from other Windows books because of its unique two-pronged approach. First, it motivates students by demonstrating why they need to learn the concepts and skills. This book teaches dBASE using a task-driven rather than a feature-driven approach. By working through the tutorials—each motivated by a realistic case—students learn how to use dBASE in situations they are likely to encounter in the workplace, rather than learn a list of features one-by-one, out of context. Second, the content, organization, and pedagogy of this book make full use of the Windows environment. What content is presented, when it's presented, and how it's presented capitalize on dBASE's power to store, maintain, and retrieve data more easily than was possible under DOS.

Features

Introductory dBASE 5 for Windows is an exceptional textbook also because it contains the following features:

■ **"Read This Before You Begin" Page** This page is consistent with Course Technology's unequaled commitment to helping instructors introduce technology into the classroom. Technical considerations and assumptions about hardware, software, and default settings are listed in one place to help instructors save time and eliminate unnecessary aggravation.

■ **Tutorial Case** Each tutorial begins with a database-related problem that students could reasonably encounter in business. Thus, the process of solving the problem will be meaningful to students.

■ **Step-by-Step Methodology** The unique Course Technology, Inc. methodology keeps students on track. They click or press keys always within the context of solving the problem posed in the Tutorial Case. The text constantly guides students, letting them know where they are in the process of solving the problem. The numerous screen shots include labels that direct students' attention to what they should look at on the screen.

■ **Page Design** Each *full-color* page is designed to help students easily differentiate between what they are to *do* and what they are to *read*. The steps are easily identified by their color background and numbered bullets. Windows default colors are used in the screen shots so instructors can more easily assure that students' screens look like those in the book.

■ **TROUBLE?** TROUBLE? paragraphs anticipate the mistakes that students are likely to make and help them recover from these mistakes. This feature facilitates independent learning and frees the instructor to focus on substantive conceptual issues rather than common procedural errors.

■ **Reference Windows and Task Reference** Reference Windows provide short, generic summaries of frequently used procedures. The Task Reference appears at the end of the book and summarizes how to accomplish tasks using the SpeedBar buttons, the menus, and the keyboard. Both of these features are specially designed and written so students can use the book as a reference manual after completing the course.

■ **Questions, Tutorial Assignments, and Case Problems** Each tutorial concludes with meaningful, conceptual Questions that test students' understanding of what they learned in the tutorial. The Questions are followed by Tutorial Assignments, which provide students with additional hands-on practice of the skills they learned in the tutorial. Finally, each tutorial (except Tutorial 1) ends with four complete Case Problems and one exploratory Case Problem (see "Exploration Exercises" below) that have approximately the same scope as the Tutorial Case.

■ **Exploration Exercises** Unlike DOS, the Windows environment allows students to learn by exploring and discovering what they can do. The Exploration Exercises are Questions, Tutorial Assignments, or Case Problems designated by an **E** that encourage students to explore the capabilities of the computing environment they are using and to extend their knowledge using the Windows on-line Help facility and other reference materials.

The CTI WinApps Setup Disk

The CTI WinApps Setup Disk bundled with the instructor's copy of this book contains an innovative Student Disk generating program designed to save instructors time. Once this software is installed on a network or standalone workstation, students can double-click the "Make dBASE 5.0 Student Disk" icon in the CTI WinApps group window. Double-clicking this icon transfers all the data files students need to complete the tutorials, Tutorial Assignments, and Case Problems to a high-density disk in drive A or B. Tutorial 1 provides complete step-by-step instructions for making the Student Disk.

Adopters of this text are granted the right to install the CTI WinApps group window on any standalone computer or network used by students who have purchased this text.

For more information on the CTI WinApps Setup Disk, see the section in this book called "Read This Before You Begin."

The Supplements

■ **Instructor's Manual** The Instructor's Manual is written by the authors and is quality assurance tested. It includes:
- Answers and solutions to all the Questions, Tutorial Assignments, and Case Problems. Suggested solutions are also included for the Exploration Exercises.
- A 3.5-inch disk containing solutions to all the Questions, Tutorial Assignments, and Case Problems.
- Tutorial Notes, which contain background information from the authors about the Tutorial Case and the instructional progression of the tutorial.
- Technical Notes, which include troubleshooting tips as well as information on how to customize the students' screens to closely emulate the screen shots in the book.
- Transparency Masters of key concepts.
■ **Test Bank** The Test Bank contains 50 questions per tutorial in true/false, multiple choice, and fill-in-the-blank formats, plus two essay questions. Each question has been quality assurance tested by students to achieve clarity and accuracy.
■ **Electronic Test Bank** The Electronic Test Bank allows instructors to edit individual test questions, select questions individually or at random, and print out scrambled versions of the same test to any supported printer.

Acknowledgments

Through their contributions, many people are responsible for the successful completion of this book. While "thank you" never seems enough, this is our thanks to each of them.

Our appreciation goes to the Course Technology production and product testing staff—particularly Catherine Griffin and Jeff Goding, and student testers Lyle Korytkowski, David Vislosky, and Christian Murphy—for working tirelessly under tight deadlines to produce a quality, professional product. Thanks to Barbara Clemens, Product Manager, for her managerial skills in guiding this product to completion.

Special thanks to Kathy Finnegan for her valuable insights and suggestions, which turned a "rough" manuscript into a quality text. Thanks also to Tony Austin for his able assistance. Finally, thanks to Joan Soderland and Anna Hommel for their help and understanding.

Charles Hommel
Roy Ageloff

Brief Contents

Contents

TUTORIAL 2   Creating a Database Table

TUTORIAL 3   Maintaining a Database

TUTORIAL 4   Querying a Database

Reference Windows

Read This Before You Begin

To the Student

To use this book, you must have a Student Disk. Your instructor will either provide you with one or ask you to make your own by following the instructions in the section "Your Student Disk" in Tutorial 1. See your instructor or lab manager for further information. If you are going to work through this book using your own computer, you need a computer system running Microsoft Windows 3.1 or later, dBASE 5.0 for Windows, and a Student Disk. *You will not be able to complete the tutorials and exercises in this book using your own computer until you have a Student Disk.*

To the Instructor

Making the Student Disk To complete the tutorials in this book, your students must have a copy of the Student Disk. To relieve you of having to make multiple Student Disks from a single master copy, we provide you with the CTI WinApps Setup Disk, which contains an automatic Student Disk generating program. Once you install the Setup Disk on a network or standalone workstation, students can easily make their own Student Disks by double-clicking the "Make dBASE 5.0 Student Disk" icon in the CTI WinApps icon group. Double-clicking this icon transfers all the data files students need to complete the tutorials, Tutorial Assignments, and Case Problems to a high-density disk in drive A or B. If some of your students will use their own computers to complete the tutorials and exercises in this book, they must first get the Student Disk. The section called "Your Student Disk" in Tutorial 1 provides complete instructions on how to make the Student Disk.

Installing the CTI WinApps Setup Disk To install the CTI WinApps icon group from the Setup Disk, follow the instructions on the Setup Disk label. By adopting this book, you are granted a license to install this software on any computer or computer network used by you or your students.

README File A README.TXT file located on the Setup Disk provides complete installation instructions, additional technical notes, troubleshooting advice, and tips for using the CTI WinApps software in your school's computer lab. You can view the README.TXT file using any word processor you choose.

System Requirements

The minimum software and hardware requirements for your computer system are as follows:

- Microsoft Windows Version 3.1 or later on a local hard drive or a network drive.
- A 386 or higher processor with a minimum of 6 MB of RAM (8 MB or more is strongly recommended).
- A mouse supported by Windows 3.1.
- A printer supported by Windows 3.1.
- A VGA 640 x 480 16-color display is recommended; an 800 x 600 or 1024 x 768 SVGA, VGA monochrome, or EGA display is also acceptable.
- 24 MB free disk space for a complete installation, 10 MB for a minimum installation.
- Student workstations with at least 1 high-density 3.5" disk drive.
- If you want to install the CTI WinApps Setup Disk on a network drive, your network must support Microsoft Windows.

Introductory
dBASE® 5.0 for
Windows™ Tutorials

OBJECTIVES

In this tutorial you will:

- Make a dBASE Student Disk
- Define the terms field, record, table, database, query, form, and report
- Start and exit dBASE
- Identify the components of the dBASE Desktop
- Open a dBASE table
- Navigate through a table
- Change a table's format using direct manipulation
- Access on-line Help
- Print a dBASE table

An Introduction to Database Concepts and dBASE 5.0 for Windows

Improving an Advertising Agency's Efficiency Through Computerization

CASE   **Wells & Martinez Advertising Agency**   Three years ago Nancy Wells and Martin Martinez founded the Wells & Martinez Advertising Agency (W&M) in Santa Fe, New Mexico. Their initial goal was to plan, prepare, and place advertising and other promotions for small to mid-sized local companies. Like many new, struggling businesses, W&M has experienced limited success providing advertising services to a few key clients. Their current client list includes a fashion boutique, a furniture designer, a caterer, a law firm, an automobile dealership, a ski resort, and the city of Santa Fe's tourism board.

Recently, in an effort to attract more clients, Nancy and Martin launched an aggressive marketing campaign that focused on their agency's strengths, creativity, flexibility, and reasonable rates. The campaign generated increased interest among local companies, but, more important, it also attracted attention from several regional companies.

Although Nancy and Martin were pleased with the success of their marketing campaign, the prospect of increasing the size of their client list presents them with some new challenges. They have a limited budget and only six employees to help run the operations and creative activities of the agency. In addition, the day-to-day administration of W&M is a time-consuming process that relies on a manual system of recordkeeping. Nancy and Martin recognize that if they don't improve their agency's efficiency, W&M might not be able to handle new business.

Martin directs the creative activities of W&M. He is responsible for generating advertising ideas and converting those ideas into print and broadcast messages. As the head of this part of W&M, Martin is primed and ready for the impending growth.

Nancy manages the administrative and production side of the agency. She has been struggling with the manual system that handles billing, payroll, and general bookkeeping. Nancy knows that W&M has outgrown this manual system, which she established three years ago. She expects to run into even more difficulty with the addition of new clients.

Martin and Nancy have identified several problems with their current administrative system. They are concerned about cash flow, and they are worried that billings to clients are not always mailed promptly. Martin and Nancy cannot easily determine whether clients are being charged correctly or whether a specific job is profitable. In addition, their system of tracking various jobs and job-related expenses is inadequate. Finally, they know that in a manual system there is a high probability of human error.

Nancy and Martin believe that computerization is the way to solve these administrative problems. But because of the cost of their recent marketing campaign, they cannot afford a software package specifically designed for advertising agencies. Before they decide how to proceed, they need to identify exactly what their computerization needs are.

First, Nancy and Martin analyze how work flows within W&M. They talk to the other employees about how each advertising job is initiated, tracked, and billed.

After studying the work flow and discussing ways to improve their administrative system, Nancy and Martin outline a possible solution. They present their ideas to the other staff members, and everyone agrees that a computerized system must contain three tables of information. First, a CLIENTS table would store the following information for each client: the client's identification (ID) code, the name of the client company, the name of the contact at the client company, the client's main telephone number, the client's fax number, and the client's address (street, city, state, and zip code). Second, a JOBS table would store information about each job a client has authorized W&M to complete. The JOBS table would include the following information for each job: job number, client ID, types of media (print, broadcast, direct mail, or other), due date, brief description of the job, and estimate of the cost to the client. The third table, EXPENSES, would include the following information for each expense: a sequential transaction number for each expense, the job number, the billing category (indicating the type of expense, such as creative meeting, typesetting, copywriting, and so on), the date, the amount, and a brief description.

Nancy and Martin decide that a database product, specifically dBASE 5.0 for Windows, meets their needs for a computerized system. They begin by creating the CLIENTS table, and they want you to help them complete and maintain the three tables in the W&M database.

Using the Tutorials Effectively

In the tutorials, you will help Martin and Nancy complete and maintain the W&M database and, by doing so, you will learn about dBASE 5.0 for Windows. The tutorials are designed to be used at your computer. Begin by reading the text that explains the concepts. Then when you come to the numbered steps, follow the steps on your computer. Read each step carefully and completely before you try it.

As you work, compare your screen with the figures to verify your results. Don't worry if your screen display differs slightly from the figures. The important parts of the screen display are labeled in each figure. Just be sure you have these parts on your screen.

Don't worry about making mistakes; that's part of the learning process. TROUBLE? paragraphs identify common problems and explain how to get back on track. You should complete the steps in the TROUBLE? paragraph *only* if you are having the problem described.

After you read the conceptual information and complete the steps, you can do the exercises found at the end of each tutorial in the sections entitled "Questions," "Tutorial Assignments," and "Case Problems." (Note: Tutorial 1 does not include Case Problems.) The exercises are carefully structured to help you review what you learned in the tutorials and apply your knowledge to new situations.

When you are doing the exercises, refer back to the Reference Window boxes. These boxes, which are found throughout the tutorials, provide you with short summaries of frequently used procedures. You can also use the Task Reference at the end of the tutorials; it summarizes how to accomplish tasks using the mouse, the menus, and the keyboard. Before you begin the tutorials, you should know how to use the menus, dialog boxes, Help facility, Program Manager, and File Manager in Microsoft Windows. Course Technology, Inc. publishes two excellent texts for learning Windows: *A Guide to Microsoft Windows* and *An Introduction to Microsoft Windows*, both available in current releases.

Your Student Disk

To complete the tutorials and exercises in this book, you must have a Student Disk. The Student Disk contains all the practice files you need for the tutorials, the Tutorial Assignments, and the Case Problems. If your instructor or technical support person provides you with your Student Disk, you can skip this section and go to the section entitled "Introduction to Database Concepts." If your instructor asks you to make your own Student Disk, you need to follow the steps in this section.

To make your Student Disk you will need:
- A blank, formatted, high-density 3.5-inch or 5.25-inch disk
- A computer with Microsoft Windows 3.1, dBASE 5.0 for Windows, and the CTI WinApps icon group installed on it.

 If you are using your own computer, the CTI WinApps icon group will not be installed on it. Before you proceed, you must go to your school's computer lab and find a computer with the CTI WinApps icon group installed on it. Once you have made your own Student Disk, you can use it to complete all the tutorials and exercises in this book on any computer you choose.

To make your dBASE Student Disk:
❶ Launch Windows and make sure the Program Manager window is open.

 TROUBLE? The exact steps you follow to launch Microsoft Windows 3.1 might vary depending on how your computer is set up. On many computer systems, type WIN then press [Enter] to launch Windows. If you don't know how to launch Windows, ask your technical support person.

❷ Label your formatted disk "dBASE Student Disk" and place it in drive A.

TROUBLE? If your computer has more than one disk drive, drive A is usually on top. If your Student Disk does not fit into drive A, then place it in drive B and substitute "drive B" anywhere you see "drive A" in the tutorial steps.

❸ Look for an icon labeled "CTI WinApps" like the one in Figure 1-1 or a window labeled "CTI WinApps" like the one in Figure 1-2.

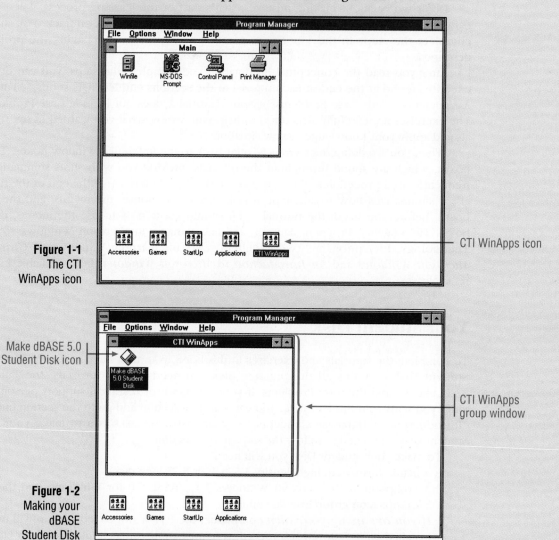

Figure 1-1
The CTI
WinApps icon

Figure 1-2
Making your
dBASE
Student Disk

TROUBLE? If you cannot find anything labeled "CTI WinApps," the CTI software might not be installed on your computer. If you are in a computer lab, ask your technical support person for assistance. If you are using your own computer, you will not be able to make your Student Disk. To make it you need access to the CTI WinApps icon group, which is, most likely, installed on your school's lab computers. Ask your instructor or technical support person for further information on where to locate the CTI WinApps icon group. Once you have made your own Student Disk, you can use it to complete all the tutorials and exercises in this book on any computer you choose.

❹ If you see an icon labeled "CTI WinApps," double-click it to open the CTI WinApps group window. If the CTI WinApps group window is already open, go to Step 5.

❺ Double-click the icon labeled "Make dBASE 5.0 Student Disk." The Make dBASE 5.0 Student Disk window opens. See Figure 1-3.

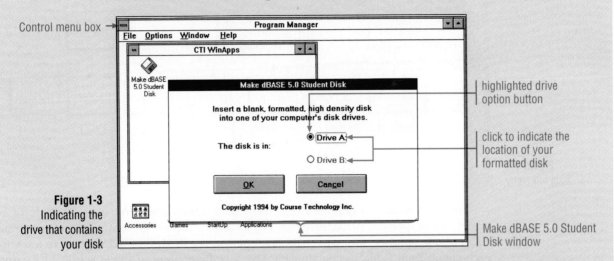

Control menu box →

Figure 1-3
Indicating the
drive that contains
your disk

highlighted drive
option button

click to indicate the
location of your
formatted disk

Make dBASE 5.0 Student
Disk window

❻ Make sure the drive that contains your formatted disk corresponds to the drive option button that is selected in the dialog box on your screen.

❼ Click **OK** to copy the practice files to your formatted disk.

❽ When the copying is complete, a message appears indicating the number of files copied to your disk. Click **OK**.

❾ To close the CTI WinApps window, double-click the **Control menu box** on the CTI WinApps window.

Introduction to Database Concepts

Before you begin working on the W&M database, you need to understand a few important database terms and concepts.

How Data Is Organized

Stored data, computerized or not, is commonly organized into a structure, or hierarchy, that starts at the bottom with fields (the smallest units of information) and builds to records, tables, and then databases (Figure 1-4). This organization of data helps you to process and retrieve information quickly and efficiently.

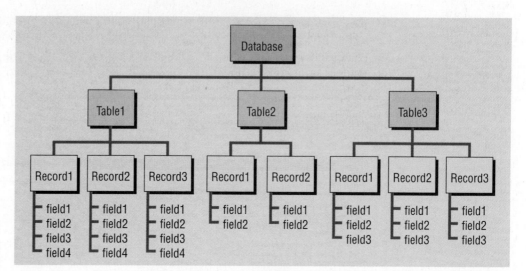

Figure 1-4
Data hierarchy

First let's look at a field. A **field**, also called a **data element**, is an attribute of an object, event, person, place, or thing. For example, the client ID number, client name, client phone number, and name of contact person are fields that W&M wants to track for each client. Each field can contain data. The specific content of a field is called its **value**. For example, the value of the field "client phone number" might be (505)883-9222, and the value of the field "contact person" might be Paul Alexander.

When related fields are grouped together, they form what is known as a record. A **record** is a collection of fields that describe an event, person, or object. For example, Figure 1-5 shows a client record for the client, Alexander Insurance. A complete client record at W&M consists of nine related fields: CLIENT_ID, NAME, CONTACT, PHONE, FAX, STREET, CITY, STATE, and ZIP.

CLIENT_ID	NAME	CONTACT	PHONE	FAX	STREET	CITY	STATE	ZIP
A01	Alexander Insurance	Paul Alexander	(505)883-9222	(505)883-9000	105 Canyon Road	Santa Fe	NM	87501

Figure 1-5   A client record

A collection of related records is called a **table**. A table is organized into horizontal rows (records) and vertical columns (fields). Figure 1-6 shows part of the CLIENTS table, which Nancy and Martin have already created. Each record in the table contains the same nine fields, but the values in those fields vary from record to record.

CONTACT field

Limelight record

records →

Figure 1-6
W&M's
CLIENTS table

fields →

CLIENT ID	NAME	CONTACT	PHONE	FAX	STREET	CITY	STATE	ZIP
A01	Alexander Insurance	Paul Alexander	(505)883-9222	(505)883-9000	105 Canyon Road	Santa Fe	NM	87501
B01	Boatslip Inn	Victor Santos	(505)432-6590	(505)432-0560	32 Commercial Street	Taos	NM	87544
B02	Bullard Inc.	Gregory Bullard	(505)642-8674	(505)342-4789	4008 Washington Road	Albuquerque	NM	87434
C01	Celebrity Catering	Linda Randall	(505)833-9922	(505)833-9921	890 Third Avenue	Santa Fe	NM	87501
C02	Castro Bicycle Co-op	Mark Salgado	(505)628-9132		314 Castro Street	Santa Fe	NM	87501
E01	Eyes Have It	Sandy Alonso	(505)728-2277	(505)267-2349	9552 East Avenue	Santa Fe	NM	87501
F01	Fire Island Realtors	Jeffrey Stryker	(505)345-9234	(505)454-3478	434 West Evelyn Road	Santa Fe	NM	87501
G01	Gauntlet	Samuel Domingo	(505)234-7878	(505)897-3897	25 Market Street	Santa Fe	NM	87501
H01	Holistic Jewelry	Susan Glover	(505)432-9366		Rural Route 5	Taos	NM	87544
I01	Industrial Light & Sound	James Musil	(505)343-5278	(505)343-5277	549 North Halsted	Albuquerque	NM	87434
L01	Lambda Engineering	Jay Sharp	(505)437-1043	(505)437-1002	613 North Clark	Albuquerque	NM	87434
L02	Limelight	Junial Montingier	(505)523-2348	(505)234-5213	3243 Fifth Avenue	Albuquerque	NM	87434
M01	Mountain Top Ski Resort	Gunther Williams	(505)432-6210	(505)432-7890	895 South Wells	Taos	NM	87544
M02	Manana Outfitters	Daniel Gibbs	(505)754-6998	(505)754-8971	735 Tropicana Drive	Santa Fe	NM	87501
M03	Meteorological Survey	Sunil Jain	(505)343-7264	(505)343-7265	PO Box 5434	Santa Fe	NM	87501
N01	Nell's Rib Pit	Janelle May	(505)343-0124	(505)343-3204	64 Lansing Boulevard	Santa Fe	NM	87501
N02	Newsday	Esther Ling	(505)433-8677	(505)433-8641	881 Commonwealth	Taos	NM	87544
R01	Rocky Mountain Tours	Helen Carson	(505)433-2432	(505)692-1234	3489 Ray Beam Drive	Albuquerque	NM	87434
S01	Santa Fe Tourist Center	Liddy Posada	(505)986-5555	(505)986-4905	12 Avenue of America	Santa Fe	NM	87501
S02	Santa Fe Properties	Wendy Falchetti	(505)988-0733	(505)988-0730	736 Hopi Avenue	Santa Fe	NM	87501
S03	Southwest Styles	Gary Higgins	(505)952-1286	(505)952-3209	632 Highland Street	Albuquerque	NM	87434
S04	Shotgun Willy's Lounge	Randy Warren	(505)439-5327	(505)439-5573	320 South Station	Taos	NM	87544
S05	Stonewall	Larry Kramer	(505)432-4534	(505)432-7812	9 Christopher Street	Taos	NM	87544
V01	Viking Auto Group	Jeff Serito	(505)984-9216		3024 Ventura Avenue	Santa Fe	NM	87501
V02	Viola d'Amore	Julie Edwards	(505)789-6344	(505)825-8232	789 Zu Zu Boulevard	Santa Fe	NM	87501

Typically a company maintains several different tables to store related data. A **database**, specifically a **relational database**, is a collection of related tables in which the relationships between tables are represented by common values. As mentioned earlier, the W&M database will include three tables: CLIENTS, to store basic data about the agency's clients; JOBS, to store data about each job W&M is completing for those clients; and EXPENSES, to track the expenses incurred by W&M as they work on the jobs. These three related tables make up the W&M database. Figure 1-7 shows the completed W&M database structure.

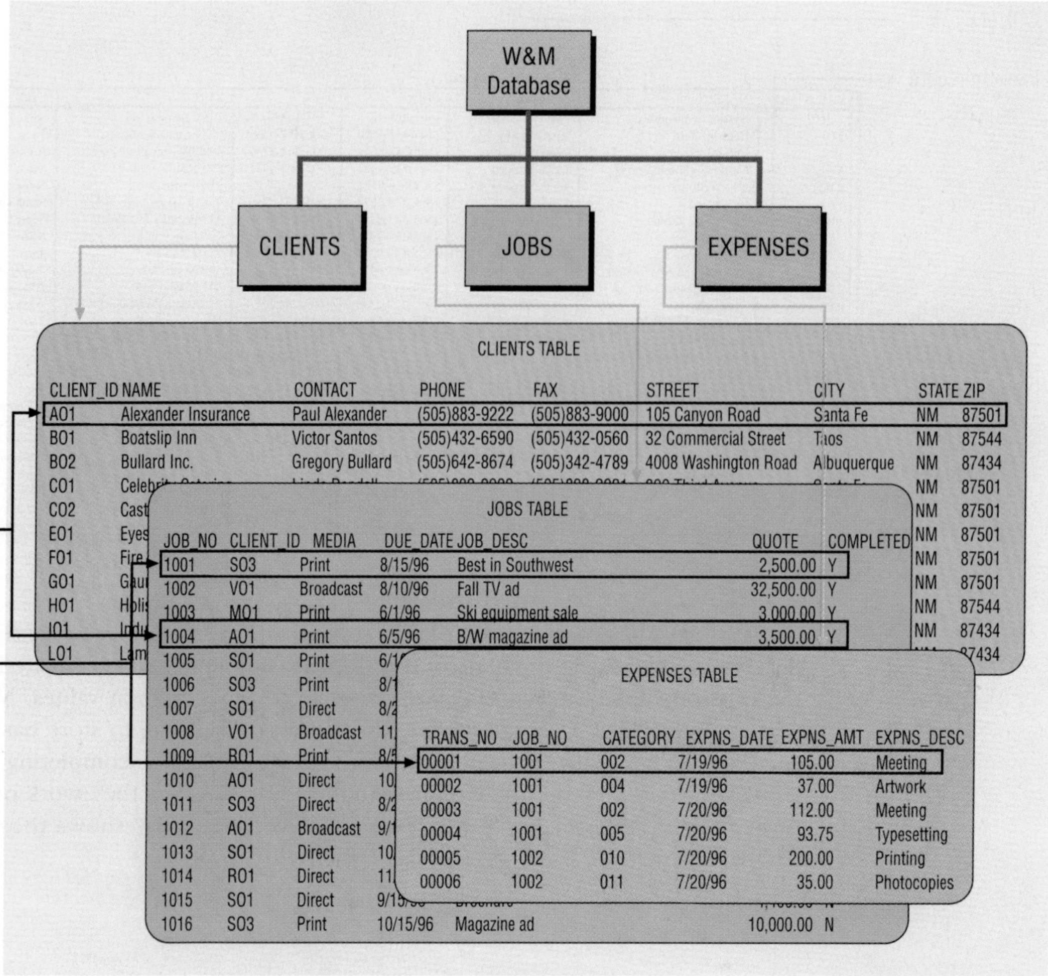

Figure 1-7
W&M's database

In a relational database, tables are related to other tables via **common fields**. This means that two or more tables contain the same field. For example, the CLIENTS table and the JOBS table both contain a CLIENT_ID field, so these tables are related via the CLIENT_ID field. With a relational database, you can link tables so that you can retrieve information from more than one table at a time.

Database Management Systems

To create and manage its database, a company often purchases a database management system. A **database management system (DBMS)** is the software that lets you create, enter, maintain, manipulate, retrieve, and output data in a database. Most current database management systems are based on the relational model. Those that are based on this model are classified as **relational database management systems (RDBMS)**.

A DBMS works as an interface; that is, it serves as an intermediary between a database and the users who are seeking data from that database (Figure 1-8). A DBMS allows you to store information in a database and retrieve information from a database conveniently and efficiently.

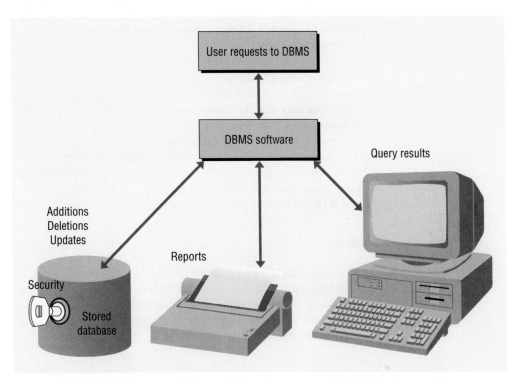

Figure 1-8
DBMS environment

Specifically, a DBMS does the following:
- It creates the structure of the database tables. In other words, it defines the fields in a record. It facilitates the initial entry of data into the database and enables you to update the database by adding, deleting, and modifying records.
- It allows you to retrieve information by issuing queries and generating reports. A **query facility** lets you obtain immediate responses to questions you ask about information in the database. You specify what you are looking for, and the DBMS searches the database and gives you the answers. The emphasis of a query is on quick response rather than well-designed output. A **report generator** allows you to develop professional-looking reports by including page numbers, report titles, column headings, and totals as part of the output.
- It has the capability of sharing data among several users with safeguards to ensure that data is updated properly.
- It provides a mechanism to protect the database from damage and unlawful use.

Overview of dBASE 5.0 for Windows

dBASE 5.0 for Windows is an RDBMS package that functions in the Windows environment. Marketed by Borland International, dBASE is designed for computer users with all levels of experience. This software enables you to work with one or more tables in order to perform a variety of database management tasks, including:

- defining a table
- adding new data to a table
- editing data in a table
- deleting data from a table
- sorting data in a table into some meaningful order
- searching a table for particular information
- creating forms to display data on the screen
- printing data from the table into a formatted report

In dBASE you create objects, such as tables, queries, forms, and reports, to help you perform these database management tasks. dBASE objects and the tools used to create them will be covered in this text. Let's now briefly review each object.

Tables

dBASE stores data in one or more tables. As mentioned earlier, a table is a collection of records containing data related to a particular person, thing, or event. A table is organized into rows and columns. Each column of information is a *field;* each row is a *record.* In Tutorial 2 you will learn how to create tables. In Tutorial 3 you will learn how to add, edit, and delete data in a table.

Queries

A **query** is a quick, interactive way to retrieve information from a database. It is the means of finding the specific records that answer a question. For example, you might want the phone number of a particular client, or a list of all clients in a particular city, or a list of all jobs due during the next month. Figure 1-9 shows a query for finding all W&M clients in Taos, New Mexico. The query instructions appear at the top of the screen. When you run a query, the results of the query appear in a separate window, and the window containing the query instructions closes. Each field with a checkmark in the query instructions is included in the display of the query results. You will learn how to query tables in Tutorial 4.

query instructions →

query results →

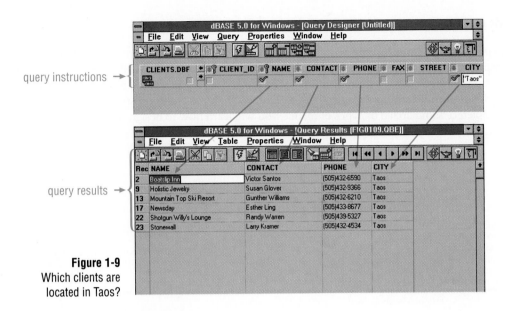

Figure 1-9
Which clients are
located in Taos?

Forms

Adding, editing, and deleting data are important database tasks. You can add, edit, and delete data directly in a table like the one shown in Figure 1-6. **Forms** offer another way to access and manipulate information in a table. Forms often display the same information as a table, but they display it in a more useful and readable format. For example, a form for data entry might look exactly like a paper form that a clerk would use to enter information about a client or a job. Figure 1-10 shows a form for entering and editing client data. You will learn how to design and use forms in Tutorial 5.

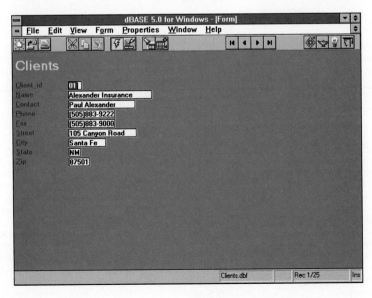

Figure 1-10
Data entry form
for clients

Reports

Reports offer another way to retrieve information from a database. Forms and queries usually display information on the screen; **reports** enable you to display carefully formatted information on the screen or in printed output. For example, you can print lists, reports with totals and subtotals, form letters, and mailing labels. Figure 1-11 shows a report listing the jobs W&M has completed, summarized by types of media. You will learn how to design reports in Tutorial 6.

Completed Jobs - By Media

Media: Broadcast

Client Name	Contact	Job No	Media	Due Date	Quote
Industrial Light & Sound	James Musil	1033	Broadcast	07/28/96	$25,000.00
Rocky Mountain Tours	Helen Carson	1040	Broadcast	08/06/96	$15,000.00
Viking Auto Group	Jeff Serito	1002	Broadcast	08/10/96	$32,500.00
				Total:	$72,500.00

Media: Direct

Client Name	Contact	Job No	Media	Due Date	Quote
Alexander Insurance	Paul Alexander	1010	Direct	10/10/96	$1,250.00
Holistic Jewelry	Susan Glover	1039	Direct	06/12/96	$4,000.00
Nell's Rib Pit	Janelle May	1022	Direct	06/05/96	$1,000.00
Santa Fe Tourist Center	Liddy Posada	1007	Direct	08/02/96	$3,000.00
Southwest Styles	Gary Higgins	1011	Direct	08/22/96	$8,450.00
Viking Auto Group	Jeff Serito	1035	Direct	06/17/96	$2,000.00
				Total:	$19,700.00

Media: Other

Client Name	Contact	Job No	Media	Due Date	Quote
Manana Outfitters	Daniel Gibbs	1030	Other	08/10/96	$4,000.00
				Total:	$4,000.00

Media: Print

Client Name	Contact	Job No	Media	Due Date	Quote
Alexander Insurance	Paul Alexander	1004	Print	06/05/96	$3,500.00
Boatslip Inn	Victor Santos	1024	Print	07/04/96	$10,000.00
Castro Bicycle Co-op	Mark Salgado	1026	Print	08/02/96	$2,500.00
Gauntlet	Samuel Domingo	1023	Print	06/27/96	$3,500.00
Limelight	Juniaf Montingier	1034	Print	08/08/96	$3,000.00
Mountain Top Ski Resort	Gunther Williams	1003	Print	06/01/96	$3,000.00
Newsday	Esther Ling	1038	Print	06/30/96	$38,000.00
Rocky Mountain Tours	Helen Carson	1009	Print	08/05/96	$2,500.00
Santa Fe Tourist Center	Liddy Posada	1005	Print	06/10/96	$22,500.00
Southwest Styles	Gary Higgins	1001	Print	08/15/96	$2,500.00
Southwest Styles	Gary Higgins	1006	Print	08/01/96	$2,200.00
Stonewall	Larry Kramer	1029	Print	07/16/96	$6,400.00
Viola d'Amore	Julie Edwards	1028	Print	07/21/96	$2,000.00
				Total:	$101,600.00

Figure 1-11 Sample report showing completed jobs summarized by media

Starting dBASE

The first step in working with dBASE is to load, or start, the software package. Let's start dBASE and take a brief tour of the package.

To start dBASE:

❶ Make sure the Windows Program Manager is on the screen. The dBASE for Windows group icon should be visible in the Program Manager window.

❷ Double-click the **dBASE for Windows group icon** to open the dBASE for Windows group window. See Figure 1-12.

dBASE for Windows program-item icon

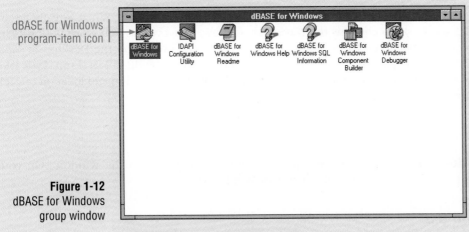

Figure 1-12
dBASE for Windows group window

❸ Double-click the **dBASE for Windows program-item icon**. After several seconds the dBASE Desktop appears. See Figure 1-13.

menu bar
SpeedBar

Navigator window

Command window tool

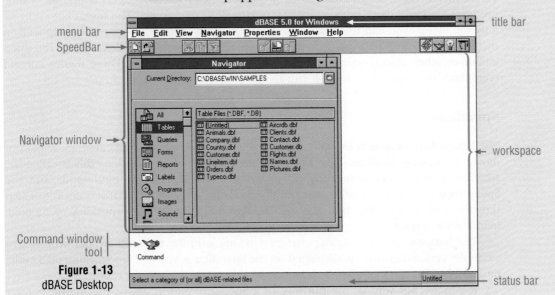

title bar

workspace

status bar

Figure 1-13
dBASE Desktop

TROUBLE? The exact procedure you need to follow to start dBASE might be slightly different from the one given here. If you have any difficulty starting dBASE, see your instructor or technical support person.

❹ Click the **Maximize button** if the dBASE 5.0 for Windows title bar is not at the top of the screen.

Your screen now displays the dBASE Desktop.

The dBASE Desktop

The dBASE Desktop is where you begin all your work in dBASE. When you first start dBASE, the Desktop contains the Navigator window. However, as you work with dBASE, objects, such as tables, forms, queries, and reports, will appear on the Desktop in separate windows. Figure 1-13 shows the main components of the dBASE Desktop. Let's take a look at these components so that you are familiar with the function and location of each one on the Desktop.

Title Bar

The **title bar** is the bar at the top of a window that identifies the window. On your screen the title bar displays "dBASE 5.0 for Windows."

Menu Bar

The **menu bar** is located directly below the title bar. The menu bar lists the available dBASE menus. Each menu contains commands you can select to open windows, configure your Desktop, work with your data, obtain Help, and so on. The menu bar contains only the menus you can use from a particular window. Initially, seven menus appear on the menu bar: File, Edit, View, Navigator, Properties, Window, and Help. When you open a table or other object, additional menus appear on the menu bar. These menus contain commands that pertain to the task you are performing.

SpeedBar

The **SpeedBar**, located below the menu bar, is a row of buttons you can click with your mouse to perform frequently used tasks. In many Windows applications this is called the *toolbar*. You can perform many of the same tasks using menu commands, but the SpeedBar usually allows you to work more efficiently. Most of the instructions in this text direct you to use SpeedBar buttons; you can, however, use the corresponding menu commands if you prefer.

The buttons on the SpeedBar change depending on the task you are performing. For example, certain buttons are displayed on the SpeedBar when you are working on a table; different buttons appear when you are working on a query, form, or report.

If you are not sure of the purpose of a SpeedBar button, move the mouse pointer over the button *without clicking*. A description of the button appears in the status bar (defined later in this section).

Workspace

The **workspace** is the area between the SpeedBar and the status bar. This is where you perform all your work in dBASE, for example, creating tables, designing forms, and entering data.

The Navigator

The dBASE **Navigator** provides an easy way to view and access your files. The file type list on the left side of the Navigator window (Figure 1-14) displays a list of database file types: tables, queries, forms, and so on. When you select a file type, the selection panel on the right side of the Navigator window lists the files of the selected type in the current directory. Using the Navigator, you can open files, create new files, and change the current directory. Note that the current directory and list of files on your screen might be different from those shown in the figure.

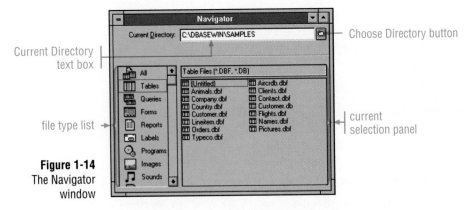

Figure 1-14
The Navigator window

Command Window Tool

The **Command window tool,** shown in Figure 1-13, gives you access to the Command window, in which you can enter and execute dBASE commands and see the results. Use of this tool is beyond the scope of this book.

Status Bar

The status bar is located at the bottom of the Desktop, as shown in Figure 1-13. The **status bar** displays information about the tasks you are working on and the current status of dBASE. Information such as descriptions of SpeedBar buttons, error messages, and which record of a table is being accessed appears in this part of the Desktop.

Working with dBASE

Now that you have a basic understanding of database terms and are familiar with the dBASE Desktop, you are ready to use dBASE to build the W&M database.

First, you'll begin by looking at the CLIENTS table, which Nancy and Martin have already created and into which they've entered data for each client. They would like you to look at the CLIENTS table to see how it is structured and to become familiar with some basic dBASE features.

The CLIENTS table is stored on your Student Disk, as are all the files you will use throughout the tutorials. You need to tell dBASE where to find the table so you can work with it. To do this, you must change the current directory.

Changing the Current Directory

When you first start dBASE, the Navigator window is open. At the top of the window, the Navigator displays the name of the current directory, as shown in Figure 1-14. The **current directory** is the disk and directory where dBASE finds and writes all the tables and associated files you will be working with during the current session. When you're working with an application such as dBASE, it's best to put all files related to the application in the same directory. Files related to other applications should be stored in different directories. This way, only files that are associated with a specific application will be displayed when you access a directory. You can change the current directory using the Navigator.

REFERENCE WINDOW

Changing the Current Directory

- Double-click in the Current Directory text box in the Navigator window.
- Type the name of the directory you want as the current directory.
- Press [Enter].

or

- Click the Choose Directory button in the Navigator window.
- In the Choose Directory dialog box, specify the drive and directory name you want as the current directory.
- Click OK.

Because all the tables and files you will use to build the W&M database are stored in the WM directory of the Student Disk, let's change the current directory to A:\WM.

To change the current directory to A:\WM:

❶ Make sure your Student Disk is in drive A.

TROUBLE? If you don't have a Student Disk, you need to get one before proceeding. Your instructor will either give you a copy of the Student Disk or ask you to make your own by following the instructions earlier in this tutorial in the section entitled "Your Student Disk." See your instructor or technical support person for information.

❷ Double-click in the **Current Directory text box** of the Navigator window. The name of the current directory is highlighted in the Current Directory text box. (The directory name in the text box on your screen might be different from the one in Figure 1-14.)

❸ Type **A:\WM** in the Current Directory text box. Note that when you begin typing, the highlighted text disappears and the new text replaces it.

If you can't remember the name of the directory where your files are located, you can click the Choose Directory button (see Figure 1-14) to search for and choose the directory you want.

❹ Press **[Enter]**. A:\WM is now the current directory. Unless you specify otherwise, all database tables and associated files that you create while working in dBASE will be stored in the current directory. See Figure 1-15.

name of current
directory

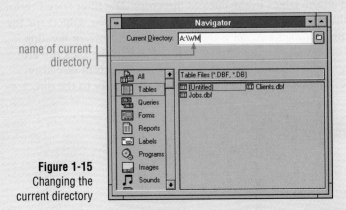

Figure 1-15
Changing the
current directory

Each time you start dBASE you should check the Current Directory text box in the Navigator window to make sure the current directory is set to the directory where your files are located.

Now that dBASE can locate the files in your current directory, you can open and view the CLIENTS table.

Opening a dBASE Table

Before you can view, add, modify, or delete data in a table, the table must be open. There are three ways to open a table: using the Navigator, using the Open button on the SpeedBar, or using the Open option on the File menu.

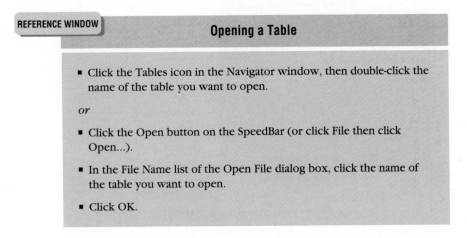

REFERENCE WINDOW

Opening a Table

- Click the Tables icon in the Navigator window, then double-click the name of the table you want to open.

or

- Click the Open button on the SpeedBar (or click File then click Open...).

- In the File Name list of the Open File dialog box, click the name of the table you want to open.

- Click OK.

Let's open the CLIENTS table and view the client data.

To open the CLIENTS table:

❶ Click the **Tables icon** in the Navigator window (if necessary). The list of dBASE tables in the current directory appears. See Figure 1-16. The current selection panel displays the names of all the tables in the current directory. The filter specifications *.DBF, *.DB identify the types of files dBASE displays in the list box. DBF is the file-name extension for dBASE tables and DB is the filename extension for Paradox tables. In the tutorials you will work with dBASE tables only. If the files you are looking for do not appear in the current selection panel, the current directory might be set to a different directory. Change the current directory to the directory you want.

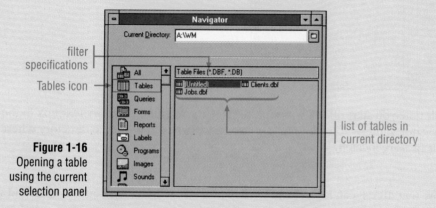

filter specifications

Tables icon

list of tables in current directory

Figure 1-16
Opening a table using the current selection panel

❷ Double-click **Clients.dbf**. dBASE displays the contents of the CLIENTS table in the Table Records window. See Figure 1-17. Notice that the title bar for the Table window specifies "Table Records: (CLIENTS.DBF)" and the options on both the SpeedBar and menu bar have changed.

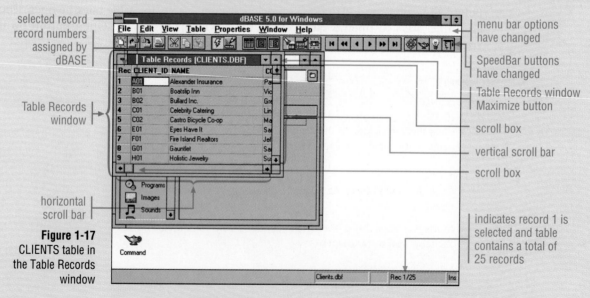

selected record
record numbers assigned by dBASE

menu bar options have changed

SpeedBar buttons have changed

Table Records window Maximize button

scroll box

vertical scroll bar

scroll box

Table Records window

horizontal scroll bar

indicates record 1 is selected and table contains a total of 25 records

Figure 1-17
CLIENTS table in the Table Records window

❸ Click the **Maximize button** to maximize the Table Records window.

When you first open a table, the table is in Browse layout. While in **Browse layout**, a table shows several records at a time, with each record displayed as a row and each field as a column. dBASE automatically places a record number in the first column of each table, as shown in Figure 1-17. A **record number** is an internal counter that dBASE uses to keep track of each record. The heading "Rec" appears at the top of this column. All the other columns have the name of the field at the top. The status bar displays the name of the table ("Clients.dbf") and the message, "Rec 1/25." This message indicates that the first record, Alexander Insurance, is the selected record, and there are 25 records in the table.

Now that the CLIENTS table is open, you can move through it to view the data it contains.

Navigating Through a Table

Although the CLIENTS table contains relatively few records, a table typically stores hundreds or thousands of records. When a table is large, all the data will not fit on the screen at one time. dBASE provides several ways to navigate through a table:

- The SpeedBar navigation buttons, described in Figure 1-18, let you move to specific records. Figure 1-19 shows the location of the navigation buttons on the SpeedBar.
- The Table menu commands, also shown in Figure 1-18, provide the same navigation capabilities as the SpeedBar buttons.
- The Table window provides a vertical scroll bar and a horizontal scroll bar (shown in Figure 1-17). The up arrow and down arrow on the Table window's vertical scroll bar let you scroll through the table one record at a time. The left arrow and right arrow on the Table window's horizontal scroll bar let you scroll through the fields of the table. The scroll box on each scroll bar allows you to scroll the Table window to view records that are not currently visible.
- The keyboard arrow keys—[↑], [↓], [←], and [→]—allow you to move through a table in the direction of the arrow.
- You can also click any field with the mouse to move to that field.

SpeedBar Button	Table Menu Command	Movement Within Table
⏮	Top Record	Move to the first record
⏪	Previous Page	Scroll up one screen
◀	Previous Record	Move up one record
▶	Next Record	Move down one record
⏩	Next Page	Scroll down one screen
⏭	Bottom Record	Move to the last record

Figure 1-18
Navigation buttons
and commands

Right now Alexander Insurance is the selected record. Let's practice different navigation methods as you move through the CLIENTS table. Note that in Browse layout any changes you make to field values are saved with the table; therefore, when navigating through the table, be careful not to change any values.

To practice moving through the CLIENTS table:

❶ Click the field for record 2 (in the Rec column) to select the second record. dBASE highlights the entire Boatslip Inn record. See Figure 1-19.

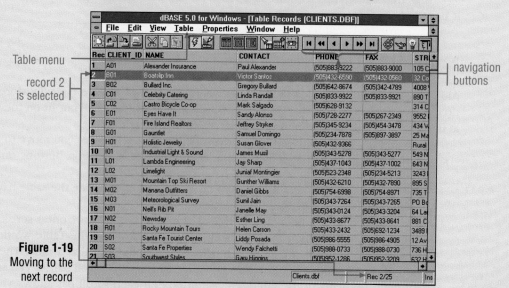

Figure 1-19
Moving to the
next record

When you click a record number in the Rec column, dBASE highlights the entire record. When you click any other field in the record, only that field is highlighted.

Now, move to the last record in the table using the Table menu.

❷ Click **Table** then click **Bottom Record**. dBASE positions the highlight on the CLIENT_ID field of the last record in the table, Viola d'Amore.

❸ Click the **NAME field (Viola d'Amore)**, then press [↑] on the keyboard three times to move up three records.

❹ Click the **right arrow** on the horizontal scroll bar four times to move to the right. The other fields in the table are now visible.

❺ Drag the horizontal scroll box left to scroll back to display the first column. Note that the highlight doesn't move.

Now, use the SpeedBar buttons to continue to move through the table.

❻ Click the **Previous Record button** ◄ to move up one record.

❼ Click the **Top button** ◄◄ to return to the first record.

Now that you know how to move through a table, Martin would like you to make a few changes to the table's format. He thinks the changes will improve the table's appearance.

Changing a Table's Format Using Direct Manipulation

Sometimes you can make a table easier to work with by changing the way the data in the table is displayed. dBASE lets you change the format of a table on the screen. For example, you can expand and reduce column widths, rearrange columns, or change the font, color, type style, and alignment of data in columns. You can change many aspects of a table's appearance—such as the width and position of columns—by using the mouse to change an object. This is called **direct manipulation**. When you move your mouse across certain areas on a table, called **hot spots**, the pointer's shape changes to indicate that you can use the mouse to manipulate the object.

Changing Column Width

Changing the width of columns can be helpful if you want to see more data on the screen at one time. Martin thinks the table would look better if the column width for the CONTACT field were narrower. He asks you to reduce the column width for CONTACT.

To reduce the column width of the CONTACT field:
- ❶ Place the pointer on the vertical grid line between the column headings for the CONTACT and PHONE fields. The pointer changes to ⬄. See Figure 1-20.

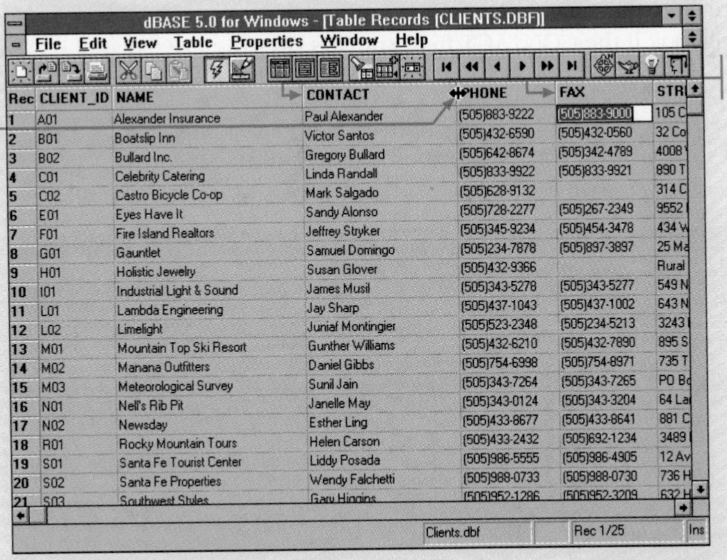

Figure 1-20
Changing the column width of the CONTACT field

- ❷ Click and drag the grid line to the left until it is beside the right-most character visible in the CONTACT column.
- ❸ Release the mouse button. The CONTACT column is now narrower. See Figure 1-21.

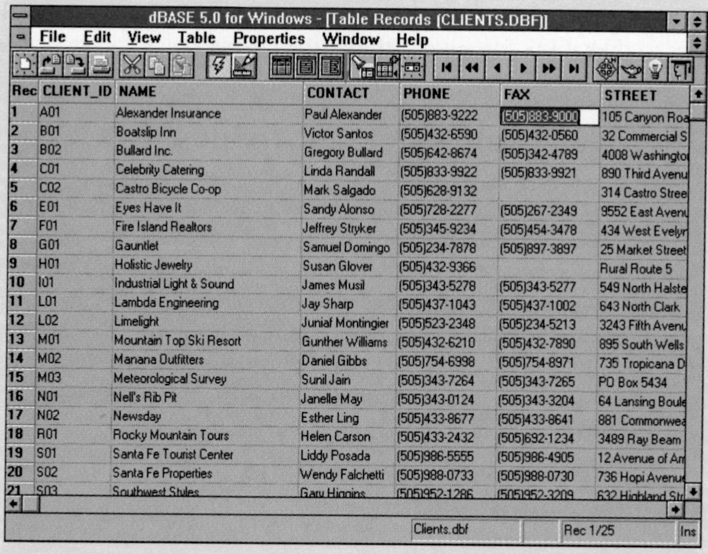

narrower column
width for
CONTACT field

Figure 1-21
Result of changing
column width

TROUBLE? If you drag the grid line too far, or not far enough, simply repeat the above steps until the CONTACT column is as wide or narrow as you want.

Moving Columns

Sometimes you might want to rearrange the columns in a table so that certain columns are closer to one another or appear in a different order. Martin wants to see how the table will look if the CONTACT field appears after the PHONE and FAX fields. Let's try it.

To move the CONTACT column after the FAX column:
❶ Place the mouse pointer on the column header for the CONTACT field. The pointer changes to 🖑. See Figure 1-22.

pointer shape for
moving column

column header for
CONTACT field

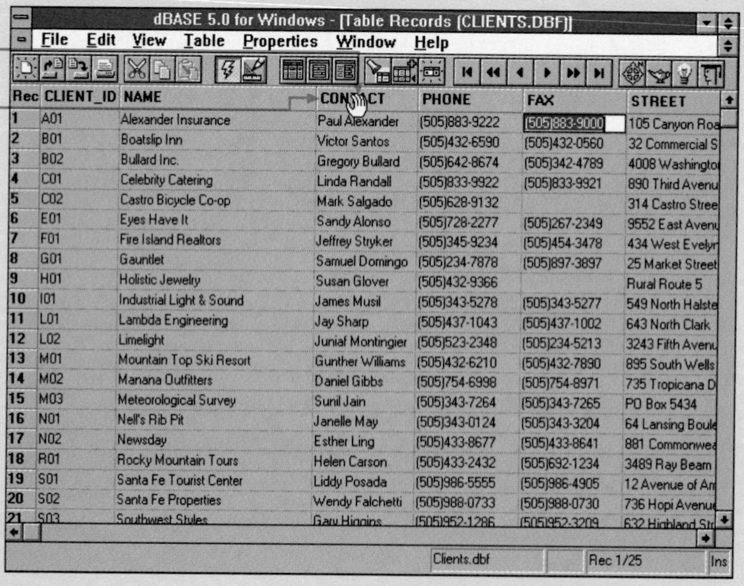

Figure 1-22
Moving the
CONTACT column

❷ Click and drag the header to the FAX column. Notice that as you drag the header over the PHONE column, the PHONE column moves left. As you drag the header over the FAX column, the FAX column also moves left.

❸ Release the mouse button. The CONTACT column moves to its new location to the right of the FAX column. See Figure 1-23.

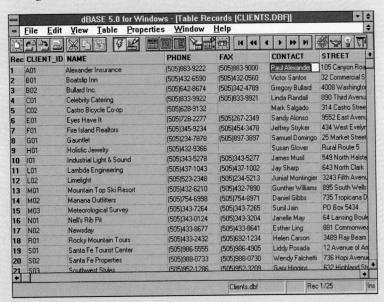

Figure 1-23
CONTACT column in
new location

Martin decides that he prefers the CONTACT column in its original location.

❹ Place the mouse pointer on the column header for the CONTACT field. The pointer changes to 🖑.

❺ Click and drag the header to the PHONE column, then release the mouse button. The CONTACT column is back in its original location, to the right of the NAME column.

Next, Martin wants to see how the table would look without the grid lines displayed. When you open a dBASE table, the table is displayed with grid lines that separate records and fields in the Table Records window. You can remove the grid lines by changing the properties of the Table Records window.

Changing the Properties of the Table Records Window

In dBASE, each element you see on the screen—such as a window, icon, or button—is an object. Each object has certain **properties** that control its appearance and behavior on the screen. Some of these objects, such as the Table Records window, have properties you can view or change. For example, you can remove the display of grid lines from the Table Records window. To do so, you use the Properties menu, which is available in all dBASE windows.

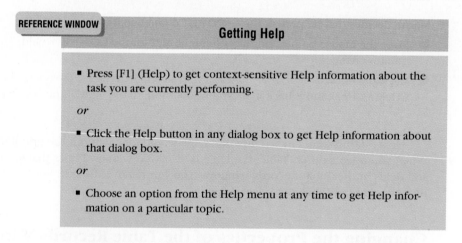

REFERENCE WINDOW

Changing an Object's Properties

- Click Properties on the menu bar.
- In the Properties menu, click the object whose properties you want to modify.
- Enter your changes in the resulting dialog box.
- Click OK.

Martin wants to see how the table would look with the grid lines removed. He suggests that you use the dBASE on-line Help system to find out how to remove the grid lines from the Table Records window.

Accessing On-line Help

dBASE has an extensive on-line Help system you can access any time you are using dBASE. For instance, if you need help understanding the current task you are working on, **context-sensitive Help** provides you with information specific to whatever you are doing at the time. In addition, you can explore any dBASE topic or refresh your memory about an object, task, or operation by using the Help menu.

REFERENCE WINDOW

Getting Help

- Press [F1] (Help) to get context-sensitive Help information about the task you are currently performing.

or

- Click the Help button in any dialog box to get Help information about that dialog box.

or

- Choose an option from the Help menu at any time to get Help information on a particular topic.

Context-Sensitive Help

You can view context-sensitive Help information by pressing the function key [F1] (Help). A Help window will open with information about the object you are currently working with or the operation you are trying to perform. For example, if you are not clear about the function of the Find Records option of the Table menu on the menu bar, you can get Help while you are using the menu.

Before you search for an answer to Martin's question, let's take a minute to look at the different ways of accessing Help. First, you'll access context-sensitive Help on the Find Records option of the Table menu.

To get Help on the Table menu:

❶ Click **Table** on the menu bar. Notice that the first menu choice, Find Records..., is highlighted.

❷ Press **[F1]** (Help). The dBASE for Windows Help window opens providing information about the Find Records... option of the Table menu. See Figure 1-24.

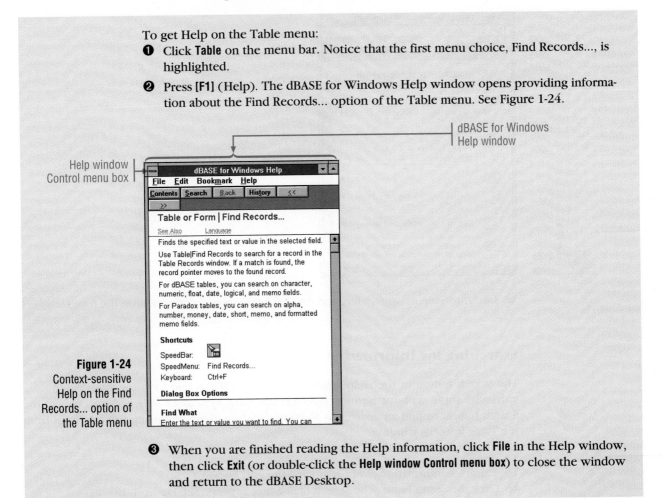

Figure 1-24
Context-sensitive Help on the Find Records... option of the Table menu

❸ When you are finished reading the Help information, click **File** in the Help window, then click **Exit** (or double-click the **Help window Control menu box**) to close the window and return to the dBASE Desktop.

Help Menu

The Help menu provides options that let you access and move through the entire Help system. For example, the Contents option displays a list of the major topics available; you can then choose the topic for which you want more information. Let's try using the Help menu.

To use the Help menu:

❶ Click **Help** then click **Contents**. The dBASE for Windows Help window opens and displays a list of the major Help topics. See Figure 1-25.

Search button

click icons or
underlined words to
move to Help topic

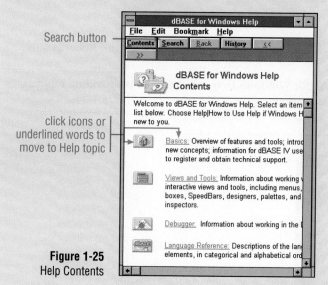

Figure 1-25
Help Contents

❷ Click any icon or any underlined text to obtain more information on the topic.

Searching for Information

The Search button in the Help window (Figure 1-25) lets you look for information on a particular topic without hunting through the Help system to find it. You can use the Search button to find an answer to Martin's question about removing the grid lines from the Table Records window.

To search for information about removing the grid lines:

❶ Click the **Search button**. The Search dialog box appears. See Figure 1-26.

type text to search
for or click a word
in topic list

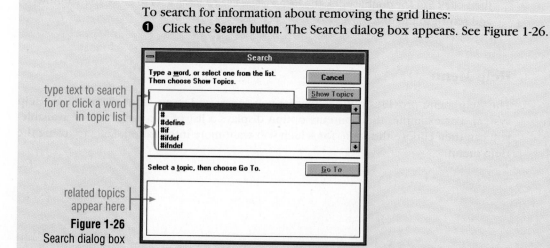

related topics
appear here

Figure 1-26
Search dialog box

You can either type the text you are searching for in the text box with the flashing cursor, or click a word in the list.

❷ Type **gr**. Although you could have typed the entire word "grid," dBASE starts scrolling the topic list as soon as you start typing. In this case the topic "grids" appears after you type the first two letters.

❸ Click **grids**.

❹ Click **Show Topics**. The list of related topics appears in the box below. Because you want information on changing a property of the Table Records window, the topic "Window Properties [Table Records Properties dialog box]" seems like an appropriate choice.

❺ Click the topic **Window Properties [Table Records Properties dialog box]**, then click **Go To**. The information on turning grid lines on and off appears. See Figure 1-27.

Help window
Control menu box

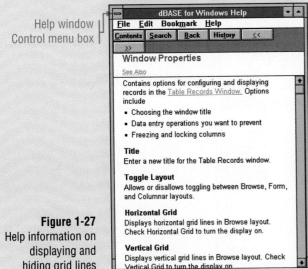

Figure 1-27
Help information on displaying and hiding grid lines

The information specifies that you can display the horizontal grid lines by checking the Horizontal Grid box in the Table Records Properties dialog box. You can display vertical grid lines by checking the Vertical Grid check box. If the boxes are already checked, clicking them will clear the boxes and the grid lines will not be displayed.

❻ When you are finished using Help, click **File** in the Help window, then click **Exit** (or double-click the **Help window Control menu box**) to close the window and return to the dBASE Desktop.

Now that you've read the Help information, let's try removing the horizontal and vertical grid lines to see if that improves the appearance of the table.

To remove the grid lines from the Table Records window:

❶ Click **Properties** in the menu bar.

❷ Click **Table Records Window...** in the Properties menu. The Table Records Properties dialog box appears. See Figure 1-28.

Figure 1-28
The Table
Records Properties
dialog box

This dialog box has three tabs: Fields, Records, and Window. The grid lines are part of the window, so you need to display the Window tab.

❸ Click the **Window tab**. The window options appear. See Figure 1-29.

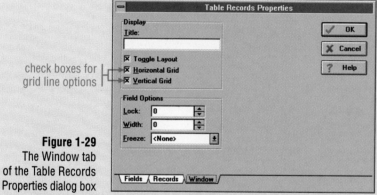

Figure 1-29
The Window tab
of the Table Records
Properties dialog box

The panel in the upper left of the dialog box contains check boxes for Horizontal Grid and Vertical Grid. These boxes are already checked.

❹ Click the **Horizontal Grid check box** to turn it off.

❺ Click the **Vertical Grid check box** to turn it off.

❻ Click **OK** to close the Table Records Properties dialog box and return to the Table Records window.

After looking at the modified table, Martin decides he prefers to have the grid lines visible. Let's turn them back on before proceeding.

To display the grid lines in the Table Records window:

❶ Click **Properties** in the menu bar.

❷ Click **Table Records Window...** in the Properties menu. The Table Records Properties dialog box appears. Notice that the Window tab is still displayed.

❸ Click the **Horizontal Grid check box** to turn it back on.

❹ Click the **Vertical Grid check box** to turn it back on.

❺ Click **OK** to close the Table Records Properties dialog box and return to the Table Records window.

The grid lines are once again visible in the Table Records window.

Meanwhile, Nancy stops by to see how things are going. She suggests that you print a copy of the CLIENTS table so that you can refer to it later when creating and working with the other tables in the W&M database.

Printing a dBASE Table

You can print the contents of a table by clicking the Print button on the SpeedBar, or by choosing Print from the File menu. If you want printed output to be formatted in a particular way, you need to design a report. You'll work with reports in Tutorial 6.

Initially, when dBASE prints a table, it uses the default printer and settings defined in the Printers option of the Windows Control Panel. One of the settings is the print orientation. dBASE provides two print orientations, portrait and landscape. The **portrait orientation** prints the table with the paper positioned so it is taller than it is wide. The **landscape orientation** prints the table with the paper positioned so it is wider than it is tall. Because of the number of fields in the CLIENTS table, it would look best printed in landscape orientation. You need to set up the printer for landscape printing.

Setting Up the Printer

To change the printer settings, you use the Print Setup dialog box. The settings are preserved from session to session in dBASE.

REFERENCE WINDOW

Modifying Printer Setup Options

- Click File then click Printer Setup... to display the Print Setup dialog box.

- Select the options you want to use.

- Click OK in the Print Setup dialog box to accept the changes you made.

Let's make sure the printer is set up for landscape orientation.

To set the orientation to landscape:

❶ Click **File** then click **Printer Setup...** to display the Print Setup dialog box. See Figure 1-30. The settings shown in this dialog box will vary based on the selected printer.

Landscape option button

Figure 1-30
Print Setup
dialog box

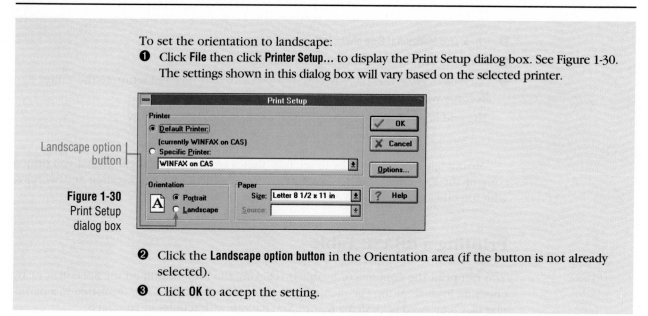

❷ Click the **Landscape option button** in the Orientation area (if the button is not already selected).

❸ Click **OK** to accept the setting.

Now that you have changed the printer setup, you can print the CLIENTS table.

Printing the Table

As mentioned earlier, you can print a table by clicking the Print button on the SpeedBar or by choosing Print from the File menu.

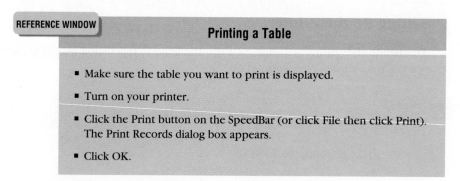

REFERENCE WINDOW

Printing a Table

- Make sure the table you want to print is displayed.
- Turn on your printer.
- Click the Print button on the SpeedBar (or click File then click Print). The Print Records dialog box appears.
- Click OK.

To print the CLIENTS table:

❶ Make sure your printer is on and contains paper.

❷ Click the **Print button** 🖨 on the SpeedBar. The Print Records dialog box appears. See Figure 1-31.

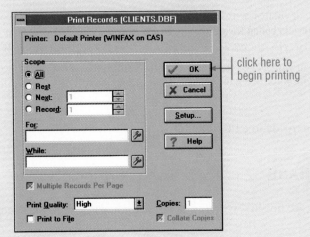

click here to
begin printing

Figure 1-31
Print Records
dialog box

❸ Click **OK** to print the CLIENTS table. The table prints in landscape orientation over two pages. Note that the grid lines displayed in the Table Records window do not appear in the printed table.

This printout is adequate for simply viewing the contents of the table. For professional, well-formatted output, you must produce a report. You will learn how to do this in Tutorial 6.

With the CLIENTS table printed, you're ready to close the table and exit dBASE.

Closing a Table

You can close a table or other objects on the Desktop by double-clicking the Control menu box of the window you want to close, or by clicking the Control menu box and choosing Close. Now that you've had a chance to view and print the CLIENTS table, you can close the table.

To close the CLIENTS table:
❶ Double-click the **Control menu box** for the Table window. *Do not double-click the Control menu box for the dBASE for Windows window; this will cause you to exit dBASE.*

TROUBLE? If you double-clicked the Control menu box for the dBASE for Windows window and exited dBASE, restart dBASE and continue with the tutorial.

The CLIENTS table closes and you return to the dBASE Desktop. Notice that the Navigator window is maximized. dBASE maximizes this window because you maximized the Table Records window. If you leave the Navigator window maximized, it will appear this way when you start dBASE again. Let's restore the window so that it is not maximized.

To restore the Navigator window:

❶ Click the **Restore button** for the Navigator window, which appears at the right end of the menu bar. *Do not click the Restore button for the dBASE for Windows window.*

TROUBLE? If you clicked the Restore button for the dBASE for Windows window, click the Maximize button for this window, then repeat Step 1.

Now you're ready to exit dBASE.

Exiting dBASE

Whenever you are finished working in dBASE, you can exit to end your dBASE session.

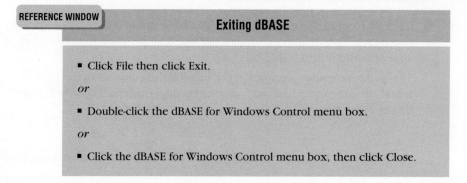

REFERENCE WINDOW

Exiting dBASE

- Click File then click Exit.

or

- Double-click the dBASE for Windows Control menu box.

or

- Click the dBASE for Windows Control menu box, then click Close.

Because you have finished your dBASE work session, you can exit dBASE.

To exit dBASE using the File menu:

❶ Click **File** then click **Exit**. You return to the Windows Program Manager.

Exiting Windows

Before you turn off your computer, it's a good idea to exit Windows so that all files are properly closed.

To exit Windows:

❶ Click **File** on the Program Manager menu bar to display the File menu.

❷ Click **Exit Windows…**. A dialog box displays the message, "This will end your Windows Session."

❸ Click **OK** to exit Windows and return to the DOS prompt.

■   ■   ■

This tutorial introduced you to database concepts and dBASE, and prepared you to help Nancy and Martin build the W&M database.

Questions

1. Define the following terms:
   a. field
   b. record
   c. table
   d. database
   e. DBMS
   f. RDBMS
   g. query

Use the data in Figure 1-32 to answer Questions 2 through 5.

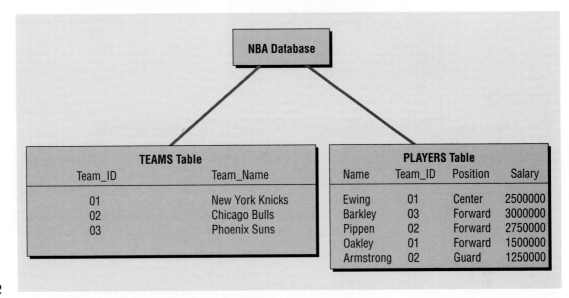

Figure 1-32

2. List all the fields in the NBA database.
3. Identify the fields in the TEAMS table.
4. How many records are in the PLAYERS table?
5. How many fields are in the PLAYERS table?
6. Explain the purpose of the following SpeedBar buttons:
   a.
   b.
   c.

7. Identify each of the labeled elements in Figure 1-33.

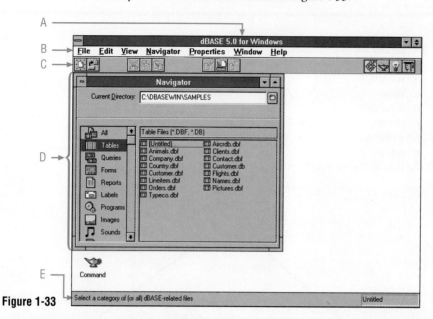

Figure 1-33

8. A dBASE table is stored in the directory C:\DEMO. Describe how you can access this table in dBASE.
9. After you open a table, the first record is selected. How would you move to the last field of the selected record using the keyboard? Using the mouse?
10. After you open a table, the first record is selected. How would you move to the second record using the keyboard? Using the mouse? Using the SpeedBar? Using the menu?
11. After opening a table, how can you quickly determine the number of records in the table?
12. Selecting the Printer Setup command on the File menu allows you to:
    a. Print the table
    b. Select the print orientation to use in printing the table
    c. Preview the table you will be printing
    d. Turn the printer on
13. How do you close a table?
E 14. Review Figure 1-34, a form used by Bryer College's Off-Campus Housing Office. Using this form, identify the fields the Housing Office might include in a HOUSING table.

```
┌─────────────────────────────────────────────────────────────┐
│                                                               │
│        AVAILABLE OFF-CAMPUS HOUSING FORM           001        │
│                                                               │
│   1.  Rental address:                                         │
│       _____        │
│       Street Address                                          │
│                                                               │
│       _____        │
│       City                                State      Zip      │
│                                                               │
│   2.  Indicate name and phone numbers of owner of rental property: │
│       _____        │
│       Last Name                    First Name                 │
│                                                               │
│       _____        │
│       Home Phone #                 Work Phone #               │
│                                                               │
│   3.  Type of rental unit available (check one):              │
│         (  ) House    (  ) Apartment                          │
│                                                               │
│   4.  # of bedrooms: _____                                   │
│                                                               │
│   5.  How many miles is unit from campus? _____      │
│                                                               │
│   6.  Length of lease required (in months)? _____    │
│                                                               │
│   7.  Rent per month? _____          │
│                                                               │
│   8.  Date available?    __ /__ /__                           │
│                                                               │
│   9.  Please check all amenities that your rental unit features: │
│         (  ) Utilities included        (  ) Washer/dryer      │
│         (  ) Furnished bedroom(s)       (  ) Dishwasher        │
│         (  ) On bus line                (  ) Pets allowed      │
│         (  ) Wheelchair accessible      (  ) Children allowed  │
│                                                               │
└─────────────────────────────────────────────────────────────┘
```

Figure 1-34

Tutorial Assignments

Start dBASE and make sure your Student Disk is in the disk drive. Then set the current directory to A:\PRACTICE.

1. Identify the database tables in this directory.
2. Use the Navigator window to open the table GRANT1.DBF, which is a table of grant applications.
3. Move to the record with the grant title, "Resume Expert System." What is the amount awarded for this grant?
4. Name all the fields in this table.
5. What is the title of the last grant in the table? Was the grant approved?
6. How many records are in the table?
7. Move the COLLEGE field to the left of the GRANTEE field.
8. Print the table in landscape orientation.
9. Close the table.

E 10. Make additional changes to the GRANT1 table's properties:
  a. Make sure the current directory is set to A:\PRACTICE.
  b. Open the GRANT1.DBF table again.
  c. Adjust the column widths so that you can view the entire table on the screen.
  d. Change the table title to GRANTS. (*Hint:* The table title is a window property of the Table Records window.)
  e. Change the column heading of the LOG_ID column to LOG ID. (*Hint:* The column heading is a field property of the Table Records window.)
  f. Reset the table title to GRANT1.DBF and reset the column heading to LOG_ID, then close the table.

E 11. The dBASE Help system provides short, easy-to-understand lessons, called Tutors, that help you proceed step-by-step through common dBASE tasks. From the dBASE Desktop, click Help then click Interactive Tutors... to begin working with the Tutors. Explore the first two lessons in the Introducing dBASE Tutor: "A Quick Look At dBASE For Windows" and "Navigating In dBASE For Windows."

12. Exit dBASE.

Creating a Database Table

Designing and Creating a Table to Track Jobs

CASE

Wells & Martinez Advertising Agency

Early one morning Martin receives a phone call from Phyllis Higgins. Phyllis and her husband, Gary, are the owners of Southwest Styles, a fashion boutique. They have been W&M clients since Martin and Nancy started the agency.

Phyllis tells Martin that she and Gary are very excited about their new line of Southwest-style denim clothing for men and women, and that they want W&M to develop an ad campaign to launch the new line. Later that day Martin tells Nancy about this new business opportunity from Southwest Styles. They decide that Martin and his creative team will put together a campaign plan. As soon as he has an outline of the plan, Martin will give the outline to Nancy so that she can estimate the cost of the job. They agree to have both the campaign plan and the cost estimate finalized and ready to present to Gary and Phyllis in two weeks.

Two weeks later Martin and Nancy meet with Phyllis and Gary and present the plan and the estimate. Phyllis and Gary are so impressed that they authorize W&M to begin work on the campaign—Best in Southwest—immediately. They sign W&M's standard Job Authorization Form (Figure 2-1), which authorizes Martin to begin working on the campaign and accepts the projected cost as Nancy has estimated it.

Figure 2-1
W&M Job
Authorization Form

Wells & Martinez Ad Agency
Job Authorization Form

Job No: 1001
Client ID: S03

Client: Southwest Styles
Address: 632 Highland Street
             Albuquerque, NM 87434

Media: Print
Due Date: 8/15/96   Quote: $2,500
Description: Best in Southwest
Accepted: *Phyllis Higgins*   Date: *June 1, 1996*

At W&M a Job Authorization Form is filled out for each job W&M does for every client. For example, if Gary and Phyllis authorized W&M to begin an advertising campaign on a new line of formal wear, someone at W&M would have to fill out another Job Authorization Form. That person could not use the same form that Nancy filled out for the Best in Southwest campaign. Having a separate authorization form for each job allows Martin and Nancy to track each job by its due date and to track costs by job rather than by client. They are able to keep a closer watch over their costs for each job and to see how actual costs compare to their original estimates.

Until now Nancy and Martin have tracked jobs manually, on paper. This has been a difficult and time-consuming process. With the new W&M database, however, Nancy and Martin can track jobs more easily and efficiently. The CLIENTS table, which Nancy already created, contains information about W&M's clients, but not about the jobs Nancy and Martin want to track. The W&M database must include a separate table relating specifically to jobs. This table will store all the data from each Job Authorization Form. Each record in the table will include the job number, client ID, types of advertising media, due date, description of job, and cost estimate (quote).

Using the information from the Job Authorization Form for the Southwest Styles job, Nancy has sketched the layout of the JOBS table, as shown in Figure 2-2.

JOBS

JOB_NO	CLIENT_ID	MEDIA	DUE_DATE	JOB_DESC	QUOTE
1001	503	Print	8/15/96	Best in Southwest	2,500.00

Figure 2-2
Sketch of JOBS table

In this tutorial you will create the JOBS table as part of the W&M database. Note, however, that you will name your table WMJOBS instead of JOBS because the completed JOBS table, which contains many records, already exists on your Student Disk. This way you would not have to enter all the data necessary to complete the table. In subsequent tutorials you will work with the completed JOBS table; in this tutorial you will work only with the WMJOBS table you create.

Guidelines for Designing a Database Table

Before you use any database software, you should plan and design the database table or tables you are going to build. If you plan first, your database is more likely to meet your expectations in solving your particular business problems.

Fields

When you design a database, follow these basic principles when defining fields:

- Identify the type of information users will need from the database. This will help you decide which data elements to track. For example, Martin and Nancy and their employees need information on their clients, the jobs their clients have authorized, and the costs associated with each job. Therefore, the completed W&M database will contain three tables: CLIENTS, JOBS, and EXPENSES.
- Group logically related fields in the same table. For example, the fields that contain the client ID, the client's name, the contact's name, and the client's phone number are data elements that describe clients and, therefore, are included in the CLIENTS table.
- If your database has more than one table, include common fields in those tables that are related. These fields act as connectors when you need to combine data from related tables. For example, the field CLIENT_ID is included in both the CLIENTS and JOBS tables and can be used to relate records in those tables. (You will work with related tables in Tutorial 4.)
- Avoid data redundancy. Include data elements in a way that eliminates the need to enter the same information many times in many files. For example, the company name, contact name, and phone number are not included in the JOBS table. These data elements are already stored in the CLIENTS table.

Key Fields and Indexes

It is important to be able to find specific records in a data table quickly and efficiently. For this reason, each record in a table must be unique. For example, it doesn't make sense to keep two records in the CLIENTS table that describe the same client. If records are duplicated, you begin to lose confidence in the accuracy of your data. It is also useful to be able to view records in whatever order suits your purpose. For example, you might want to view the records in a personnel table in order by employee Social Security number, by employee last name, or by date of hire.

To find records and to view them in a particular order, you must designate key fields for each table. A **key field** is a field whose values dBASE can use to search for, sort, and update the records in the table.

To help you avoid having duplicate records in a table, you should designate a key field known as the primary key. The **primary key** is the field or fields whose values uniquely identify each record in a table. In other words, the value in the primary key field (or fields) cannot be the same for two different records in the same table. A table that has a primary key is referred to as a **keyed table**. For example, a personnel table might use an employee's Social Security number as the primary key because no two employees can have the same Social Security number. Note that dBASE does not designate a field as the primary key; that is, it does not ensure that each value entered in a primary key field is, in fact, unique. However, your database design should include a primary key field so that you can avoid duplicate records.

Sometimes two or more fields are required to uniquely identify a record in a table. In such a case, the primary key is referred to as a **composite key**. For example, a table tracking an airline's flight schedule might use a combination of the flight number and date to form the primary key because flight numbers are often repeated several days a week.

dBASE also lets you designate other fields in a table as **alternate key fields**. For example, the employee name field might be a good choice for an alternate key. Although there is a possibility that employee names might not be unique, it would be useful to search a table by employee name or to see the records in alphabetical order by name. Like the primary key, an alternate key can be composed of two or more fields (a composite key).

You can designate as many key fields as you want for a table. For each key you create, dBASE creates an index. An **index** is a sorted list of the values in a key field. For each value in the list, dBASE records the position of the corresponding record in the table. As you add or delete records, dBASE updates each index. Because an index is always sorted, dBASE can search it quickly to find the information you want. After dBASE finds the appropriate key value in the index, it can retrieve the record immediately from the table. This method of searching for records is much more efficient than searching an unsorted table sequentially from beginning to end.

Indexes are also useful for viewing records in sorted order. For example, if you want to view employee records in order by Social Security number, you simply tell dBASE to use the Social Security number index as the master index. The **master index** controls the order in which records are displayed. At any time, you can designate another index as the master index. This makes it easy to view records in any order you want.

Although indexes are very convenient, they do require extra space in the memory of your computer and on the disk. Extra processing time is required to keep them updated as records are added, deleted, and edited. For these reasons, you should carefully choose which fields to designate as key fields. Each table should have a primary key and an alternate key for any field you will search frequently or for any field whose values you want to sort in a particular order.

Validating Data

Another important part of planning your database is ensuring that the data in the tables is accurate. A common complaint of users of computerized systems is that the data is inaccurate or inconsistent. The database must provide checks against inaccuracies. For example, a field storing the gender of an employee should be defined to contain only the letter "M" for male or "F" for female. Or, a field storing U.S. state abbreviations should not allow an abbreviation for a nonexistent state. Similarly, a field for age should have minimum and maximum limits, and a customer name field in a customer table should not be allowed to be left blank.

To ensure that data in tables is accurate, you must include a way to validate your data. In many database management systems, you can define validity checks that prevent incorrect data from being accepted into the database. **Validity checks** are criteria you can specify to limit the data values that are accepted into a table. In dBASE, you can define validity checks in two ways:

- By including validity checks as field properties of the Table Records window, you define rules that control the viewing and entry of data in the Table Records window. These validity checks are stored with the copy of dBASE installed on the computer you use when you define them. In other words, these validity check definitions are *not* stored with the table. You will define validity checks in this way in Tutorial 3.
- When you design a form for viewing, editing, and entering data, you can include validity checks for fields in the form. These validity checks apply to the form only and are recorded with the form description file. If you view or edit the data using a different form, the validity checks are not enforced. You will define validity checks in this way in Tutorial 5.

When you design a database table, you might want to define some rules that specify what values are acceptable in each field. The following are some of the questions you could consider:

- Should a value in this field be rejected if it is above or below an acceptable range? What is the minimum acceptable value? What is the maximum acceptable value?
- Should the contents of this field be restricted to only certain types of characters, such as uppercase letters or digits?
- Should the contents of this field have a specific format, such as three digits followed by a hyphen, followed by four digits?

In addition to following the basic guidelines for designing a database, you must also consider the rules of the database software you are using.

Rules for Creating a dBASE Table

When you design a table, you must decide on the fields to be included in a record, the type of data to be stored in each field, and for some fields, the amount of space to be allotted to the field. This information makes up the table's structure. dBASE has rules for naming fields and for handling data input to the tables. Let's look at these rules now.

Naming Fields

You've already seen that each table is made up of records. For example, the JOBS table will contain a record for each job W&M undertakes. Each of these records is made up of fields, and you must name each field. A **field name** identifies the data stored in each field. According to Nancy's sketch (see Figure 2-2), the fields in the JOBS table will be named JOB_NO, CLIENT_ID, MEDIA, DUE_DATE, JOB_DESC, and QUOTE. Field names help you work more easily with the data in a table.

The rules for naming fields in dBASE are as follows:
- A field name can be up to 10 characters long.
- A field name can contain letters, numbers, and underscores. Spaces are *not* allowed in a field name.
- A field name must start with a letter.
- A field name must be unique within a table, although it can be used again in another table.

Assigning Field Types

For each field, dBASE requires that you assign a **field type**, that is, the type of data the field can contain. Each field stores data based on only one field type. Your choice of field type determines how data is displayed on the screen, the kind of operations that can be performed on the data, and how much data the field can store.

The following is a description of the field types available in dBASE.

Character

The **character** field type is the most commonly used field type because it contains strings consisting of letters, numbers, blank spaces, and special symbols, such as + – % $ &. The contents of a character field can be anywhere from 1 to 254 characters in length.

Numeric

The **numeric** field type stores positive or negative numbers. The only characters permitted within a numeric field are the digits 0 to 9, a decimal point (.), a plus sign (+), and a minus sign (–). Parentheses, commas, and dollar signs are not permitted; however, you can add these as formatting options. You assign the numeric field type to fields that you want to use in calculations. A numeric field can store a number up to 20 digits in length (including the plus sign, minus sign, and decimal point).

Date

The **date** field type is used to store any valid date. The default format for dates is: MM/DD/YY (month, day, year). Dates stored using the date field type can be used in calculations. For example, suppose that the due date for a W&M job is 30 days after the job was authorized. This due date can be computed by adding 30 to the date the Job Authorization Form was signed. You could also store the date as a character field type, but then the date could not be used in calculations.

Logical

The **logical** field type stores a single character value indicating "true" or "false." For example, a personnel file might contain a logical field indicating whether an employee is a U.S. citizen. The value "Y" would indicate U.S. citizenship. The only legal values for a logical field are T or t (for True), Y or y (for Yes), F or f (for False), and N or n (for No). The values T, t, Y, and y are all equivalent, as are N, n, F, and f. A logical field cannot be indexed.

Memo

The **memo** field type stores large blocks of descriptive text. Although similar to the character field type, the memo field type is used for fields that must contain a large amount of text. For example, an abstract of a book or a medical diagnosis would be stored as a memo field type. A memo field cannot be indexed.

Binary

The **binary** field type stores data in a binary format, such as graphic images or digitized sound recordings. For example, an employee table might contain a binary field that displays the employee's picture. A binary field cannot be indexed.

Float

The **float** field type is the same as the numeric field type. It appears here for compatibility with older versions of dBASE. You should use the numeric field type.

OLE

The **OLE** (object linking and embedding) field type contains objects created in other Windows applications that support OLE, enabling you to use data from more than one program in a table. For example, a dBASE table could contain a field whose value is taken from a spreadsheet.

Determining Field Width

In dBASE, you must indicate the **field width**, or number of characters, for character and numeric field types. For some fields, deciding the width is a straightforward process. For example, W&M uses a combination of a letter and two digits as the client identification, so the width of the CLIENT_ID field is 3. On the other hand, job descriptions vary in length. So the length of the JOB_DESC field must be based on your knowledge of the data. Most descriptions are shorter than the Santa Fe Tourist Center's "4-page color ad in Southwest Magazine" description. Accordingly, a width of 40 characters for the JOB_DESC field should provide enough room to allow each entry to be meaningful.

You must also specify a field width for numeric fields, such as the QUOTE field in the JOBS table. Most of the quotes W&M has offered in the past are on the order of thousands or tens of thousands of dollars. So a field width that allows numbers up to 999999.99 should be adequate, specifically, a field width of 9 (six digits, the decimal point, two digits). dBASE predefines the width of date, logical, memo, binary and OLE fields.

Preparing a File Layout Sheet

When you design a database table, you should document the structure of the records you will include in the table by preparing a file layout sheet. A **file layout sheet** is a document that describes the field name, field type, and width of every field in a record. You can also use the file layout sheet to identify the key fields.

Nancy has prepared a file layout sheet for the JOBS table, as shown in Figure 2-3. Note that the JOB_NO field is the primary key for the JOBS table. Nancy and Martin know that each W&M job is assigned a unique number; therefore, the JOB_NO field is an appropriate choice for the primary key. (Remember, dBASE does not indicate which key field is the primary key; however, your table design should include a field or fields whose values will be unique, to avoid duplicate records.) The CLIENT_ID field is an alternate key. Also notice the number 2 in parentheses in the Width column for QUOTE; this identifies the number of decimal places for the QUOTE field. The number 9 represents the total width—that is, 6 digits, plus the decimal point, plus the two digits after the decimal point.

Field Name	Type	Width	Key
JOB_NO	Character	4	Yes (Ascend)
CLIENT_ID	Character	3	Yes (Ascend)
MEDIA	Character	9	
DUE_DATE	Date		
JOB_DESC	Character	40	
QUOTE	Numeric	9(2)	

Figure 2-3
File layout sheet for
the JOBS table

Using Nancy's file layout sheet as a reference, you can now create the JOBS table.

Creating a Table

Creating a dBASE table involves defining the fields of the table and saving the table structure. Let's start dBASE and then create the JOBS table.

Note: When you create the JOBS table in the following procedures, you need to do so in one work session; no breaks are included. Therefore, make sure you have enough time to finish creating the table—which takes you up to the section, "Modifying the Structure of a Table"—before you begin.

To start dBASE and create the JOBS table:
❶ Place your Student Disk in the disk drive.
❷ Start dBASE.
❸ Make sure the current directory is A:\WM.

TROUBLE? The current directory is displayed in the Current Directory text box of the Navigator window. If the current directory is not A:\WM, double-click in the Current Directory text box, then type A:\WM.

❹ Click the **Tables icon** in the Navigator window to display the list of tables in the current directory.

❺ Click **Untitled** in the current selection panel, then click the **Design button** 🖼️ on the SpeedBar. The Table Structure window appears. See Figure 2-4.

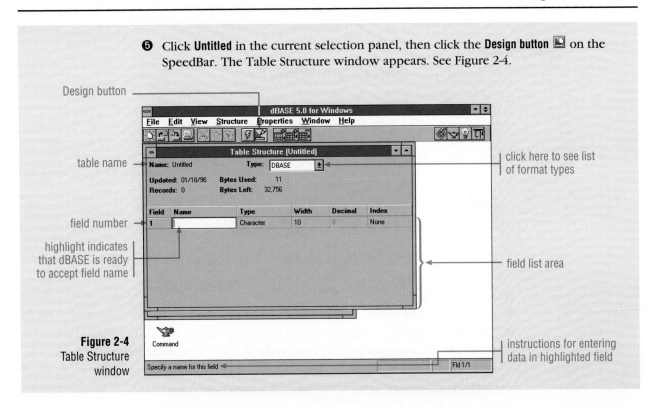

Design button

table name

field number

highlight indicates
that dBASE is ready
to accept field name

click here to see list
of format types

field list area

instructions for entering
data in highlighted field

Figure 2-4
Table Structure
window

The window contains two main areas. The upper area defines the characteristics of the table, including the table name and type. In this area you can select the type of database format for your table. The Type list box indicates that this table will use the dBASE format. Although you can create a table in a different format (a Paradox table), in this text you will create only dBASE for Windows tables. The lower area, called the field list area, defines the characteristics of the fields in the table. In this area you enter the definition of each field. Each row holds information about one field, including the field name, the field type, the width of the field, the number of decimal digits (for a numeric field), and whether you want to create an index for the field—in other words, make it a key. Note that dBASE assigns a field number to each field in the list.

As shown in Nancy's file layout sheet (Figure 2-3), the JOBS table will contain six fields: JOB_NO, CLIENT_ID, MEDIA, DUE_DATE, JOB_DESC, and QUOTE. You will use the information from the file layout sheet to define each field in the JOBS table.

Defining Fields

To define the fields of the table, you complete the following steps for each field:

1. Name the field.

2. Assign a field type.

3. Indicate the field width (for character and numeric fields only).

4. Specify if the field should be indexed (that is, if you want it to be a key field).

REFERENCE WINDOW

Creating a Table: Defining Fields

- In the Navigator window, click the Tables icon, click Untitled, then click the Design button on the SpeedBar to display the Table Structure window.

- Select the type of table you want to create from the Type list box.

- In the field list area of the Table Structure window, enter the field name, type, width, decimal, and index selection for each field, as appropriate.

The first field in Nancy's file layout sheet (Figure 2-3) is JOB_NO. Let's define this field.

To define the JOB_NO field:

❶ Click in the **Name column** for field number 1 (if necessary).

❷ Type **JOB_NO** then press **[Enter]** or **[Tab]**. The Type column is now highlighted. (Alternatively, you can click the **Type column** to move to it after entering the field name.) See Figure 2-5.

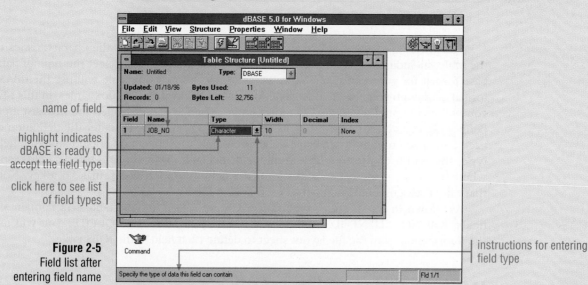

name of field

highlight indicates dBASE is ready to accept the field type

click here to see list of field types

instructions for entering field type

Figure 2-5
Field list after entering field name

TROUBLE? If you make a typing error, you can correct it by clicking in the field containing the error, then use [Backspace] or [Del] to remove the incorrect characters, then type the correct text and press [Enter].

Because the job numbers will not be used for calculations, you can assign the character field type instead of the number field type. This is the default type chosen for you automatically by dBASE. To see the list of available field types, you can click the Type list down arrow. See Figure 2-6.

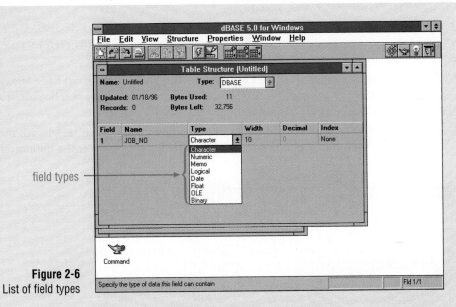

field types

Figure 2-6
List of field types

The Character field type is already selected.

❸ Press **[Enter]** to accept the selected field type (Character). Because you chose the Character field type, which requires that you specify the field width, the highlight now appears in the Width column. When you choose a field type that does not require a width, such as Date, dBASE skips the Width column.

Now enter the field width, the maximum number of characters the field can store. The default width for a character field is 10 characters, so 10 shows in the Width spin box when you select Character as the field type. You can change the width for a column by using the spin arrows to increase or decrease the value in the spin box, or you can double-click the current value and enter a new value. To use the spin arrows to set the field, click the up arrow to increase the width of the column, or click the down arrow to decrease the width. As shown in Figure 2-3, the width of the JOB_NO field is 4.

❹ Click the **down arrow** in the spin box until **4** is displayed, then press **[Enter]**. Because this field is not numeric, the highlight skips the Decimal column and moves to the Index column. See Figure 2-7.

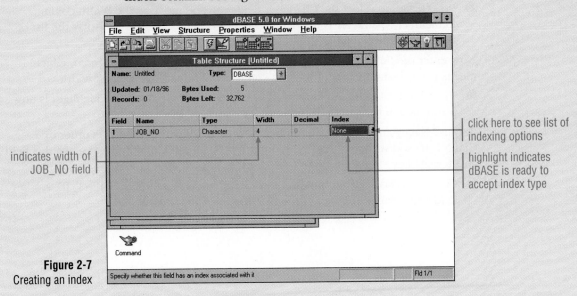

indicates width of
JOB_NO field

click here to see list of
indexing options

highlight indicates
dBASE is ready to
accept index type

Figure 2-7
Creating an index

As noted earlier, Nancy and Martin want the JOB_NO field to be the primary key for the JOBS table because each W&M job is assigned a unique number. Therefore, you need to specify this field as a key field.

❺ Click the **Index list down arrow**, then click **Ascend**. This identifies the field as a key field and creates an index for it. "Ascend" means that the job numbers will be sorted in ascending order. (You can also specify descending order.)

❻ Press **[Enter]**. The definition of the first field is complete, and the highlight advances to the Name column in the next row. dBASE waits for you to enter the definition of the second field. See Figure 2-8.

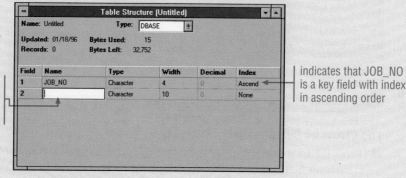

highlight indicates dBASE is ready for the name of the second field

indicates that JOB_NO is a key field with index in ascending order

Figure 2-8
Completed definition for JOB_NO

Nancy's file layout sheet shows that CLIENT_ID is the second field in the JOBS table. The CLIENT_ID field is a character field, and the width is 3. Let's define this second field.

To define the CLIENT_ID field:

❶ Type **CLIENT_ID** in the highlighted Name column, then press **[Enter]**. The highlight moves to the Type column.

W&M uses the first letter of the company name followed by a two-digit sequential number as the CLIENT_ID. So you will select Character as the field type for the CLIENT_ID field.

❷ Press **[Enter]** to select the Character field type and move to the Width column. Remember, Character is the default field type. You can always display the list of types available by clicking the list button.

Now enter the field width. Note that the default width is already selected, which means you can simply type the width you want to replace the default width.

❸ Type **3** to replace the default width of 10, then press **[Enter]**. The highlight is now positioned in the Index column.

Because Nancy and Martin will frequently want to view the records in order by CLIENT_ID and will be querying the table by CLIENT_ID, they want to make this field an alternate key.

❹ Click the **Index list down arrow**, then click **Ascend**. This specifies CLIENT_ID as a key field and creates an index of the field in ascending order.

❺ Press [Enter] to complete the definition of the CLIENT_ID field. The highlight advances to the next row, where you will enter the definition of the third field. See Figure 2-9.

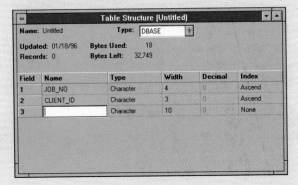

Figure 2-9
Table Structure
dialog box after
defining two fields

Using Nancy's file layout sheet in Figure 2-3, you can now complete the remaining field definitions.

To define the remaining fields of the JOBS table:
❶ Type **MEDIA** in the highlighted Name column, then press [Enter].
❷ Press [Enter] to select the Character field type and move to the Width column.
❸ Set the field width to **9**, then press [Enter] to move to the Index column.
Because you do not want to create an index for MEDIA, you can move to the next row.
❹ Press [Enter] to move to the Name column of the next row.
❺ Type **DUE_DATE** in the highlighted Name column, then press [Enter].
Because this field will contain date information, you will choose the Date field type. You could choose Character for the field, but then you would not be able to use the field in calculations or take advantage of the different date formats available to date field types.
❻ Click the **Type list down arrow** to display the list of field types.
❼ Click **Date** to select the Date field type, then press [Enter]. Notice that the highlight skips the Width column (the width of a date field type is fixed at 8 characters) and moves to the Index column. You do not want to create an index for the DUE_DATE field.
❽ Press [Enter] to move to the next row.
❾ Follow the same procedure to define the next field, JOB_DESC, which is a character field with a width of 40. Do not specify an index for this field.

To define the final field, QUOTE, which is a numeric field, you must specify both the width and the number of digits after the decimal point.

To define the QUOTE field:

❶ Type **QUOTE** in the highlighted Name column, then press **[Enter]**.

❷ Click the **Type list down arrow** to display the list of field types.

❸ Click **Numeric** to select the Numeric field type, then press **[Enter]**.

❹ Set the width to **9**, then press **[Enter]**.

The highlight is now in the Decimal column for the QUOTE field. This allows you to specify the number of digits you want to appear after the decimal point for all QUOTE field values. Because W&M's quotes are in dollars and cents, you will specify two digits after the decimal.

❺ Set Decimal to **2**, then press **[Enter]**.

❻ Press **[Enter]** to move the highlight from the Index column to the Name column of the next line.

Now that you have defined each field, the structure of the JOBS table is complete. Look at your screen. The Table Structure dialog box should be identical to the one in Figure 2-10.

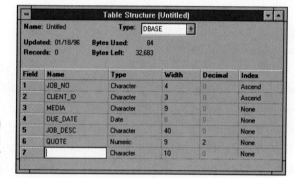

Figure 2-10
Table Structure
dialog box after
defining all six fields

Before saving the table structure, you should correct any errors you might have made in the field definitions.

Correcting Errors in the Field Definitions

If you make an error while dBASE is displaying the Table Structure dialog box, you can use one of the techniques listed in Figure 2-11 to correct it.

Type of Modification	Steps to Take
Correcting a field name, type, width, or decimal setting	Make sure the field you want to correct is highlighted, then click where you want to start correcting. Use [Backspace] or [Del] to remove characters. Type the correct text, then press [Enter].
Deleting a field	Click anywhere in the field definition of the field you want to delete, then click the Delete Field button on the SpeedBar.
Inserting a field	Click anywhere in the field definition above which you want the new field inserted, then click the Insert Field button on the SpeedBar. The fields below the point of insertion move down one row, and an empty row appears. Type the new field definition in the empty row.
Changing the order of fields	Move the pointer to the number of the field you want to move. The pointer changes to a hand. Click and drag the field definition to its new location, then release the mouse button.
Removing an index	Click the Index column for the field, click the Index list down arrow, then click None.
Starting over from scratch	Double-click the Control menu box for the Table Structure window, then click No when dBASE asks if you want to save the table structure.

Figure 2-11
Correcting errors in
the field definitions

Let's intentionally make an error in a field definition so that you can correct it. For example, suppose you change your mind and decide that you do not want to include the MEDIA field in the table. You can remove it from the field definitions. Let's try it.

To remove the MEDIA field definition from the field list:
❶ Click anywhere in the field definition for MEDIA.
❷ Click the **Delete Field button** 🖳 on the SpeedBar. The MEDIA field definition is removed from the field list. See Figure 2-12.

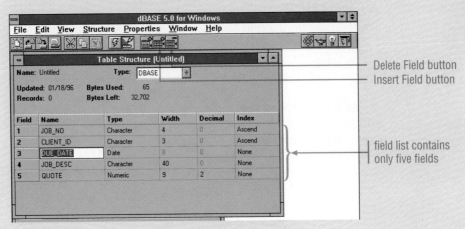

Figure 2-12
Field list after
deleting MEDIA field

Now insert the MEDIA field definition back into the field list.

❸ Click anywhere in the field definition for DUE_DATE (if necessary), then click the **Insert Field button** 📇 on the SpeedBar. An empty row is inserted above the DUE_DATE field, and the Name column is highlighted.

❹ Type **MEDIA** in the highlighted Name column, then press **[Enter]**.

❺ Press **[Enter]** to select Character and move to the Width column.

❻ Set the field width to **9**, then press **[Enter]** to move to the Index column.

❼ Press **[Enter]** to complete the field definition.

If you made any errors when you defined the fields for the JOBS table, make the necessary corrections now so that your field definitions match those shown in Figure 2-10.

Saving the Table Structure

The last step in creating a table is to name and save the table's structure on disk. Once the table structure is saved, you can use it to enter the data for the table.

When naming a table, it is best to choose a descriptive name that helps you identify the table's contents. For example, the names CLIENTS and JOBS are appropriate because they identify the data that W&M plans to store in these tables.

In dBASE, a table name can contain up to eight letters, numbers, and/or certain special characters, such as _ – $ % &. No spaces are permitted. This restriction is based on the eight-character limit for DOS filenames.

REFERENCE WINDOW

Saving the Table Structure

- Click File then click Save As... to display the Save Table dialog box.

- In the Save Table dialog box, type the name of the table in the File Name text box.

- Make sure the directory path indicates the correct disk and directory for saving the file.

- Click OK.

As mentioned at the beginning of this tutorial, you will use the name WMJOBS instead of JOBS for the table you save. This is because the completed JOBS table already exists on your Student Disk.

To name and save the table structure:

❶ Click **File** then click **Save As...**. The Save Table dialog box appears. See Figure 2-13. Any tables already saved in the current directory are listed in the file list. Notice that the JOBS.DBF table is listed. Also, notice that the File Name text box is highlighted, indicating that dBASE is ready for you to type the table name.

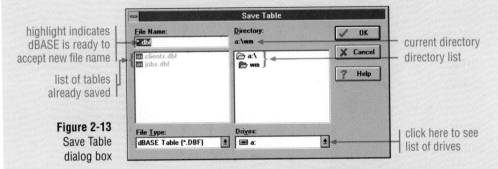

highlight indicates dBASE is ready to accept new file name

list of tables already saved

Figure 2-13
Save Table
dialog box

current directory
directory list

click here to see
list of drives

❷ In the File Name text box, type **wmjobs**.

The Save Table dialog box indicates the disk and directory where your table will be saved. The default entry is the current directory. Unless you specify otherwise, your table will be saved to the current directory. If the current directory is not where you want to store your table, double-click the correct directory name in the directory list.

❸ Click **OK**. The table's structure is saved to the current directory.

dBASE automatically added the extension ".DBF" to the WMJOBS filename. The table is stored on your Student Disk as the file WMJOBS.DBF. This file stores the structure of the table, as well as any data you enter in the table. dBASE might also create other files automatically, depending on the options selected in the Table Structure dialog box. In this case, dBASE created an additional file when you saved the WMJOBS.DBF file. That file, named WMJOBS.MDX, stores information about the indexes for the fields you specified as key fields.

If you no longer need a table or if its structure is incorrect and you want to start over, you can delete the table file. To delete a table, click the table name in the Navigator window, then press [Del]. The Delete Table dialog box appears to confirm that you want to delete the table. Click Yes to delete the table and the index file associated with it.

After you save the structure of the WMJOBS table, the Table Structure window is still open on the Desktop. To add records to the table, you must change to the Table Records window. Let's add a record to the table now. Figure 2-14 shows the Job Authorization Form for the first job. Let's enter this record in the WMJOBS table.

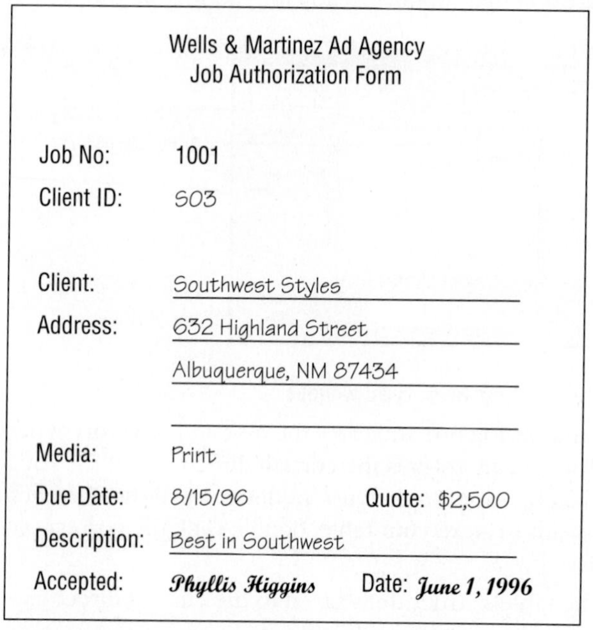

```
┌─────────────────────────────────────────────────────┐
│            Wells & Martinez Ad Agency                │
│               Job Authorization Form                 │
│                                                      │
│                                                      │
│     Job No:      1001                                │
│     Client ID:   S03                                 │
│                                                      │
│                                                      │
│     Client:      Southwest Styles                    │
│     Address:     632 Highland Street                 │
│                  Albuquerque, NM 87434               │
│                                                      │
│                                                      │
│     Media:       Print                               │
│     Due Date:    8/15/96          Quote: $2,500      │
│     Description: Best in Southwest                   │
│     Accepted:    Phyllis Higgins    Date: June 1, 1996│
└─────────────────────────────────────────────────────┘
```

Figure 2-14
Job Authorization
Form for the first job

Adding a Record to the WMJOBS Table

The Table Structure window allows you to define or modify the structure of a table. You cannot add, delete, or modify records using this window. To add a new record, change an existing record, or delete a record, you must change to the Table Records window.

To change to the Table Records window:

❶ Click the **Run Table button** 🗗 on the SpeedBar (or click **View** then click **Table Records**). The Table Records window displays the current contents of the WMJOBS table. Because this is a new table, no records are displayed. To add a record to the table, you must switch to Append mode.

❷ Click the **Add Record button** 🖽 on the SpeedBar to switch to Append mode. The first field, JOB_NO, is highlighted. See Figure 2-15.

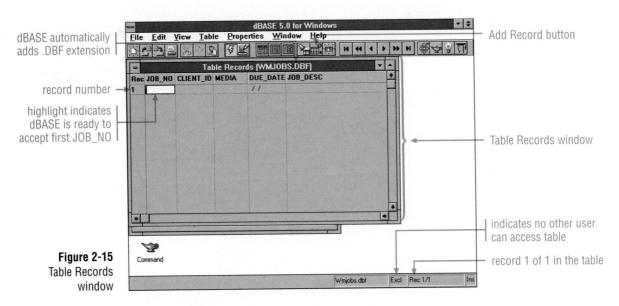

dBASE automatically adds .DBF extension

record number

highlight indicates dBASE is ready to accept first JOB_NO

Add Record button

Table Records window

indicates no other user can access table

record 1 of 1 in the table

Figure 2-15
Table Records window

The status bar indicates that you are editing the first record. The notation "Excl" in the status bar means that you have exclusive use of the table; no other users can access the table at this time. More than one user can access the same database table if the users' systems are connected in a network environment. dBASE excludes others from using the table until you close the Table Structure window.

Now that you are in Append mode, you can enter information in the table by typing a value in each field. Let's add the record for the first job using Figure 2-14 for reference.

To add the first record:

❶ Type **1001** *but do not press [Enter]*. dBASE beeps to let you know that you have filled the field, and the highlight moves to the CLIENT_ID field. If you press [Enter] after typing an entry that fills a field, the highlight will skip the next field, so make sure that you do not press [Enter] after typing the job number.

TROUBLE? If you make a typing error before you fill the field, use [Backspace] to erase characters. If you have filled the field and moved to the next field, click the field you want to change so that you can retype the entry.

TROUBLE? If you pressed [Enter] after typing the job number, the highlight skips the CLIENT_ID field. Click in the CLIENT_ID field, then continue with the tutorial.

❷ In the CLIENT_ID field, type **S03**. The highlight moves to the MEDIA field.

❸ Type **Print**. Because this entry doesn't fill the field (which can hold up to 9 characters), you must press [Enter] to move to the next field.

❹ Press **[Enter]** to move to the DUE_DATE field. When typing the value for a date field, you type only the numbers; dBASE automatically fills in separators (such as the slash, /). Also, when typing the number for a one-digit month (such as "8" for August), you must include a 0 (as in "08") in order for dBASE to accept the entry.

❺ In the DUE_DATE field, type **081596**. Notice that dBASE automatically separates the month, day, and year with slashes (/). The highlight moves to the JOB_DESC field, and the window scrolls to the right.

⑥ Type **Best in Southwest** then press **[Enter]**. The highlight moves to the QUOTE field.

⑦ Type **2500** then press **[Enter]**. The highlight moves to a new blank record. See Figure 2-16.

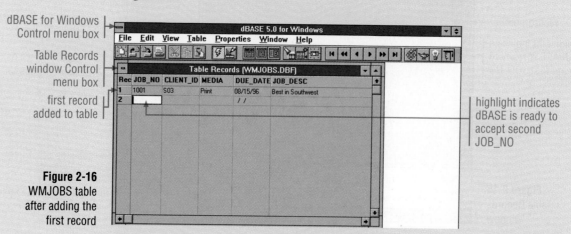

dBASE for Windows Control menu box

Table Records window Control menu box

first record added to table

highlight indicates dBASE is ready to accept second JOB_NO

Figure 2-16
WMJOBS table after adding the first record

Once you press [Enter] after completing the last field of any record, the record is stored. In this case, the record you entered is stored in the WMJOBS.DBF file in the current directory.

The QUOTE field is not currently visible on the screen. Let's scroll the window to view the QUOTE field value.

⑧ Click the **right arrow** on the horizontal scroll bar to scroll to the right until you see the QUOTE field. Notice that the data in the QUOTE field automatically appears with two decimal places, as specified in the field definition.

⑨ Click the **left arrow** on the horizontal scroll bar to display the JOB_NO field again.

Because there was only one record to add, you can close the table.

To close the WMJOBS table:

① Double-click the **Control menu box** for the Table Records window. See Figure 2-16 for the location of this Control menu box. *Do not double-click the dBASE for Windows Control menu box (in the upper-left corner of your screen)*, or you will exit dBASE. The WMJOBS table closes, and the Navigator window appears on the Desktop.

TROUBLE? If you accidentally double-clicked the dBASE for Windows Control menu box and exited dBASE, don't worry. dBASE closes the table automatically when you exit.

If you want to take a break and resume the tutorial at a later time, you can exit dBASE by double-clicking the dBASE for Windows Control menu box. When you resume the tutorial, make sure your Student Disk is in the disk drive, start dBASE, make sure the current directory is A:\WM, then continue with the tutorial.

After reviewing the structure of the JOBS table, Martin realizes that it would be helpful if the table indicated which jobs were completed. The current structure of the table has no field to enable users to distinguish between completed jobs and on-going jobs. Martin asks Nancy if there is any way to add a field to the table. Nancy informs Martin that dBASE does allow you to change the table's structure, and she asks you to modify the table to add the new field.

Modifying the Structure of a Table

Perhaps the data you originally planned for your database will not adequately handle a particular business problem. Or, perhaps a field is not long enough to store certain data values. You can return to the Table Structure window to change the structure of the table. In this way, you can add and delete fields and change a field's name, type, or width.

Martin wants to add a field to the JOBS table that will indicate which jobs are completed. Nancy modifies her original file layout sheet, as shown in Figure 2-17, to include a new field called COMPLETED after the QUOTE field.

Field Name	Type	Width	Key
JOB_NO	Character	4	Yes (Ascend)
CLIENT_ID	Character	3	Yes (Ascend)
MEDIA	Character	9	
DUE_DATE	Date		
JOB_DESC	Character	40	
QUOTE	Numeric	9(2)	
COMPLETED	Logical		

Figure 2-17
Modified file layout
sheet for the JOBS table

The COMPLETED field will use the value Y to indicate that a job is complete, and the value N to indicate that a job is not complete. Therefore, the COMPLETED field can be defined as a logical field type.

REFERENCE WINDOW

Modifying a Table's Structure

- Make sure the table you want to modify is open.
- Click the Design button on the SpeedBar.
- Click Open Exclusive in the Table Not Exclusive dialog box.
- Make the modifications you want to the table's structure.
- Click File then click Save to save the new structure.

You'll use the Design button to add the COMPLETED field to the WMJOBS table. Remember, the finished JOBS table, which includes the COMPLETED field, is already on your Student Disk so that you can work with it in later tutorials.

To add the COMPLETED field to the WMJOBS table:

❶ From the dBASE Desktop, click the **Tables icon** in the Navigator window to display the list of files in the current directory.

❷ Double-click **Wmjobs.dbf** in the current selection panel to open the WMJOBS table. The Table Records window for the WMJOBS table appears.

❸ Click the **Design button** 🖼 on the SpeedBar. dBASE displays the Table Not Exclusive dialog box, which notifies you that you must have exclusive access to the table in order to modify its structure. See Figure 2-18. This prevents other users (in a networked environment) from using the table while you are modifying its structure. This issue is only relevant in a networked environment.

Figure 2-18
Table Not Exclusive
dialog box

❹ Click **Open Exclusive** in the Table Not Exclusive dialog box. The current structure of the WMJOBS table appears in the Table Structure window. See Figure 2-19.

Add Field button —

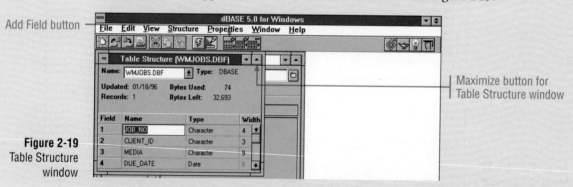

Maximize button for
Table Structure window

Figure 2-19
Table Structure
window

Now you can add the new field to the table's structure. You'll add the COMPLETED field after QUOTE, the last field in the table.

❺ Click the **Maximize button** on the Table Structure window to see the complete table structure.

❻ Click the **Add Field button** 🖼 on the SpeedBar. An empty row for field 7 appears in the field list. See Figure 2-20.

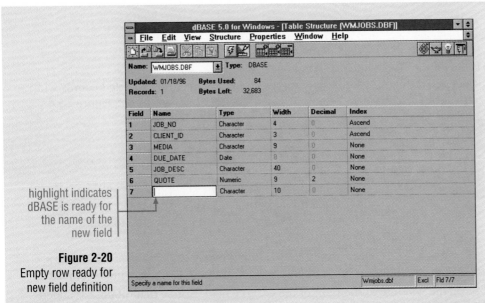

highlight indicates
dBASE is ready for
the name of the
new field

Figure 2-20
Empty row ready for
new field definition

TROUBLE? If an empty row appears at the top of the field list instead of at the bottom, you probably clicked the Insert Field button ▦ instead of the Add Field button ▦. To delete the empty row at the top of the field list, position the pointer in the row, then click the Delete Field button ▦ on the SpeedBar and repeat Step 6.

❼ Type **COMPLETED** in the Name column, then press **[Enter]**. The highlight advances to the Type column.

❽ Click the **Type list down arrow** to display the list of field types.

❾ Click **Logical** then press **[Enter]**. Because a logical field type has a fixed width and cannot be indexed, this completes the definition of the COMPLETED field. A new row appears below the row containing the COMPLETED field.

Look at the Table Structure window on your screen. It should look like Figure 2-21. If it does not, move to the COMPLETED field definition and make the appropriate corrections. You can use any of the methods listed in Figure 2-11 to make corrections.

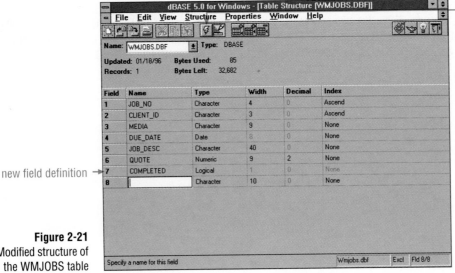

— Run Table button

new field definition →

Figure 2-21
Modified structure of
the WMJOBS table

Now let's view the modified table in the Table Records window.

To switch to the Table Records window:

❶ Click the **Run Table button** 🗲 on the SpeedBar to switch to the Table Records window. The Changes Made - Table Structure dialog box appears. See Figure 2-22.

Figure 2-22
Changes Made -
Table Structure
dialog box

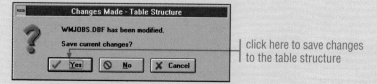

click here to save changes
to the table structure

Because you changed the structure of the table, dBASE asks you to confirm that you want the changes recorded.

❷ Click **Yes** in the Changes Made - Table Structure dialog box to save the changes. dBASE records the new table structure, and the Table Records window appears.

❸ Scroll the window to the right of the QUOTE field. Notice that dBASE has added the COMPLETED field to the existing record and entered a value of N for this field. This is because N is the default value for a logical field. You can change this value; however, in this case, the record is for a new job, so the value N is appropriate.

❹ Click the **Restore button** in the upper-right corner of the Table Records window to restore the window to its original size.

You've completed your work in dBASE for the moment, so you can close the WMJOBS table and exit dBASE.

To close the table and exit dBASE:

❶ Double-click the **Control menu box** for the Table Records window to close it.

❷ Double-click the **Control menu box** for the dBASE window (or click **File** then click **Exit**) to exit dBASE.

Figure 2-23 shows what has taken place on your Student Disk. You stored WMJOBS.DBF on your Student Disk, but you changed its structure from that of the original database table. Your new version includes the COMPLETED field.

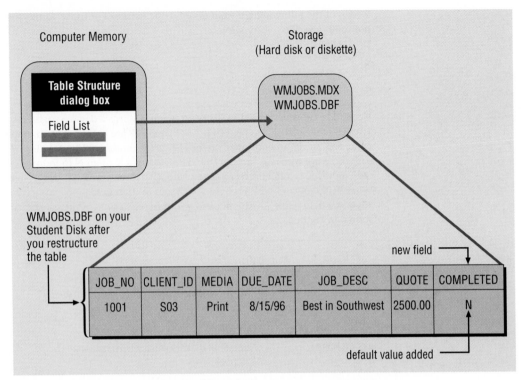

Figure 2-23
After modifying the
WMJOBS table
structure

Martin and Nancy are pleased with the addition of the JOBS table to the W&M database. They know that the JOBS table will help them track jobs and monitor their associated costs more efficiently.

Questions

1. Which of the following are valid dBASE field names? For those names that are not valid, give the reason why.
   a. CUST#
   b. CUSTOMER_NUMBER
   c. CUSTOMER
   d. CUST->NUM
   e. CUST{95}
   f. 1STQTR
   g. PERIOD[1]
   h. #
   i. NET PROFIT(LOSS)
2. What field type(s) can be used for arithmetic operations?
3. Jim defines a phone number using the numeric field type, with a field width of 10 digits (zero after the decimal). Frank defines a phone number using the character field type, specifying a width of 14. Which method is preferable, and why? How would each enter phone numbers? Give an example of a phone number that Jim would enter. Give an example of a phone number that Frank would enter.
4. What is the purpose of creating an index for a field?

5. Which of the following are valid dBASE table names? For those names that are not valid, give the reason why.
   a. SALES HISTORY
   b. SALES95
   c. 95SALES
   d. SALESHISTORY
   e. SALES
6. What file extension does dBASE assign when it stores a database table?
7. The fields SSN, HIRE_DATE, FULL_TIME, and ZIP are included in an employee table. SSN stores an employee's Social Security number, HIRE_DATE stores the date the employee was hired, FULL_TIME stores a Y or an N to indicate whether the employee is a full-time employee, and ZIP stores the employee's zip code. What field type and width would you assign to each field?
8. Suggest a field name, field type, and width for each field in the inventory file shown in Figure 2-24.

Field	Description
Product ID	First two characters are letters, next two are numbers
Product Name	Longest name is 30 characters
Units on Hand	Number of units is usually between 0 and 325 (inclusive)
Unit Price	Highest price is $55.00
Date of Last Sale	
Taxable Item	Values are Yes and No

Figure 2-24

Place your Student Disk in the disk drive, start dBASE, and set the working directory to A:\PRACTICE. Then answer Questions 9 and 10.

9. Determine the structure of the GRANT1.DBF table. Fill in the file layout sheet below for each field.

Field Name	Type	Width	Key

10. Modify the structure of the GRANT1.DBF table:
    a. Change the field name LOG_ID to GRANT_ID.
    b. Insert a new field, DEPARTMENT, between the TITLE and GRANTEE fields. The field type for DEPARTMENT is character, and the field width is 25.
    c. Save the table as GRANT2.DBF.

E 11. Figure 2-25 represents a structure for a table intended to keep track of employee skills.

Field Name	Type	Width
EMP_ID	C	5
EMP_NAME	C	20
DEPARTMENT	C	20
JOB_TITLE	C	20
SKILL1	C	25
SKILL2	C	25
SKILL3	C	25
SKILL4	C	25
SKILL5	C	25

Figure 2-25

  a. Using Figure 2-23 as a guide, make a sketch of this structure. Include two records in the table as test data.

  b. List any problems users might encounter with data entry, queries, or reports using this structure.

  c. Suggest an alternative structure. Sketch your new structure and include the test data you entered in Question 11-a.

  d. What advantages does your new structure have over the original structure with regard to data entry, queries, and reports?

E   12. The dBASE Help system provides short, easy-to-understand lessons, called Tutors, that help you work step-by-step through common dBASE tasks. From the dBASE Desktop, click Help, then click Interactive Tutors to begin working with the Tutors. Explore all of the Tutors in the "Building a Database" category.

Tutorial Assignments

Place your Student Disk in the disk drive, start dBASE, and set the working directory to A:\WM.

1. Determine the structure of the CLIENTS table. Fill in the file layout sheet below for each field.

   Field Name   Type   Width   Key

2. Create an EXPENSES table for the third table in the W&M database system. Each record in this table will represent an expense that W&M has incurred for a client, and each expense will be assigned to a specific category. Figure 2-26 shows the file layout sheet for the EXPENSES table.

Field Name	Type	Width	Key
TRANS_NO	C	5	Yes (Ascend)
JOB_NO	C	4	Yes (Ascend)
EXPNS_CODE	C	3	
EXPNS_DATE	D		
AMOUNT	N	9(2)	
EXPNS_DESC	C	30	

Figure 2-26

3. Save the table as EXPENSES.
4. Add the expenses shown in Figure 2-27 to the EXPENSES table.

	Record 1	Record 2	Record 3
TRANS_NO	00001	00002	00003
JOB_NO	1001	1001	1001
EXPNS_CODE	002	004	002
EXPNS_DATE	7/19/96	7/19/96	7/20/96
AMOUNT	210.00	94.00	125.75
EXPNS_DESC	Meeting	Artwork	Meeting

Figure 2-27

5. Print the contents of the EXPENSES table. (Refer to Tutorial 1 if you need to review printing.)
6. Modify the EXPENSES table structure to change the field name EXPNS_CODE to CATEGORY.
7. Save and close the EXPENSES table.
 8. Explore the dBASE Help system to become more familiar with database terms and concepts. From the Help menu, choose Contents. Then use the Glossary to find definitions for the following: append, data type, field, key field, record, and table.

Case Problems

1. Inventory of State-owned Land

Malcolm Fiere works in the State Division of Planning in Rhode Island. This state agency is responsible for tracking all parcels of land owned by the state. Malcolm has just been assigned the task of setting up a database using dBASE. This database will consist of two tables: LNDUSE, which will store data identifying the parcels of land; and STATELND, which will store more descriptive data about the land. Use dBASE to create the two tables in the database.

Place your Student Disk in the disk drive, start dBASE, and set the working directory to A:\LAND.

1. Create a table named LNDUSE using the file layout sheet shown in Figure 2-28.

Field Name	Type	Width	Key
USE_CODE	C	2	Yes (Ascend)
USE_DESC	C	30	

Figure 2-28

2. After you create the table structure, add the data shown in Figure 2-29.

Figure 2-29

USE_CODE	USE_DESC
01	Institutional

3. Create a table named STATELND using the file layout sheet in Figure 2-30.

Field Name	Type	Width	Key
LAND_ID	C	4	Yes (Ascend)
DIVISION	C	25	
USE_CODE	C	2	
ACQUIRED	N	4(0)	
ACREAGE	N	10(1)	
VALUE	N	12(2)	
LAND_DESC	C	30	

Figure 2-30

4. After you create the table structure, add the data shown in Figure 2-31.

LAND_ID	DIVISION	USE_CODE	ACQUIRED	ACREAGE	VALUE	LAND_DESC
0001	Administration	03	1971	16.5	5000000	State House

Figure 2-31

5. Modify the structure of the STATELND table to increase the width of the DIVISION field from 25 to 40 characters. Save the table.
6. Print the LNDUSE and STATELND tables. Close both tables.

E 7. You're considering changing the name of the ACQUIRED field in the STATELND table and changing its width at the same time. Explore the dBASE Help system to see if this is a good idea. Use the Search dialog box to find information on modifying file structures, and look at the rules for modifying table structures. Why should you be careful about making more than one change at a time to a table's structure?

2. FINSTAT Inc.

FINSTAT Inc., an electronic information service, provides financial information to its clients. One of the databases it offers contains financial data on the leading U.S. corporations for the past several years. This database consists of two tables: COMPANY, which stores general data about each company, and FINANCE, which tracks the yearly financial data for each company. Using dBASE, create the two tables for the FINSTAT database.

Place your Student Disk in the disk drive, start dBASE, and set the working directory to A:\FINANCE.

1. Create a table named COMPANY using the file layout sheet shown in Figure 2-32.

Field Name	Type	Width	Key
COMPANY_ID	C	3	Yes (Ascend)
COMP_NAME	C	30	Yes (Ascend)
INDUSTRY	C	2	
SYMBOL	C	6	Yes (Ascend)

Figure 2-32

2. After you create the structure, add the data shown in Figure 2-33. Save the table.

	Record 1	Record 2
COMPANY_ID	C01	G01
COMP_NAME	Chrysler	General Motors
INDUSTRY	CA	CA

Figure 2-33

3. Print the COMPANY table, then close it.
4. Create a table named FINANCE using the file layout sheet shown in Figure 2-34.

Field Name	Type	Width	Key
COMPANY_ID	C	3	Yes (Ascend)
YEAR	N	4(0)	Yes (Ascend)
SALES	N	6(0)	
ASSETS	N	6(0)	

Note: Values for sales and assets are rounded to the nearest million.

Figure 2-34

5. After you create the structure, add the data shown in Figure 2-35.

	Record 1	Record 2
COMPANY_ID	C01	G01
YEAR	1992	1992
SALES	25501	132429
ASSETS	40653	185115

Figure 2-35

6. Add a new field named PROFITS at the end of the FINANCE table. Assign the numeric field type to the PROFITS field. Values for profits are rounded to the nearest million. Allow for values up to 10 billion dollars. Save the table.
7. Print the FINANCE table, then close it.
8. Use the Search dialog box in dBASE's Help system to search for the word "tables." Explore the topic "About Tables" and the underlined topic "Table Design Guidelines." In your own words, summarize the guidelines for designing a table.

3.   Marine Diving Equipment, Inc.

Marine Diving Equipment, Inc. sells diving supplies to dive shops around the world. Using dBASE, create a database containing two tables: the CUST table, which stores data about Marine Diving Equipment's customers, and the ORD table, which stores data about customer orders for the company.

Place your Student Disk in the disk drive, start dBASE, and set the working directory to A:\MARINE.

1. Create a table named CUST using the file layout sheet shown in Figure 2-36.

Field Name	Type	Width	Key
CUST_NO	C	4	Yes (Ascend)
CUST_NAME	C	30	Yes (Ascend)
STREET	C	30	
CITY	C	15	
ST_OR_PROV	C	20	
POST_CODE	C	10	
COUNTRY	C	20	
PHONE	C	15	
CONT_DATE	D		

Figure 2-36

2. After you create the table structure, add the data shown in Figure 2-37.

Field Name	Record 1	Record 2
CUST_NO	1221	1231
CUST_NAME	Kauai Dive Shoppe	Unisco
STREET	4-976 Sugarloaf Hwy	PO Box z-547
CITY	Kapaa Kauai	Freeport
ST_OR_PROV	HI	
POST_CODE	94766	
COUNTRY	U.S.A.	Bahamas
PHONE	808-555-0269	809-555-3915
CONT_DATE	04/03/90	02/28/91

Figure 2-37

3. Create a table named ORD using the file layout sheet shown in Figure 2-38.

Field Name	Type	Width	Key
ORD_NO	C	4	Yes (Ascend)
CUST_NO	C	4	Yes (Ascend)
SALE_DATE	D		
SHIP_VIA	C	7	
INV_AMT	N	10(2)	
AMT_PAID	N	10(2)	

Figure 2-38

4. After you create the table structure, add the data shown in Figure 2-39.

	Record 1	Record 2
ORD_NO	1001	1002
CUST_NO	1221	1231
SALE_DATE	04/03/88	04/05/88
SHIP_VIA	UPS	FedEx
INV_AMT	7320	10154
AMT_PAID	7320	10154

Figure 2-39

5. Modify the structure of the ORD table to add a new field named PAY_METHOD. The PAY_METHOD field will be a 7-character field. Add this field after the AMT_PAID field. Save the table.
6. Print the CUST and ORD tables. Close both tables.

E 7. Use the Search dialog box in dBASE's Help system to search for the topic "backup files." Read the entire topic "Using the Table Designer—Overview." What files does dBASE automatically make backup copies of? Why do you need to have exclusive use of a table?

4. Teaching Activity

Sandy Kruck, assistant dean at a local university, has created a database to track faculty members and the courses they teach. The university has a centralized system that keeps track of faculty, courses in the catalog, and the courses faculty members have taught, but Sandy has been frustrated because each of her requests for information has been met with excuses or delays. Out of necessity, she designs a system to capture the data she needs. The database consists of three tables: FACULTY, which stores one record per faculty member; COURSES, which stores one record for each course offered at the university; and TEACH, which stores one record for each section a faculty member has taught. Using dBASE, create the three tables for the Teaching Activity database.

Place your Student Disk in the disk drive, start dBASE, and set the working directory to A:\TEACH.

1. Create a table named FACULTY using the file layout sheet shown in Figure 2-40.

Field Name	Type	Width	Key
FAC_ID	C	3	Yes (Ascend)
LAST_NAME	C	15	Yes (Ascend)
FIRST_NAME	C	12	
RANK	C	4	
DEPT	C	3	
SALARY	N	9(2)	

Figure 2-40

2. After you create the table structure, add the data shown in Figure 2-41.

	Record 1	Record 2
FAC_ID	A10	C10
LAST_NAME	ABLE	COHEN
FIRST_NAME	RON	SIMON
RANK	ASST	ASST
DEPT	MGS	MGS
SALARY	55500	53000

Figure 2-41

3. Create a table named COURSES using the file layout sheet shown in Figure 2-42.

Field Name	Type	Width	Key
COURSE_NO	C	6	Yes (Ascend)
TITLE	C	30	Yes (Ascend)
DEPT	C	3	

Figure 2-42

4. After you create the table structure, add the data shown in Figure 2-43.

COURSE_NO	TITLE	DEPT
MGS207	INTRO TO COMPUTING	MGS
MGS306	ADV QUANT METHODS	MGS

Figure 2-43

5. Create a table named TEACH using the file layout sheet shown in Figure 2-44.

Field Name	Type	Width	Key
FAC_ID	C	3	Yes (Ascend)
COURSE_NO	C	6	Yes (Ascend)
SECTION	C	2	Yes (Ascend)
YEAR	N	4(0)	Yes (Ascend)
TERM	C	1	Yes (Ascend)
ENROLLMENT	N	3(0)	

Figure 2-44

6. After you create the table structure, add the data shown in Figure 2-45.

FAC_ID	COURSE_NO	SECTION	YEAR	TERM	ENROLLMENT
A10	MGS306	01	1992	F	37
A10	MGS306	02	1992	F	32

Figure 2-45

7. Print the TEACH table, then close it.
8. Modify the structure of the FACULTY table to include a new field named YEAR_HIRED. The new field will be a numeric field with 4 digits after the decimal. Insert the YEAR_HIRED field between the DEPT and SALARY fields. Save the table.
9. Print the FACULTY table, then close it.

E 10. Why does it take five fields to form the primary key in the TEACH table? Give some examples of teaching assignments that support the need for five fields. Recall that the primary key must uniquely identify the records in a table, and that it may comprise more than one field. Explore the dBASE Help system to read about the distinction between simple indexes and complex indexes.

E 5. CD-ROMS Inc.

Place your Student Disk in the disk drive, start dBASE, and set the working directory to A:\PRACTICE.

CD-ROMS Inc. is a specialty software store selling software that is available only on CD-ROM. Figure 2-46 is a sample invoice the company generates from its computerized invoicing system. Based on Figure 2-46, design the database tables that CD-ROMS Inc. might have used to prepare this invoice. For each table, fill out a file layout sheet with the column headings "Field Name," "Type," "Width," and "Key" (as in Figure 2-44). Use dBASE to create the tables.

```
                        CD-ROMS INC.                    Page 1
                    24 BLUEBERRY HILL RD
                    WINDHAM, NH 03087
                       (603)  888-8049
                    FAX # : (603)888-3007




                    * * * * * INVOICE * * * * *


        Customer # : SAL                    Invoice # : 30009

        Purch Ord # : 101
        Salesperson : LARRY                 Bill Date : 5/28/96
        Shipped VIA : UPS                   Ship Date : 5/28/96

        BILL TO:                      SHIP TO :

           Kim Sally                     Kim Sally
           802 Main Street               802 Main Street
           Cranston, RI 02889-6000       Cranston, RI 02889-6000
```

Qty Ord	Item Code	Item Description	Qty Ship	Item Cost	Exp Amount
1	VGT7GV1	The Seventh Guest	1	55.00	55.00
1	CMPIAENDY	Comptons Interactive Ency	1	99.00	99.00
1	LORGEXP	Global Explorer	1	89.00	89.00
1	TWANMPC	The Animals MPC	1	22.00	22.00
1	MAYO	Mayo Clinic MPC	1	27.00	27.00
1	CMPGA	Grammy Awards 1995	1	22.00	22.00
1	CQUEST	Composer Quest	1	39.00	39.00

```
                            Subtotal          353.00
                            Sales Tax           24.70
                            Freight Charges      5.00
                            Please Remit      $382.70
```

Figure 2-46

Maintaining a Database

Updating the CLIENTS and JOBS Tables

OBJECTIVES

In this tutorial you will:

- Add records using Browse layout, Form layout, and Columnar layout
- Specify the master index to change the order in which records are displayed
- Edit records using Columnar layout
- Define validity checks
- Handle validity check violations
- Search for records within a table
- Delete a record
- Make a backup copy of a table

CASE **Wells & Martinez Advertising Agency**
After you created the JOBS table, Martin and Nancy entered the data from all the Job Authorization Forms they had. Therefore, to this point, the CLIENTS and JOBS tables of the W&M database are current and complete.

Nancy also filled out file layout sheets for the CLIENTS and JOBS table structures and placed them in a folder for easy reference (Figures 3-1 and 3-2 on the following page). Keeping file layout sheets for the tables will help the other W&M employees understand the structure of the tables and how to use them to enter and modify data.

Field Name	Type	Width	Key
CLIENT_ID	Character	3	Yes (Ascend)
NAME	Character	25	Yes (Ascend)
CONTACT	Character	20	
PHONE	Character	13	
FAX	Character	13	
STREET	Character	20	
CITY	Character	11	
STATE	Character	2	
ZIP	Character	5	

Figure 3-1
File layout sheet for
the CLIENTS table

Field Name	Type	Width	Key
JOB_NO	Character	4	Yes (Ascend)
CLIENT_ID	Character	3	Yes (Ascend)
MEDIA	Character	9	
DUE_DATE	Date		
JOB_DESC	Character	40	
QUOTE	Numeric	9(2)	
COMPLETED	Logical		

Figure 3-2
File layout sheet for
the JOBS table

Today, Nancy and Martin hold a staff meeting to let the employees know what's going on at W&M.

The meeting starts on time, and as usual, Martin begins by reporting any good news or success stories. Martin is happy to announce that W&M's marketing campaign has brought in two new clients: a local restaurant chain, Taco Heaven, and a retail shop that specializes in custom-made goose down comforters, Peaches & Ice. Taco Heaven has given W&M approval to start planning an advertising campaign. Peaches & Ice has signed on as a W&M client but has not yet authorized W&M to begin a job.

Martin then informs everyone that despite W&M's efforts, one of their clients, Eyes Have It, a specialty eyeglass store, has gone out of business.

Finally Martin asks if there are any other announcements. Nancy doesn't have any announcements, but she wonders if anyone has recently heard from Gunther Williams—W&M's contact person at Mountain Top Ski Resort. Ann Lightfeather responds that the owner of Mountain Top Ski Resort called yesterday and told her that Gunther had resigned and Victor Juarez had taken over for him. Victor's phone number is (505)783-6220.

After the meeting, Martin stops by your office to give you the changes that need to be made to the W&M database. He gives you three items: a note with the client information for the two new clients, another note with the changes to the Mountain Top Ski Resort record, and the Job Authorization Form for Taco Heaven (Figure 3-3).

New client info:

Client ID: P01	Client ID: T01
Name: Peaches & Ice	Name: Taco Heaven
Contact: Alice Beaumont	Contact: Bert Clinton
Phone: (505)728-5176	Phone: (505)728-1295
Fax: (505)728-9911	Fax: (505)728-1595

Address: 101 Canyon Drive
        Santa Fe, NM 87501
	Address: 1065 El Hombre Drive,
	        Santa Fe, NM 87501

Changes for Mountain Top Ski Resort:

New Contact: Victor Juarez

New Phone: (505)783-6220

Wells & Martinez Ad Agency
Job Authorization Form

Job No: 1041

Client ID: T01

Client: Taco Heaven

Address: 1065 El Hombre Drive

             Santa Fe, NM 87501

Media: Broadcast

Due Date: 12/15/95   Quote: $14,000

Description: TV Ad

Accepted: *Bert Clinton*   Date: *10/1/95*

Figure 3-3
Changes to
W&M's database

What do all the changes in Figure 3-3 have in common? They affect the accuracy of the data in the W&M database. W&M, like any other business, must keep the contents of its database tables up to date and accurate so that the output from the tables is meaningful and helpful in making business decisions.

Using dBASE, you'll make the changes necessary to keep the W&M database up to date.

Updating Database Tables

Database maintenance—adding, changing, and deleting records—is a basic function you must perform when you have a DBMS. In this tutorial you will learn how to use a variety of dBASE commands and features to update your database tables.

First, you need to start dBASE.

To start dBASE and set the current directory:

❶ Place your Student Disk in the disk drive.

❷ Start dBASE.

❸ Make sure the current directory is A:\WM.

You will begin by adding the two new clients to the CLIENTS table. As discussed in Tutorial 1, before you can view, add, modify, or delete data in a table, the table must be open. So, let's open the CLIENTS table.

To open the CLIENTS table:

❶ Click the **Tables icon** in the Navigator window to display the list of tables in the current directory (if necessary).

❷ Double-click **Clients.dbf** to open the CLIENTS table. dBASE displays the contents of the CLIENTS table in the Table Records window. The status bar indicates that there are 25 records in the table.

❸ Click the **Maximize button** on the Table Records window to display more of the data. See Figure 3-4.

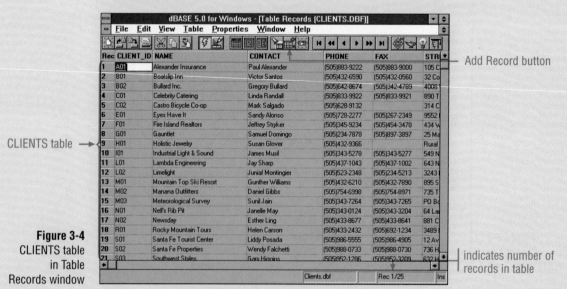

Figure 3-4
CLIENTS table
in Table
Records window

Now that you have opened the CLIENTS table, you can add the two new client records.

Adding Records to a Table

dBASE provides three ways to enter data into a table: using Browse layout, Form layout, or Columnar layout. When you first open a table, dBASE displays the data in **Browse layout**, which shows data in a tabular format with as many rows and columns as will fit in the Table Records window. **Form layout** displays all the fields of one record horizontally on a single screen (or several screens if all the fields cannot fit on one screen). Each field name appears above the field data. **Columnar layout** displays a single record vertically on a single screen, with field names on the left and data values on the right. In some ways, the choice of one view over the other is simply a matter of personal preference. As you will see, each view offers an advantage.

In Browse layout, the advantage is that you see several records displayed at once, so a table with just a few columns can fit on one screen. Form layout's advantage is that you focus on all the relevant information for one record. In most cases, a table with many fields will show all the fields on one screen. Columnar layout displays one field per line, making it easy to see each individual field. Let's try all three methods so that you can decide which you prefer.

Adding a Record Using Browse Layout

First, let's use Browse layout to enter the record for the new client, Peaches & Ice, in the CLIENTS table. As explained in Tutorial 2, you must change to Append mode to add records to a table.

REFERENCE WINDOW

Changing to Append Mode

- Click the Add Record button on the SpeedBar.

  or

- Click Table then click Add Records.

  or

- In Browse layout, go to the bottom record, then press [↓].

Let's switch to Append mode so that you can add the new record.

To switch to Append mode:

❶ Click the **Add Record button** 🖾 on the SpeedBar (or click **Table** then click **Add Records**). See Figure 3-4 for the location of the Add Record button. A blank record, number 26, appears and the CLIENT_ID field is highlighted. See Figure 3-5.

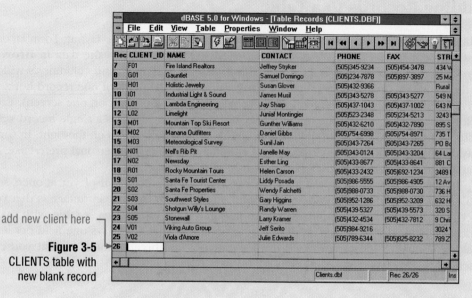

Figure 3-5
CLIENTS table with
new blank record

add new client here

Now you can enter data into the new record by typing a value in each field and pressing [Enter], [Tab], or the cursor movement keys; or you can click the mouse button to move the highlight to the next field.

Figure 3-6 summarizes the keystroke combinations you can use when entering data.

Keystroke	Action
[Tab]	Move to next field
[Enter]	Move to next field
[→]	Move to next character
[←]	Move to previous character
[Shift][Tab]	Move to previous field
[Page Up]	Move up one screen
[Page Down]	Move down one screen
[Ctrl][Page Up]	Move to first record
[Ctrl][Page Down]	Move to last record
[Ctrl][Home]	Move to first field
[Ctrl][End]	Move to last field

Figure 3-6
Data entry
keystrokes

Refer to Figure 3-3 and add the data for the new client, Peaches & Ice.

To add the data for Peaches & Ice:

❶ Type **P01** *but do not press [Enter]. Make sure you type a zero and not the capital letter O.* dBASE beeps and the highlight moves to the NAME field.

TROUBLE? If you make a typing error and your cursor is still in the field containing the error, use [Backspace] to erase characters. If you have left the field, use [Shift][Tab] to return to it so that you can retype the entry.

TROUBLE? If you pressed [Enter] after typing the Client ID, the highlight will skip the NAME field. Click in the NAME field, then continue with the tutorial.

❷ With the highlight in the NAME field, type **Peaches & Ice** then press **[Enter]**. The highlight moves to the CONTACT field.

❸ Type **Alice Beaumont** then press **[Enter]**. The highlight moves to the PHONE field.

❹ Type **(505)728-5176**. dBASE beeps and the highlight moves to the FAX field.

❺ Enter the remaining values, as follows:

FAX: **(505)728-9911**

STREET: **101 Canyon Drive**

CITY: **Santa Fe**

STATE: **NM**

ZIP: **87501**

When you finish entering the record, dBASE automatically creates a new blank record, number 27, in the Table Records window. The Peaches & Ice record is added as record 26 at the end of the table.

Before you enter the second new record in the CLIENTS table, Martin asks to see the records displayed in order by CLIENT_ID. You need to use an index to display the records in a particular order. Let's move the highlight back to the data already entered and exit Append mode.

To exit Append mode:

❶ Press [↑] to move the highlight to the CLIENT_ID field of the record you just entered. See Figure 3-7.

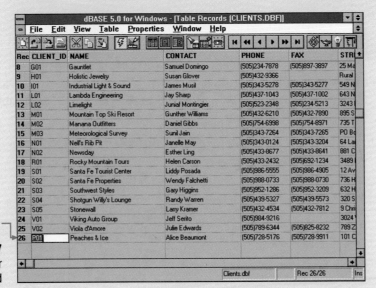

new client record

Figure 3-7
CLIENTS table after
new record added

Using Indexes to Display Records in Order

When you open a table, dBASE displays the records in **natural order**—the order in which they were entered and physically recorded on the disk. However, you might want to display records in order by a particular field, as in this case where Martin wants to see the records displayed in order by CLIENT_ID. Reordering records for display or manipulation is one of the functions of an index.

The CLIENTS table has two indexes: one for the CLIENT_ID field and another for the NAME field. These fields were designated as key fields when the CLIENTS table was created; therefore, they also have indexes. To display the records in the CLIENTS table in order by CLIENT_ID or by NAME, you specify the appropriate index as a **master index**. At any time, you can switch to another master index or to natural order for displaying records.

To display the records in order by CLIENT_ID, you need to specify CLIENT_ID as the master index.

To specify CLIENT_ID as the master index:

❶ Click **Table** then click **Table Utilities** to display the Table Utilities submenu. See Figure 3-8.

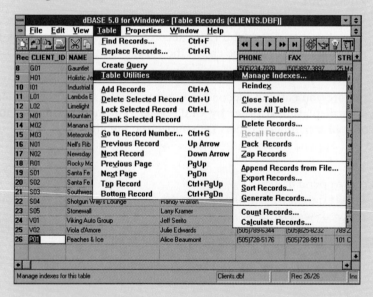

Figure 3-8
Table Utilities
submenu of the
Table menu

❷ Click **Manage Indexes...** to display the Manage Indexes dialog box. The Manage Indexes dialog box displays a list of the indexes for the CLIENTS table. See Figure 3-9.

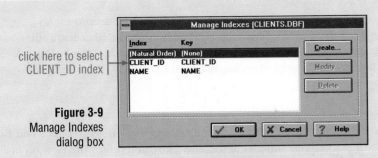

click here to select
CLIENT_ID index

Figure 3-9
Manage Indexes
dialog box

The Index column lists the available indexes for the table. The Key column identifies the field or fields that make up the key for a particular index.

❸ Click **CLIENT_ID** to select the CLIENT_ID index. (Note that you can click either occurrence of CLIENT_ID to select the index.) CLIENT_ID is now the master index for the CLIENTS table.

❹ Click **OK** to close the Manage Indexes dialog box and return to the Table Records window.

dBASE reorders the records in the Table Records window. The new record for Peaches & Ice (CLIENT_ID P01) now appears immediately after the record for Newsday (CLIENT_ID N02) instead of at the end of the table. See Figure 3-10.

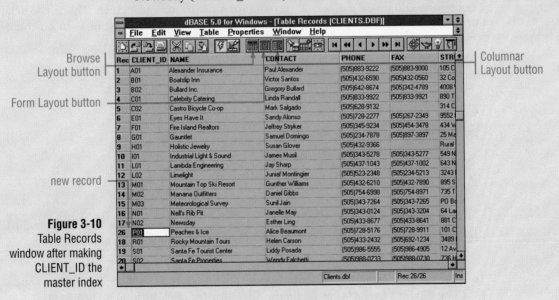

Browse
Layout button

Form Layout button

new record

Figure 3-10
Table Records
window after making
CLIENT_ID the
master index

Columnar
Layout button

The Rec column of the Table Records window indicates that the record for Peaches & Ice is record number 26. That is, it is physically recorded as the 26th record in the table. However, when CLIENT_ID is the master index, the Peaches & Ice record is displayed immediately after the record for Newsday, its logical position in the table.

Now that you have displayed the CLIENTS table in order by CLIENT_ID, let's add the second new record to the table. This time we'll use Form layout to enter the new record.

Entering Data Using Form Layout

When you enter data in Browse layout, you cannot see all the fields in a record at one time unless your table contains only a few fields. In a table with many fields, the left-most field scrolls off the screen as you enter data in fields to the right. This can be confusing, especially when columns with identifying information—such as an identification number or a name—are not on the screen when you enter data in fields that appear in the right-most columns of the table.

In Form layout the fields for one record are arranged horizontally, using multiple lines if necessary. Often you can see all the data for a record on one screen. This is the default form, but if this form doesn't meet your needs, you can create your own customized forms. You will create customized forms in Tutorial 5.

REFERENCE WINDOW

Switching to Form Layout

- Click the Form Layout button on the SpeedBar.

  or

- Click View then click Form Layout.

Let's use Form layout to add the record for Taco Heaven to the CLIENTS table. Just as in Browse layout, you must switch to Append mode before you can add a record.

To enter the new record using Form layout:
❶ Click the **Form Layout button** 🔳 on the SpeedBar (or click **View** then click **Form Layout**). The Table Records window changes to display the current record in Form layout. In this case, the record for Peaches & Ice is displayed. See Figure 3-11.

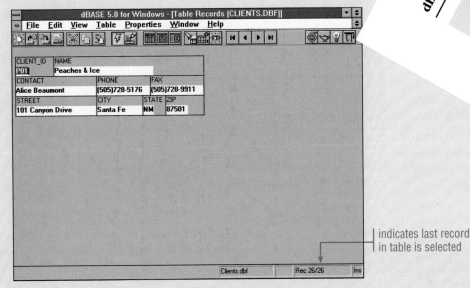

Figure 3-11
Current record
displayed in
Form layout

indicates last record
in table is selected

Now change to Append mode to enter the new record in a blank form.

❷ Click the **Add Record button** on the SpeedBar to change to Append mode. Notice that the form is now blank.

With the empty form displayed, you can enter the data that Martin gave you for the new client, Taco Heaven (refer to Figure 3-3).

To enter the data for Taco Heaven using Form layout:

❶ Type **T01** in the CLIENT_ID field. *Make sure you type a zero and not the capital letter O.* The cursor moves to the NAME field.

   TROUBLE? If you make a typing error and your cursor is still in the field containing the error, use [Backspace] to erase characters. If you have left the field, click the field, then retype the entry.

❷ Type **Taco Heaven** then press [Enter]. The cursor moves to the CONTACT field.

❸ Type **Bert Clinton** then press [Enter]. The cursor moves to the PHONE field.

❹ Type **(505)728-1295**. The cursor moves to the FAX field.

❺ Enter the remaining values, as follows:

   FAX: **(505)728-1595**

   STREET: **1065 El Hombre Drive**

   CITY: **Santa Fe**

   STATE: **NM**

   ZIP: **87501**

   After you enter the last digit for the ZIP field, dBASE beeps and displays a new blank form on the screen.

Let's move back to the record you just entered.

❻ Press **[Page Up]** to display the record you just entered (record 27). Your completed record should look like Figure 3-12.

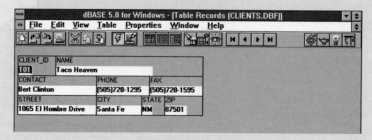

Figure 3-12
New record in
Form layout

Remember, in Form layout, you can see only one record at a time. To get an overview of the data, you can always view the table by switching to Browse layout. Let's switch from Form layout to Browse layout so that you can see all the records currently in the CLIENTS table.

To switch to Browse layout:

❶ Click the **Browse Layout button** 🔳 on the SpeedBar. The table is again displayed in Browse layout.

❷ Use the vertical scroll bar to scroll through the table to see the two new records you added—the record for Peaches & Ice (CLIENT_ID P01) and the record for Taco Heaven (CLIENT_ID T01). Notice that the record for Taco Heaven appears immediately after the record for Stonewall (CLIENT_ID S05). This is because you sorted the records by CLIENT_ID. See Figure 3-13.

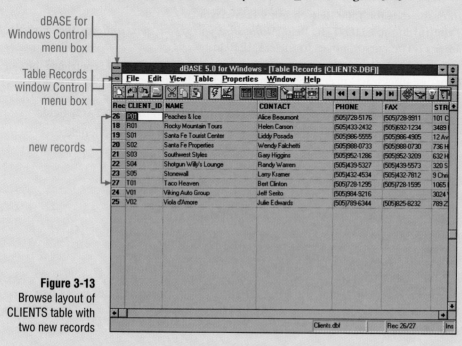

dBASE for
Windows Control
menu box

Table Records
window Control
menu box

new records

Figure 3-13
Browse layout of
CLIENTS table with
two new records

The CLIENTS table is now updated with the two new client records. Your next task is to add the new job authorized by Taco Heaven to the JOBS table. Because you don't need to keep the CLIENTS table open, let's close it.

To close the CLIENTS table:

❶ Double-click the **Control menu box** of the Table Records window. *Do not double-click the dBASE for Windows Control menu box.* See Figure 3-13 for the location of the Table Records window Control menu box.

The Table Records window closes and the dBASE Desktop now shows the Navigator window, which appears maximized. This is because the Table Records window was maximized.

TROUBLE? If you accidentally double-click the dBASE for Windows Control menu box, this will close the CLIENTS table and exit dBASE. Restart dBASE, set the current directory to A:\WM, and continue with the tutorial.

If you want to take a break and resume the tutorial at a later time, click the Restore button in the upper-right corner of the Navigator window to restore it to its original size, then exit dBASE by double-clicking the Control menu box in the upper-left corner of the screen. When you resume the tutorial, place your Student Disk in the disk drive, start dBASE, make sure the current directory is A:\WM, then continue with the tutorial.

◼   ◼   ◼

Your next database maintenance task is to add W&M's new job for Taco Heaven to the JOBS table. In Tutorial 2 you created the WMJOBS table to learn how to create a database table. The JOBS table has the same structure as the WMJOBS table, but all the records in the table—40 records in all—were entered for you. You'll work with the JOBS table in this tutorial.

Before you enter the new record, Martin and Nancy want you to define some validity checks for the JOBS table to ensure that data entered in the table meets certain criteria.

Defining Validity Checks

As explained in Tutorial 2, validity checks let you define the conditions that the values in a field must meet before they are added to a table. dBASE provides several types of validity checks. You can:

- Specify a minimum acceptable value for a field. For example, the minimum allowable value of a credit card charge might be $1.00.
- Specify a maximum acceptable value for a field. For example, the maximum allowable value for a credit card charge might be $100,000.00.
- Create a picture template of the format that entries must match before the record is accepted. For example, a Social Security number field might be restricted to digits only. A telephone number field might contain parentheses and a hyphen to make the data more readable.
- Link the contents of one field to the contents of another field. For example, entering a value in a spouse's name field might require that a marital status field be set to "Married."
- Define an expression that determines whether an entry in the field is valid. For example, the values in a field might be restricted to 1, 3, and 5.

Picture Template Validity Checks

A **picture template validity check** is a data entry format that specifies what type of characters are allowed in a field. A picture template consists of a combination of formatting (picture template) symbols and constant data characters (literals). A picture template symbol is a character that dBASE uses to represent a particular type of character or arrangement of characters. When you enter data in a field assigned a picture template validity check, dBASE uses the picture symbols to determine whether your entry is valid.

Figure 3-14 shows the picture template symbols permitted in dBASE.

Picture Symbol	Definition
9	In character fields, allows a numeric digit in this position; in numeric fields, allows a numeric digit, "+", or "–"
A	Restricts entry to letters only
X	Allows any character
N	Allows any letter or numeric digit
L	Allows only T, t, F, f, Y, y, N, or n and converts to uppercase
Y	Allows only T, t, F, f, Y, y, N, or n; T, t, Y, and y are displayed as Y; F, f, N, and n are displayed as N
#	Allows numeric digits, spaces, periods, and signs
!	Converts letters to uppercase
$	Displays a dollar sign instead of leading blanks
*	Displays asterisks in place of leading blanks
.	Indicates position of the decimal point
,	Indicates separation of thousands with a comma
@A	Allows any string of letters only
@!	When placed at the beginning of a picture template string, converts any letters entered to uppercase

Figure 3-14
Symbols used in
picture template
validity checks

The @ symbol identifies a function that applies to the entire format. So @! means that any letter in the value entered will be converted to uppercase. If you use this symbol, separate it from the rest of the template with a space. @A means that only letters are allowed in the field.

For example, a picture template for a Social Security number field could be defined as 999-99-9999. The 9 symbol is a picture symbol that ensures only digits are allowed in the field. The hyphen is a literal because it is not one of the characters listed in Figure 3-14. dBASE automatically inserts a literal in its specified position in the field.

Figure 3-15 illustrates some examples of picture template validity checks and their uses.

Picture Validity Check	Use
(999)999-9999	Phone number
99999	Zip code
!AAA	First character, if a letter, will be converted to uppercase; the remaining characters must be letters
@! AAA999	An ID consisting of three uppercase letters followed by three digits

Figure 3-15
Examples of picture template validity checks

Martin and Nancy want you to define validity checks for four fields in the JOBS table: JOB_NO, CLIENT_ID, DUE_DATE, and COMPLETED. Let's enter these validity checks.

Entering Validity Checks

Recall from Tutorial 2 that you can define validity checks as field properties of the Table Records window. By doing so, you define rules that control the viewing and entry of data in the Table Records window. These validity checks are stored with the copy of dBASE installed on the computer you use when you define them. In other words, these validity check definitions are *not* stored with the table.

Important: If another student already completed this tutorial on the computer you're using, the validity checks for the JOBS table will already be defined and stored on that computer. You can walk through the steps in this section without actually completing them, or ask your instructor or technical support person for assistance.

REFERENCE WINDOW

Defining Validity Checks

- Click Properties then click Table Records Window....
- Click the Fields tab.
- Click the field for which you want to define validity checks.
- Click Properties....
- Specify the validity checks you want for the selected field.
- Click OK.

First, you'll define the validity checks for the JOB_NO field. Nancy and Martin want to specify 1000 as the minimum acceptable value for a job number because the prenumbered Job Authorization Form begins at 1000. To minimize the chance of a data entry error, Nancy and Martin want to make the maximum allowed value for a job number 9999.

To define validity checks for the JOB_NO field in the JOBS table:

❶ Double-click **Jobs.dbf** in the Navigator window. The JOBS table appears in the Table Records window.

❷ If necessary, maximize the Table Records window. Notice that the table contains 40 records. See Figure 3-16.

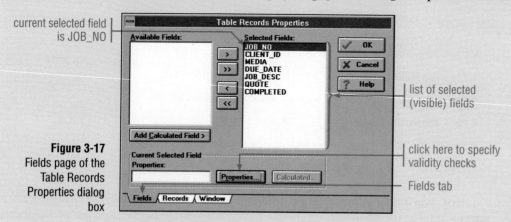

Figure 3-16
JOBS table in Table
Records window

table contains
40 records

❸ Click **Properties** then click **Table Records Window...** to display the Table Records Properties dialog box.

❹ Click the **Fields tab** to display the page containing the options for fields. See Figure 3-17.

current selected field
is JOB_NO

Figure 3-17
Fields page of the
Table Records
Properties dialog
box

list of selected
(visible) fields

click here to specify
validity checks

Fields tab

The Fields page shows the names of the fields that appear in the Table Records window. By default, all field names appear in the Selected Fields list box. Selected fields are visible in the Table Records window. The highlighted field is known as the "current selected field." You can set properties for this field by clicking the Properties... button.

You need to define validity checks for the JOB_NO field.

❺ If necessary, click **JOB_NO** to make it the current selected field.

❻ Click **Properties...** to display the Field Properties dialog box. See Figure 3-18.

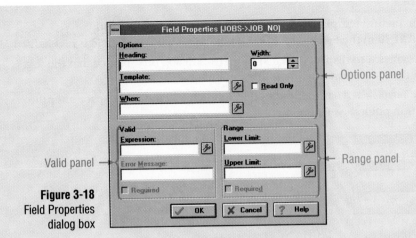

Figure 3-18
Field Properties
dialog box

Valid panel

Options panel

Range panel

The Field Properties dialog box contains three panels. The Options panel allows you to change the appearance of the field in the Table Records window, to define a picture template validity check, and to link the values of two fields. The Valid panel lets you define expressions that determine the validity of a field's value. The Range panel lets you set minimum (lower limit) and maximum (upper limit) allowable values for a field. You must specify lower and upper limits together; you cannot specify one without the other.

The first validity check for JOB_NO is to specify 1000 as the smallest job number that dBASE will accept, and the second is to specify 9999 as the largest number. Because these represent a lower limit and an upper limit, you can use the Range panel.

❼ Click the **Lower Limit text box** in the Range panel, then type **1000**.

❽ Click the **Upper Limit text box** in the Range panel, then type **9999**. See Figure 3-19.

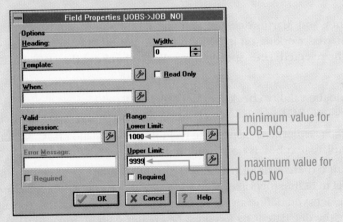

Figure 3-19
Validity checks for
the JOB_NO field

minimum value for
JOB_NO

maximum value for
JOB_NO

❾ Click **OK** to save these validity checks and return to the Fields page of the Table Records Properties dialog box.

W&M uses a specific structure for client IDs. The first character of the ID is always an uppercase letter—the first letter of the client's name—and the next two characters are sequential numbers. Nancy and Martin want you to specify a picture template validity check for the CLIENT_ID field to ensure that any entries in this field conform to this structure.

To define the picture template validity check for the CLIENT_ID field:

❶ Click **CLIENT_ID** in the Selected Fields list box. The CLIENT_ID field is highlighted.

❷ Click **Properties...** to display the Field Properties dialog box. Notice that the text boxes in the Range panel are now blank.

❸ Click the **Template text box** then type **@! A99**. Be sure to include a space after the exclamation point. See Figure 3-20.

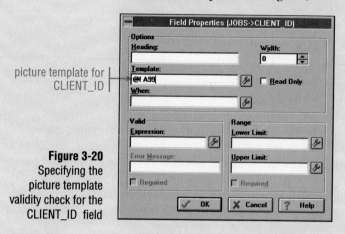

picture template for CLIENT_ID

Figure 3-20
Specifying the picture template validity check for the CLIENT_ID field

This picture template specifies that the first character must be a letter. If the letter is entered as lowercase, dBASE will automatically change it to uppercase. The next two characters must be digits.

❹ Click **OK** to save this validity check and return to the Fields page of the Table Records Properties dialog box.

Nancy and Martin decided that the JOBS table should include only those jobs that W&M started working on in 1996, nothing earlier. Therefore, a due date before 01/01/96 should be rejected. Let's specify this validity check for the DUE_DATE field.

To define the validity check for the DUE_DATE field:

❶ Click **DUE_DATE** in the Selected Fields list box. The DUE_DATE field is highlighted.

❷ Click **Properties...** to display the Field Properties dialog box. Notice that the Template text box is now blank.

Because there is no upper limit for the DUE_DATE field, you cannot use the Range panel to define this validity check. Instead, let's use the Valid panel. The Valid panel lets you define an expression that determines whether a value is valid. In this case, the due date for a job must be greater than or equal to 01/01/96. The expression for this is DUE_DATE>={01/01/96}. Notice that dBASE uses braces ({}) to signify that the characters represent a date rather than a text string.

❸ Click the **Expression text box** then type **DUE_DATE>={01/01/96}**. No date before 01/01/96 will be accepted.

The Valid panel also allows you to specify an error message dBASE will display if a user enters an invalid value. Let's have dBASE display the message "Date must be 01/01/96 or later" when a user enters an invalid due date.

❹ Click the **Error Message text box** then type **Date must be 01/01/96 or later**. See Figure 3-21.

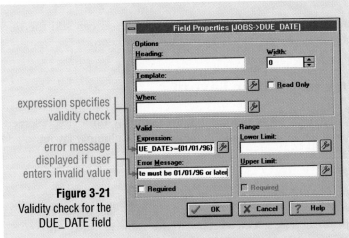

expression specifies
validity check

error message
displayed if user
enters invalid value

Figure 3-21
Validity check for the
DUE_DATE field

❺ Click **OK** to save this validity check and return to the Fields page of the Table Records Properties dialog box.

Finally, Nancy and Martin want to make sure that only the values Y or N are entered in the COMPLETED field. Let's create a picture template for this field.

To define the validity check for the COMPLETED field:

❶ Click **COMPLETED** in the Selected Fields list box.

❷ Click **Properties...** to display the Field Properties dialog box.

❸ Click in the **Template text box** then type **Y**. Recall that this template will cause dBASE to display the contents of the COMPLETED field as a Y (for Y, y, T, or t) or N (for N, n, F, or f). See Figure 3-22.

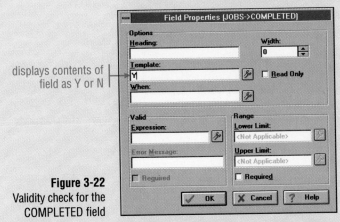

displays contents of
field as Y or N

Figure 3-22
Validity check for the
COMPLETED field

❹ Click **OK** to save this validity check and return to the Fields page of the Table Records Properties dialog box.

You have now specified all four validity checks for the JOBS table. Remember that these validity checks apply *only* when you work with the JOBS table on the computer on which you defined them.

❺ Click **OK** to close the Table Records Properties dialog box and return to the Table Records window.

Now that you've defined validity checks for the JOBS table, you can add the new record for Taco Heaven. Let's use Columnar layout to add the new record.

Entering Data Using Columnar Layout

As noted earlier, Columnar layout displays a single record vertically on a single screen, with field names on the left and data values on the right. Let's use Columnar layout to add the new record for Taco Heaven at the end of the JOBS table.

To add the record in Columnar layout:

❶ Make sure that the record for job number 1001 is selected, then click the **Columnar Layout button** 🔲 on the SpeedBar. The selected record in the Table Records window, job number 1001, appears in Columnar layout. The record is displayed in two columns, with one field per line. The field names appear on the left, and the values for the selected record appear on the right. See Figure 3-23.

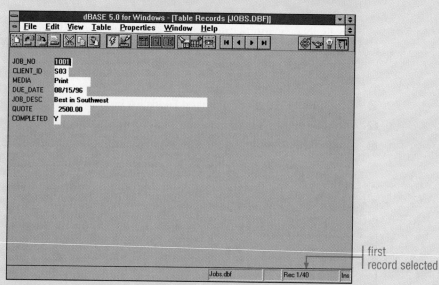

Figure 3-23
JOBS table in
Columnar layout

first record selected

❷ Click the **Add Record button** 🔲 on the SpeedBar. A blank record appears in Columnar layout. See Figure 3-24.

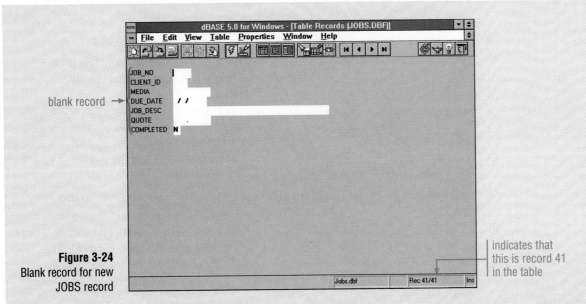

blank record →

Figure 3-24
Blank record for new
JOBS record

indicates that
this is record 41
in the table

Notice that the DUE_DATE field displays slashes as separators for the date. This is the format of the date field type. Also, notice that the default value "N" appears in the COMPLETED field.

Now you can enter the data for the new JOBS record. When you enter the data, you will make intentional errors. This is so that you can see how dBASE indicates validity check violations and learn how to handle them.

Handling Validity Check Violations

You can occasionally encounter problems when you add data in a table. For example, a common error is to enter a value that does not match the picture template for that field. In the following steps, you will enter a CLIENT_ID that does not match the picture template for the CLIENT_ID field (one letter followed by two digits). Then you'll enter a due date that violates the minimum acceptable date specified as a validity check for the DUE_DATE field.

When an entry violates a validity check, dBASE will not let you continue until you correct it. If you can't figure out how to correct a validity check violation, you can "escape" the screen by selecting Undo from the Edit menu. dBASE will undo the current entry and restore the table to the state it was in before you started entering the current record.

The correct CLIENT_ID for the new Taco Heaven record is T01. You'll attempt to enter 501 as an intentional error. The correct DUE_DATE for the new record is 12/15/96. You'll enter 12/15/93 as an intentional error.

To enter the data for the new job:

❶ Type **1041**. dBASE beeps and the cursor moves to the CLIENT_ID field.

❷ Type **5**. Notice that the 5 does not appear in the field on the screen. The picture template for the CLIENT_ID field requires a letter as the first character. dBASE will accept only a letter entered as the first character.

TROUBLE? If you can't remember what validity checks have been defined for a table, you can select the Table Records Window... command from the Properties menu. Then click the Fields page to review the validity checks for the fields in the table.

❸ Type **T01** to enter the correct value for the CLIENT_ID field. dBASE beeps and the cursor moves to the MEDIA field.

❹ Type **Broadcast** in the MEDIA field. dBASE beeps and the cursor moves to the DUE_DATE field.

❺ Type **121593**. Because you have entered a complete date, dBASE beeps and checks the date you entered against the validity checks you specified for this field. The date entered predates the earliest date allowed for this field. Therefore, dBASE displays the Alert dialog box with the message "Date must be 01/01/96 or later." See Figure 3-25.

unacceptable date

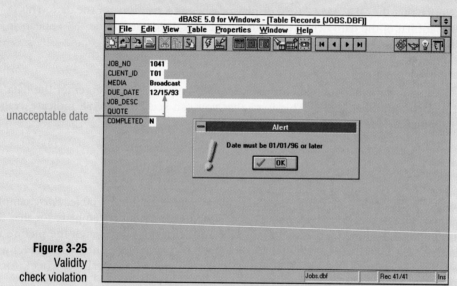

Figure 3-25
Validity
check violation

When an entry fails a validity check, you are notified immediately and must correct the error before you can move to the next field.

❻ Click **OK**. The Alert dialog box disappears, and the cursor appears before the first character in the DUE_DATE field.

Now, correct the error by changing the date from 12/15/93 to 12/15/96.

❼ Press [→] five times to move the cursor to a position immediately before the 3, press **[Delete]** to delete the 3, then type **6**. You have corrected the error. dBASE beeps and the cursor moves to the JOB_DESC field.

❽ Type **TV ad** then press **[Enter]**. The cursor moves to the QUOTE field.

❾ Type **14000** then press **[Enter]**. The cursor moves to the COMPLETED field.

Notice that the value in the QUOTE field is displayed with two decimal places, as specified in the field definition. Also, notice that the COMPLETED field already contains the value N, the default value for a logical field. You would make an entry in the COMPLETED field only if you wanted to change this value.

❿ Press **[Enter]** to leave the COMPLETED field. A new blank record appears with the cursor in the JOB_NO field. dBASE has saved the new record.

Now that you have entered data for the new job, you will not need the JOBS table anymore in this tutorial. Let's restore the Table Records window to its original size, then close it.

To close the Table Records window:
❶ Click the **Restore button** in the upper-right corner of the Table Records window.
❷ Double-click the **Control menu box** for the Table Records window. The Table Records window closes, and you return to the Navigator window on the dBASE Desktop.

If you want to take a break and resume the tutorial at a later time, you can exit dBASE by double-clicking the Control menu box in the upper-left corner of the screen. When you resume the tutorial, place your Student Disk in the disk drive, start dBASE, make sure the current directory is A:\WM, then continue with the tutorial.

■   ■   ■

Now you can continue to update the W&M database by making the necessary changes to existing records.

Making Changes to Records

You usually need to make changes and corrections to data that is already in a table. That is the case with the data in the Mountain Top Ski Resort record. The contact person has changed. You need to remove the name Gunther Williams and replace it with Victor Juarez. You also have to change the phone number for Mountain Top Ski Resort. To make these changes, you must open the CLIENTS table again.

To open the CLIENTS table:
❶ Click the **Tables icon** in the Navigator window to display the list of tables in the current directory (if necessary).
❷ Double-click **Clients.dbf** in the Navigator window to open the CLIENTS table.
❸ Click the **Maximize button** for the Table Records window to see more of the data.

Just as you did when you entered new records, you can use either Browse layout, Form layout, or Columnar layout to change the data in existing records.

Changing a Record Using Columnar Layout

Let's use Columnar layout to change the contact person and phone number for the Mountain Top Ski Resort record.

To switch to Columnar layout:

❶ Click the **Columnar Layout button** 🔳 on the SpeedBar. The first record in the table, Alexander Insurance, appears in the Table Records window. The first field, CLIENT_ID, is highlighted.

The current record in the Table Records window is Alexander Insurance, but the record you want to edit is Mountain Top Ski Resort. You can use the navigation buttons on the SpeedBar to find the Mountain Top Ski Resort record. In a small table with few records, using the navigation buttons to locate a record is a reasonable approach. In a larger table, however, searching for records using the navigation buttons can be slow. dBASE offers other tools to help you find records.

Finding Records

The Find feature helps you quickly find a record with a specific value in a field.

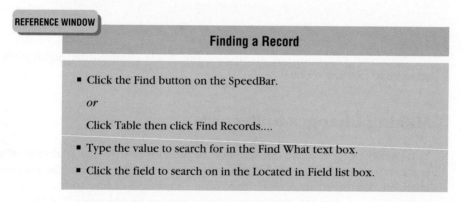

REFERENCE WINDOW

Finding a Record

- Click the Find button on the SpeedBar.

  or

  Click Table then click Find Records....
- Type the value to search for in the Find What text box.
- Click the field to search on in the Located in Field list box.

Let's have dBASE search the CLIENTS table to find the Mountain Top Ski Resort record. To find the record, you'll ask dBASE to search for the client name in the NAME field. Because the NAME field is a key field and, therefore, is indexed, dBASE can search for the name more efficiently if you first make NAME the master index for this table. (Although you might not notice this increased efficiency when searching a small table like the CLIENTS table, searching a master index is much faster when the table contains many records.)

Let's first specify NAME as the master index, then find the Mountain Top Ski Resort record.

To specify NAME as the master index and locate the Mountain Top Ski Resort record:

❶ Click **Table**, click **Table Utilities**, then click **Manage Indexes...** to display the Manage Indexes dialog box.

❷ Click **NAME** to select the NAME index.

❸ Click **OK** to close the Manage Indexes dialog box.

With the master index specified, you can now locate the record quickly.

❹ Click the **Find button** 🖼 on the SpeedBar (or click **Table** then click **Find Records...**). The Find Records dialog box appears. See Figure 3-26.

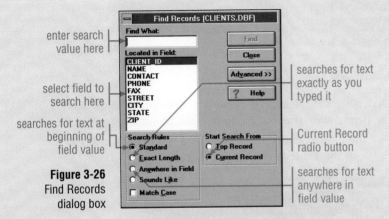

enter search value here

select field to search here

searches for text at beginning of field value

searches for text exactly as you typed it

Current Record radio button

searches for text anywhere in field value

Figure 3-26
Find Records dialog box

In the Find What text box, you type the value you want dBASE to search for. In the Located in Field list box, you specify the field you want dBASE to search through to find the value. First, enter the value that you want dBASE to search for.

If the Top Record button in the Start Search From panel is selected, dBASE starts the search at the beginning of the table. If dBASE finds a record that matches the value you specified, but it's not the record you're looking for, you can click the Current Record radio button in the Start Search From panel to find the next record that matches the value you are searching for. If dBASE does not find a record that matches your criteria, it displays an Alert dialog box with the message "Value was not found."

❺ Click the **Find What text box**, then type **Mou**. You do not have to type the entire entry—Mountain Top Ski Resort—in the Find What text box. By typing Mou, you're asking dBASE to find all client names that begin with the letters "Mou."

If you want dBASE to search for the text exactly as you typed it in the Find What text box, you must click the Exact Length radio button in the Search Rules panel.

Now select the field you want to search. Notice that the Located in Field list box displays all the fields in the table and that the CLIENT_ID field is highlighted. You need to search the NAME field.

⑥ Click **NAME** in the Located in Field list box. See Figure 3-27.

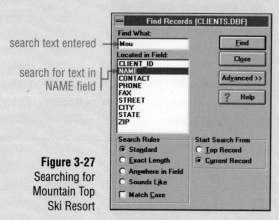

search text entered

search for text in NAME field

Figure 3-27
Searching for
Mountain Top
Ski Resort

⑦ Click **Find**. dBASE performs the search and finds the first record in the CLIENTS table whose name begins with the letters "Mou"—the Mountain Top Ski Resort.

⑧ Click **Close** to close the Find Records dialog box. The Mountain Top Ski Resort record is now visible in the Table Records window. See Figure 3-28.

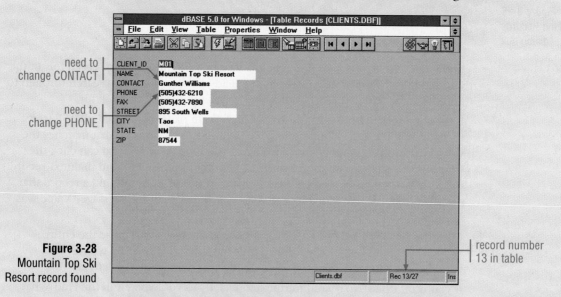

need to change CONTACT

need to change PHONE

record number 13 in table

Figure 3-28
Mountain Top Ski
Resort record found

TROUBLE? If the Alert dialog box appears with the message "Value was not found," check the Find What text box in the Find Records dialog box. You most likely did not enter the letters "Mou" correctly, or the Exact Length radio button is selected. Click OK in the Alert dialog box, then repeat Steps 5 through 8.

Now update the record by changing the contact person to Victor Juarez.

To change the value in the CONTACT field to Victor Juarez:

❶ Click anywhere in the name Gunther Williams in the CONTACT field.

❷ Click **Edit** then click **Select All**. The name Gunther Williams is highlighted.

❸ Type **Victor Juarez** then press **[Enter]**. The new entry replaces the existing one, and the PHONE field is highlighted. See Figure 3-29. Notice that as soon as you typed the first letter of the new value, the previous value was erased and you replaced the entire field.

new CONTACT name

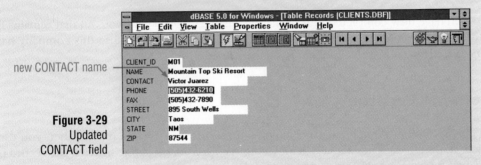

Figure 3-29
Updated
CONTACT field

TROUBLE? If you make a typing error, or if you decide not to change the record after you've made changes, you can choose Undo from the Edit menu to undo all changes to the current record. If you have moved to another record and discover an error in a previous record, you must reenter changes. (Changes cannot be undone once you move to another record.)

Next, you'll change the phone number for this record. The existing value for the phone number is (505)783-6210. You need to change the value to (505)783-6220. You can use the same procedure as above to reenter the entire phone number, or you can edit the existing value to change the single digit in the phone number that needs updating. Let's edit the existing phone number.

To change the value in the PHONE field:

❶ Move the pointer so that it is between the 2 and the 1 in the phone number, then click to position the insertion point.

❷ Press **[Delete]** to delete the 1.

❸ Type **2** to insert the new digit in the phone number.

❹ Press **[Enter]** to complete editing the value in the PHONE field. The cursor moves to the FAX field. See Figure 3-30.

new PHONE number

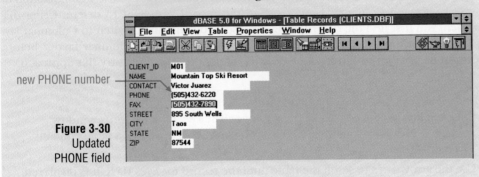

Figure 3-30
Updated
PHONE field

Now that you have changed the contact person and corrected the phone number, you can save the record.

To save the updated Mountain Top Ski Resort record:
❶ Click the **Next Record button** ▶ on the SpeedBar. The next record, N01, appears and the changes to the Mountain Top Ski Resort record are saved to the CLIENTS table.

You have now completed four of the five changes Martin gave you. All that remains is to delete the record for Eyes Have It from the CLIENTS table. Because this company has gone out of business, you no longer need the record.

Deleting Records

To delete a record from a database table, you must first select the record, then you can delete it. dBASE does not actually remove the record from the table. Instead, the record is *marked* for deletion. If you accidentally delete the wrong record, you can recall it. To permanently remove a record from the table, you must pack the records. When you **pack** the records, dBASE makes a copy of the table excluding the records marked for deletion. Then dBASE deletes the original table and renames the copy of the table, which does not contain the deleted records, using the name of the original table.

In the following steps, you will delete the record for Eyes Have It from the CLIENTS table and then recall it. Then you will delete the record again and pack the records to permanently remove the deleted record.

REFERENCE WINDOW

Deleting a Selected Record

- Click Table then click Delete Selected Record.

  or

- Press [Ctrl][U].

First, you need to find the record to be deleted. Instead of using the Find Records dialog box to find the record, let's try a different approach. You can use a combination of Browse layout and Columnar layout to find the record you want to delete. Using this approach, you first find the record using Browse layout and then switch to Columnar layout before deleting the record. Viewing the entire record in Columnar layout before deleting it helps to ensure that you're deleting the right record. Let's try this approach.

To find the record in Browse layout and then delete it:
❶ Click the **Browse Layout button** ▦ on the SpeedBar. The Table Records window appears in Browse layout. As noted in the status bar, the CLIENTS table contains 27 records.
❷ Use the arrow keys to scroll the table until the record for Eyes Have It is displayed.

❸ Click the record number for Eyes Have It. The record is selected. Note that the records are displayed in alphabetical order by name. This is because you defined the NAME field as the master index. See Figure 3-31.

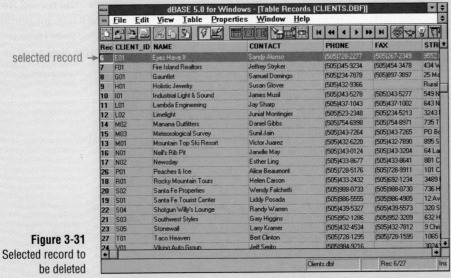

selected record →

Figure 3-31
Selected record to
be deleted

Now switch to Columnar layout to verify that you have selected the correct record.

❹ Click the **Columnar Layout button** on the SpeedBar. The selected record, Eyes Have It, appears in the Table Records window in Columnar layout. See Figure 3-32.

Figure 3-32
Selected record in
Columnar layout

After verifying that this is the record you want to delete, you can delete the record.

❺ Click **Table** then click **Delete Selected Record** (or press **[Ctrl][U]**). dBASE deletes the record and displays the next record in the CLIENTS table.

Has the record been deleted? Let's move back to Browse layout so that you can get an overview of the data in the CLIENTS table.

To switch to Browse layout:

❶ Click the **Browse Layout button** 🖿 on the SpeedBar.

❷ Click the **Top button** ⏮ on the SpeedBar to move to the top of the table. Notice that the record for Eyes Have It, which was displayed immediately after the record for Celebrity Catering, is no longer visible in the CLIENTS table. dBASE has not renumbered the records after the one you deleted, because the record for Eyes Have It (record 6) is still available for recall. The status bar still indicates that there are 27 records in the CLIENTS table. See Figure 3-33.

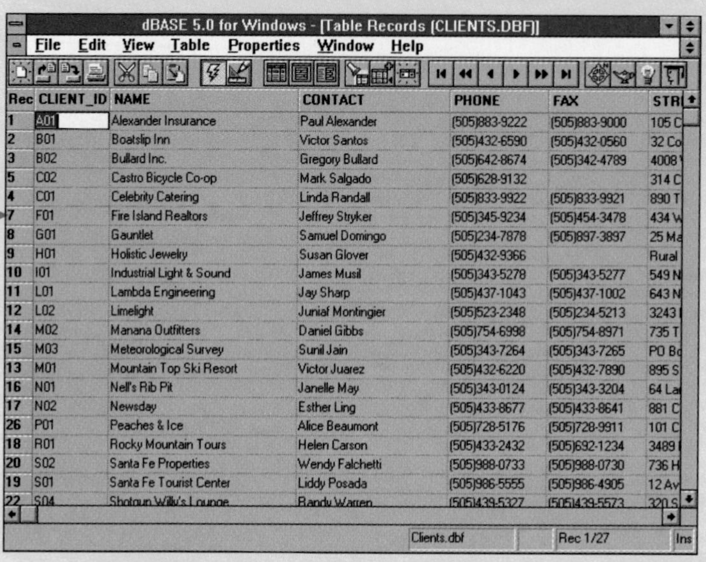

Eyes Have It record
no longer visible

Figure 3-33
CLIENTS table after
deleting record

To remove the Eyes Have It record from the table permanently, you must pack the records. If you had deleted the Eyes Have It record by mistake, you could recall it now or anytime before you pack the records. Let's recall the Eyes Have It record, then delete it again and pack the records.

Although the Eyes Have It record is still in the table, it is not visible in the Table Records window. To recall the record, you must first make it visible. The visibility of deleted records is a Desktop property.

REFERENCE WINDOW

Recalling a Deleted Record

- Make sure the table containing the deleted record is displayed in Browse layout in the Table Records window.

- Click Properties then click Desktop....

- Click the Table tab to display the Table page of the Desktop Properties dialog box.

- Click the Deleted check box to deselect this option.

- Click OK.

- Locate the record you want to recall.

- Click in the Del column to clear the "x" marking the deleted record.

  or

  Click Table then click Recall Selected Record.

  or

  Press [Ctrl][U].

Let's make the Eyes Have It record visible.

To make the record marked for deletion visible:

❶ Click **Properties** then click **Desktop....** The Desktop Properties dialog box appears.

❷ Click the **Table tab** to display the Table page of the Desktop Properties dialog box. See Figure 3-34.

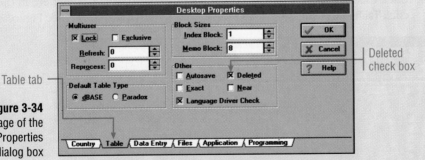

Table tab

Figure 3-34
Table page of the
Desktop Properties
dialog box

Deleted
check box

The Deleted check box in the Other panel controls the display of deleted records. By default, this box is checked (marked with an x), meaning that deleted records are not visible in the Table Records window (nor are they available for operations such as searching and editing). To make deleted records visible, you must clear the x from the Deleted check box.

❸ Click the **Deleted check box** to clear the x.

❹ Click **OK** to close the Desktop Properties dialog box and return to the Table
Records window. See Figure 3-35.

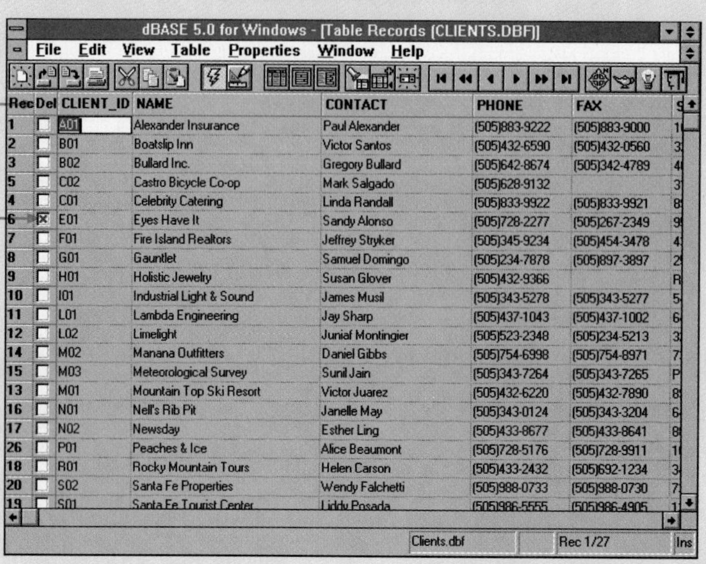

Del column visible —

Eyes Have It record
marked for deletion

Figure 3-35
Table Records
window after
making deleted
records visible

Notice that a new column, labeled Del, has been added to the window between the
record number column and the CLIENT_ID column. The Del column contains a check
box for each record. A record marked for deletion is indicated by an x in the box. The
record for Eyes Have It is now visible in the window, and the Del check box for it contains an x. Let's clear the x now to recall the record.

To recall the deleted Eyes Have It record:
❶ Click the **Del check box** for the Eyes Have It record (or click anywhere in the record,
click **Table**, then click **Recall Selected Record**). The x disappears. See Figure 3-36.

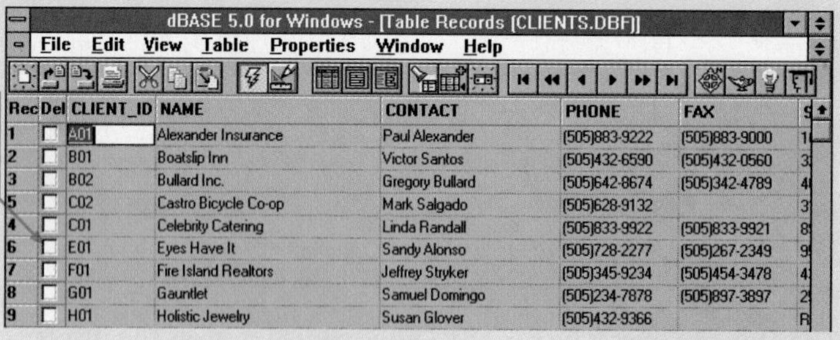

Del check
box cleared

Figure 3-36
Table Records
window after
recalling the Eyes
Have It record

TROUBLE? After you click the Del check box, if your screen shows some text superimposed on
the table, close the Table Records window. Then open the CLIENTS table again and repeat Step 1.

The Eyes Have It record is part of the CLIENTS table again. You can recall a deleted
record in this way, provided that you haven't packed the table. When the Del column is
visible in the Table Records window, you can also use it to mark records for deletion.
Records marked for deletion are removed from the table permanently by packing the
records. Let's mark the Eyes Have It record for deletion again and then remove it from the
table permanently.

To mark the Eyes Have It record for deletion and pack the table:

❶ Click the **Del check box** for the Eyes Have It record. An x appears in the box, indicating that the record is marked for deletion.

❷ Click **Table** then click **Table Utilities** to display the Table Utilities submenu.

❸ Click **Pack Records** to remove all records marked for deletion. Because packing the records involves copying the entire table, dBASE displays the Exclusive Access Required dialog box. See Figure 3-37.

Figure 3-37
Exclusive Access
Required dialog box

❹ Click **Yes** to open the file in exclusive mode and pack the records. Notice that the message "Packing records: 27" appears in the status bar. The Eyes Have It record is no longer in the table. dBASE renumbers the remaining records. The status bar shows that there are now 26 records in the table, and the records are displayed in natural order.

Now that the record is deleted, you can remove the display of the Del column. Typically you won't work with the Del column displayed and deleted records visible. Let's return to the Desktop Properties dialog box to reset the Deleted check box.

To remove the display of the Del column:

❶ Click **Properties** then click **Desktop....** The Desktop Properties dialog box appears with the Table page still visible.

❷ Click the **Deleted check box** to select this option.

❸ Click **OK** to close the Desktop Properties dialog box and return to the Table Records window.

❹ Click the **Restore button** in the Table Records window to restore it to its original size.

You have now completed all the necessary updates to the W&M database.

After making changes to database tables, it is a good practice to make backup copies of the updated database file.

Backing Up a Database File

The process of making a duplicate copy of each database table is called **backing up** the table. You do this to protect the data in case the original table is lost, stolen, damaged, or destroyed. Should any of these events occur, you can use your backup file in place of the original table. To back up your table in dBASE, you can use the Export Records option on the Table Utilities submenu of the Table menu.

Backing Up a Database File

- Click Table then click Table Utilities.
- Click Export Records... to display the Export Records dialog box.
- Type the name of the backup file in the File Name text box.
- Click OK.

In this tutorial you will store backup files on the same disk as the original files in order to reduce the number of disks needed for this course. Normally you would store a backup file on a separate disk. Then, if the original disk is lost or destroyed, you have a usable copy on a separate disk.

Let's back up the CLIENTS table.

To make a backup copy of the CLIENTS table:
❶ Click **Table** then click **Table Utilities**.
❷ Click **Export Records...**. The Export Records dialog box appears. See Figure 3-38.

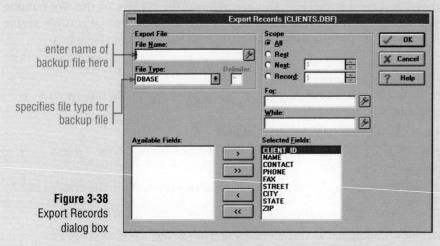

enter name of backup file here

specifies file type for backup file

Figure 3-38
Export Records dialog box

Notice that the File Type text box contains the entry "DBASE," which specifies that the backup copy will be a dBASE file.

Enter a name for the backup copy in the File Name text box. The letters "BK" are often used in filenames to specify a backup copy of a file.

❸ Click the **File Name text box**, then type **CLIENTBK.DBF**.

If you want your backup copy to be stored in a different drive or directory, you must specify the drive letter and directory path in addition to the filename. For example, to copy the CLIENTS.DBF file to a disk in drive B, you would type "B:\CLIENTBK.DBF" in the File Name text box.

❹ Click **OK**. dBASE copies the database table to the current directory (A:\WM). The message "Records copied: 26" appears in the status bar.

You have now made a backup copy of the CLIENTS table. Let's close the Table Records window and exit dBASE.

To close the Table Records window and exit dBASE:
❶ Double-click the **Control menu box** for the Table Records window. The window closes and you return to the Navigator window on the Desktop.
❷ Click **File** then click **Exit** to exit dBASE and return to the Program Manager.

■   ■   ■

The CLIENTS and JOBS tables are now up to date. Nancy and Martin feel certain that the database maintenance features of dBASE will enable them to keep the W&M database current easily and efficiently.

Questions

1. To get an overview of the data in a table, what layout should you use?
2. What are the differences between Browse layout, Form layout, and Columnar layout?
3. How do you know which record is the active (selected) record when data is displayed in Browse layout?
4. Give two different approaches for finding a specific record in a table.
5. Why should you specify a master index when finding a record using an indexed field?
6. What keystrokes do you use to delete a record?
7. Describe the steps necessary to display records marked for deletion.
8. If you want to make sure you are deleting the correct record, would you use Browse layout or Columnar layout?
9. What is the difference between marking records for deletion in a table and packing the table?
10. What menu options do you select to make a backup copy of a database table?
11. Why should you make a backup copy of a database table? Why should you use a separate disk for this backup copy?
12. A dBASE user wants to add a new client record to the CLIENTS table, but is unable to do so. First, the user opened the CLIENTS table and clicked the Add Record button on the SpeedBar. A blank record appeared after the last record in the table. The cursor was in the CLIENT_ID field. The user tried to enter "402" as the CLIENT_ID, but nothing appeared in the CLIENT_ID field. Why wasn't the user able to add a new client record?
13. A dBASE user wants to add a new client record to the CLIENTS table. The CLIENT_ID for this client is K01. After the user opens the CLIENTS table and enters the record, it appears at the end of the table, not in its logical position by CLIENT_ID. Why is the new record not displayed in logical position by CLIENT_ID?

14. Place your Student Disk in the disk drive, start dBASE, and set the current directory to A:\PRACTICE.
    a. Open the GRANT1 table.
    b. In what sequence are the records displayed? Why?
    c. Switch to Columnar layout using the Columnar Layout button.
    d. The amount awarded the Desktop Publishing Workshop grant should be $2,200. Change this amount.
    e. The Debate Team grant was withdrawn. Delete the record for this grant.
    f. Use the Find button to find all grants with the word "School" as the first word in the title. What grant title(s) did you find?

E
    g. Use the Find button to find all grants with the word "Survey" anywhere in the title. What grant title(s) did you find?

E 15. Open the GRANT1 table from the PRACTICE directory on your Student Disk. The records are arranged by record number (the order in which they were entered). What if you want to display the records in the GRANT1 table in order by College? Explore the Sort Records option on the Table Utilities submenu of the Table menu, then display the records by College. (*Note:* dBASE must create a new table, called the "target table," to store the sorted data. Name this table SORTGRNT.) What is one advantage of sorting a table over creating an index for it? (*Hint:* Explore dBASE Help and look up "sorting.") Close the table.

E 16. Open the GRANT1 table from the PRACTICE directory on your Student Disk. Examine the structure of the table. Display the records in order by GRANTEE. What is one advantage of using an index for a table over sorting it? (*Hint:* Explore dBASE Help and look up "sorting.") Close the table.

E 17. The PRACTICE directory of your Student Disk contains two tables, named KEYED and UNKEYED.
    a. Examine the structure of each table. How do the structures differ?
    b. Add the following record to each table:

STUDENT_ID	ST_NAME	SEX	MAJOR	GPA
415	MURRAY	F	MKT	3.4

    c. Comment on where the new record is displayed in Browse layout for each table.
    d. Make STUDENT_ID the master index for the KEYED table. Comment on where the new record is displayed in Browse layout for the table now.

E 18. The PRACTICE directory on your Student Disk contains a Paradox file named PDOX.DB. Open this file and print its contents. (*Hint:* Use the Open Table dialog box.)

E 19. The PRACTICE directory on your Student Disk contains a Lotus worksheet file named LOTUS.WK1. Convert this file to a dBASE table and print the contents of the file. Explore the File Import dialog box in the Help system.

Tutorial Assignments

Place your Student Disk in the disk drive, start dBASE, and set the current directory to A:\WM.

For the EXPENSES table you created in the Tutorial Assignments section of Tutorial 2, do the following:

1. Open the EXPENSES table and define the following validity checks:

Field Name	Validity Checks
TRANS_NO	Numbers only
JOB_NO	>=1000
CATEGORY	Numbers only
EXPNS_DATE	>=01/01/96

2. Add the records shown in Figure 3-39.

	Record 1	Record 2	Record 3
TRANS_NO	00004	00005	00006
JOB_NO	1001	1002	1002
CATEGORY	005	010	011
EXPNS_DATE	7/20/96	7/20/96	7/20/96
AMOUNT	93.75	200.00	35.05
EXPNS_DESC	Typesetting	Printing	Typesetting

Figure 3-39

3. The amount for transaction number 00001 was entered as 210. The correct amount is 150. Correct this entry.
4. Delete transaction number 00002. W&M decided not to bill the client for this expense. Pack the records to remove this record permanently.
5. Print the EXPENSES table.
6. Close the EXPENSES table.

For the JOBS table, do the following:
7. Print all the records in the JOBS table.
8. Make a backup copy of the JOBS table on your Student Disk. Name the backup copy BKUPJOBS.DBF.
9. Close the JOBS table.
E 10. Set the current directory to A\:PRACTICE and open the GRANT1 table. Set the master index to GRANTEE to display the records in order by GRANTEE. Close the GRANT1 table and reopen it. Are the records still displayed in order by GRANTEE?

Case Problems

1. Inventory of State-Owned Land

Place your Student Disk in the disk drive, start dBASE, and set the current directory to A:\LAND.
For the STATELND and LNDUSE tables you created in Tutorial 2, do the following:
1. Open the STATELND table and define the following validity checks:

Field Name	Validity Check
LAND_ID	Digits only
ACQUIRED	After 1950
ACREAGE	0 or greater
VALUE	0 or greater

2. Add the three records shown in Figure 3-40 to the STATELND table.

	Record 1	Record 2	Record 3
LAND_ID	0002	0003	0004
DIVISION	Education	Education	Administration
USE_CODE	02	02	05
ACQUIRED	1971	1971	1973
ACREAGE	1.1	2.0	2.1
VALUE	20000	82000	28800
LAND_DESC	Vocational School	URI extension	Cranston Armory

Figure 3-40

3. Change the value of the parcel LAND_ID 0002 from 20000 to 25000.
4. Print the STATELND table, then close it.
5. Open the LNDUSE table and add the two records shown in Figure 3-41 to the table.

USE_CODE	LAND_DESC
02	Educational
03	Offices

Figure 3-41

6. Print the LNDUSE table, then close it.
7. Make a backup copy of the STATELND table. Name the backup file STALNDBK.DBF.

8. You want to see the property records in the STATELND table in order by DIVISION. Because this reordering of the records is for a one-time use, you decide to sort the table instead of creating an index. Use the Sort Records option on the Table Utilities submenu of the Table menu to create a new table sorted by DIVISION. Call this new table STASORT. Open this table to see the sorted records.

2.   FINSTAT Inc.

Place your Student Disk in the disk drive, start dBASE, and set the current directory to A:\FINANCE.
For the COMPANY and FINANCE tables you created in Tutorial 2, do the following:
1. Open the COMPANY table, then define the following validity checks:

Field Name	Validity Check
COMPANY_ID	Character 1 uppercase; characters 2 & 3 numeric
INDUSTRY	Letters only

2. Add the two records shown in Figure 3-42 to the COMPANY table.

	Record 1	Record 2
COMPANY_ID	H01	K01
COMP_NAME	Home Depot	Kmart
INDUSTRY	DI	DI
SYMBOL	HmeDp	Kmart

Figure 3-42

3. Print the COMPANY table.
4. Open the FINANCE table, then define the following validity checks:

Field Name	Validity Check
COMPANY_ID	Character 1 uppercase; characters 2 & 3 numeric
YEAR	>=1991

5. Add the records shown in Figure 3-43 to the FINANCE table.

	Record 1	Record 2
COMPANY_ID	H01	H01
YEAR	1992	1991
SALES	7148	5142
ASSETS	3932	2504
PROFITS	362	247

Figure 3-43

6. Change the SALES value for Chrysler in 1992 from 25501 to 35501.
7. Print the FINANCE table.
8. Make a backup copy of the FINANCE table. Name the backup file FINBK.DBF.

E

9. The COMPANY table contains the field INDUSTRY, which stores a two-character industry code. The following data identifies each industry code and associated industry:

Code	Industry
AP	Apparel
BV	Beverages
CA	Cars
CH	Chemicals
DI	Discount Retailing
PE	Personal Care

Do the following:

a. Create a new table to store the industry codes and industry names. Name this table INDCODES. You determine the structure.

b. Print the INDCODES table so that a user can have a reference sheet for the industry codes and industry names.

c. Add the following company to the COMPANY table: F02, Fruit of the Loom, Apparel industry, FruitL. Use your reference sheet to find the correct industry code for this record. (In the next tutorial, you will learn the steps necessary to get dBASE to display the industry name in the same form as the COMPANY record.)

3. Marine Diving Equipment, Inc.

Place your Student Disk in the disk drive, start dBASE, and set the current directory to A:\MARINE.
For the CUST and ORD tables you created in Tutorial 2, do the following:

1. Open the CUST table, then define the following validity check:

Field Name	Validity Check
CUST_NO	Digits only

2. Add the three records shown in Figure 3-44 to the CUST table.

Field Name	Record 1	Record 2	Record 3
CUST_NO	1351	1354	1356
CUST_NAME	Sight Diver	Cayman Divers World Unlimited	Tom Sawyer Diving Centre
STREET	1 Neptune Lane	PO Box 541	632-1 Third Frydenhoj
CITY	Kato Paphos	Grand Cayman	Christiansted
ST_OR_PROV			St. Croix
POST_CODE			00820
COUNTRY	Cyprus	British West Indies	U.S. Virgin Islands
PHONE	357-687-6708	809-555-8576	809-555-7281
CONT_DATE	04/12/90	04/17/90	04/20/90

Figure 3-44

3. Change the POST_CODE value for CUST_NO 1356 to 08200.
4. Print the CUST table.
5. Open the ORD table, then define the following validity check:

Field Name	Validity Check
SHIP_VIA	Letters only

6. Add the two records shown in Figure 3-45 to the ORD table.

	Record 1	Record 2
ORD_NO	1003	1004
CUST_NO	1351	1354
SALE_DATE	03/28/91	04/02/91
SHIP_VIA	UPS	FedEx
INV_AMT	$6,885	$3,525
AMT_PAID	$6,885	$3,525
PAY_METHOD	Check	Check

Figure 3-45

7. Print the ORD table, then close it.
8. Make a backup of the CUST table. Name the backup file CUSTBK.DBF.

E 9. You need to find those customers from the Bahamas. Use the Find Records option on the Table menu to find these records. Find the first customer from the Bahamas, then search again from the current record to find the next. Continue until you have found every customer from the Bahamas.

4. Teaching Activity

Place your Student Disk in the disk drive, start dBASE, and set the current directory to A:\TEACH. For the FACULTY, COURSES, and TEACH tables you created in Tutorial 2, do the following:

1. Open the FACULTY table, then define the following validity checks:

Field Name	Validity Check
FAC_ID	Character 1 uppercase letter; characters 2 & 3 digits
RANK	Letters only
DEPT	Letters only
SALARY	>=0

2. Add the two records shown in Figure 3-46 to the FACULTY table.

	Record 1	Record 2
FAC_ID	S10	K10
LAST_NAME	SELDON	KELLY
FIRST_NAME	CHARLENE	RUPERT
RANK	PROF	PROF
DEPT	MGT	MGS
YEAR_HIRED	1975	1977
SALARY	61000	59000

Figure 3-46

3. Change the rank of RON ABLE from ASST to ASSO.
4. Change the salary of SIMON COHEN from 53000 to 54000.
5. Print the FACULTY table.
6. Open the COURSES table, then define the following validity check:

Field Name	Validity Check
COURSE_NO	Characters 1 through 3 uppercase letters; characters 4 through 6 digits

7. Add the three records shown in Figure 3-47 to the COURSES table.

COURSE_NO	TITLE	DEPT
OMT309	OPERATIONS MANAGEMENT	MGS
ACC201	ELEMENTARY ACCOUNTING I	ACC
ACC202	ELEMENTARY ACCOUNTING II	ACC

Figure 3-47

8. Change the course title of course MGS306 to QUANT METHODS II.
9. Print the COURSES table, then close it.
10. Open the TEACH table and add the two records shown in Figure 3-48 to the table.

FAC_ID	COURSE_NO	SECTION	YEAR	TERM	ENROLLMENT
K10	OMT309	01	1992	F	52
K10	OMT309	02	1992	F	45

Figure 3-48

11. Print the TEACH table, then close it.

E 12. You want to display the FACULTY records so that they are arranged by salary (low to high). To display the records in this order, explore the Sort Records command on the Table Utilities submenu of the Table menu. You'll need to create a new table in which to place the sorted records. Name this new table SORTFAC.

E **5. Off-Campus Housing**

Place your Student Disk in the disk drive, start dBASE, and set the current directory to A:\PRACTICE.

David Abelson is a sophomore at Breyers University. He works in the university's Housing Office, where he maintains a manual system for tracking the availability of off-campus housing. When landlords have vacancies, they call or visit the Housing Office to list their rental properties with David. University students come in to seek off-campus housing. Using the current system, students look through the Housing Office's book of available off-campus housing units and try to find units that match their needs.

Although students do find available rentals, the system hasn't worked very smoothly. David has found that the system has several flaws. One problem is that too few copies of the housing book are available to meet student demands. In addition, housing units that have been recently rented tend to remain in the book. Also, students can't get a list of housing units that meet their specific criteria, and they are forced to read every listing to find what they want. It would be helpful if students could specify their needs—such as maximum monthly rent, number of bedrooms, and distance from campus—to find the units that meet their needs more quickly.

David has recently completed a computer course, and he believes that this system is a perfect candidate for computerization. He suggests to his manager that the Housing Office create a database of available off-campus housing. Students would then be able to get lists of available units based on their specific needs.

Do the following:

1. Create a database table named HOUSING based on the case description and the 12 off-campus housing forms shown in Figure 3-49 on the following pages.
   Create an index for the field that contains the city name.

2. Add the data in Figure 3-49 to the table.
3. Display the first record using Form layout.
4. In Browse layout, display the records in order by city.

AVAILABLE OFF-CAMPUS HOUSING FORM   001

1. Rental Address:

39 Rippling Road

Street Address

Narragansett   RI   02894

City   State   Zip

2. Indicate name and phone numbers of owner of rental property

Panza   Ronald

Last Name   First Name

(401)555-9912

Home Phone #   Work Phone #

3. Type of rental unit available (check one)

   (X) House   ( ) Apartment

4. # of bedrooms: 3

5. How many miles is unit from campus? 8

6. Length of lease required (in months)? 9

7. Rent per month? 510

8. Date Available? 9/01/96

9. Please check all amenities that your rental unit features:

   ( ) Utilities included   ( ) Washer/dryer

   (X) Furnished bedroom(s)   ( ) Dishwasher

   ( ) On bus line   (X) Pets allowed

   ( ) Wheelchair accessible   (X) Children allowed

AVAILABLE OFF-CAMPUS HOUSING FORM   002

1. Rental Address:

28 Main Street

Street Address

Wakefield   RI   02893

City   State   Zip

2. Indicate name and phone numbers of owner of rental property

Scalia   Vinnie

Last Name   First Name

(401)555-8923   (401)555-4444

Home Phone #   Work Phone #

3. Type of rental unit available (check one)

   (X) House   ( ) Apartment

4. # of bedrooms: 4

5. How many miles is unit from campus? 7

6. Length of lease required (in months)? 6

7. Rent per month? 500

8. Date Available? 9/03/96

9. Please check all amenities that your rental unit features:

   ( ) Utilities included   (X) Washer/dryer

   (X) Furnished bedroom(s)   ( ) Dishwasher

   (X) On bus line   ( ) Pets allowed

   ( ) Wheelchair accessible   (X) Children allowed

AVAILABLE OFF-CAMPUS HOUSING FORM   003

1. Rental Address:

1 High Street

Street Address

Narrangansett   RI   02882

City   State   Zip

2. Indicate name and phone numbers of owner of rental property

Margolis   Jeanne

Last Name   First Name

(401)555-2109

Home Phone #   Work Phone #

3. Type of rental unit available (check one)

   ( ) House   (X) Apartment

4. # of bedrooms: 1

5. How many miles is unit from campus? 7

6. Length of lease required (in months)? 3

7. Rent per month? 350

8. Date Available? 9/03/96

9. Please check all amenities that your rental unit features:

   (X) Utilities included   ( ) Washer/dryer

   (X) Furnished bedroom(s)   ( ) Dishwasher

   ( ) On bus line   ( ) Pets allowed

   ( ) Wheelchair accessible   ( ) Children allowed

AVAILABLE OFF-CAMPUS HOUSING FORM   004

1. Rental Address:

61 Cheery Drive

Street Address

Narrangansett   RI   02882

City   State   Zip

2. Indicate name and phone numbers of owner of rental property

Ross   Maude

Last Name   First Name

(401)555-9822   (401)555-2291

Home Phone #   Work Phone #

3. Type of rental unit available (check one)

   (X) House   ( ) Apartment

4. # of bedrooms: 4

5. How many miles is unit from campus? 8

6. Length of lease required (in months)? 9

7. Rent per month? 600

8. Date Available? 9/05/96

9. Please check all amenities that your rental unit features:

   ( ) Utilities included   ( ) Washer/dryer

   ( ) Furnished bedroom(s)   (X) Dishwasher

   (X) On bus line   ( ) Pets allowed

   (X) Wheelchair accessible   (X) Children allowed

Figure 3-49

AVAILABLE OFF-CAMPUS HOUSING FORM   005

1. Rental Address:

915 Maple Street

Street Address

Wakefield   RI   02894

City   State   Zip

2. Indicate name and phone numbers of owner of rental property

Glass   Fred

Last Name   First Name

(401)555-9345

Home Phone #   Work Phone #

3. Type of rental unit available (check one)

( ) House   (X) Apartment

4. # of bedrooms: 1

5. How many miles is unit from campus? 7

6. Length of lease required (in months)? 3

7. Rent per month? 400

8. Date Available? 9/03/96

9. Please check all amenities that your rental unit features:

(X) Utilities included   (X) Washer/dryer

(X) Furnished bedroom(s)   (X) Dishwasher

(X) On bus line   ( ) Pets allowed

(X) Wheelchair accessible   ( ) Children allowed

AVAILABLE OFF-CAMPUS HOUSING FORM   006

1. Rental Address:

Crossways Apartments

Street Address

Wakefield   RI   02879

City   State   Zip

2. Indicate name and phone numbers of owner of rental property

Howard   Frank

Last Name   First Name

(401)555-9821   (401)555-0982

Home Phone #   Work Phone #

3. Type of rental unit available (check one)

( ) House   (X) Apartment

4. # of bedrooms: 1

5. How many miles is unit from campus? 1

6. Length of lease required (in months)? 9

7. Rent per month? 350

8. Date Available? 10/01/96

9. Please check all amenities that your rental unit features:

(X) Utilities included   ( ) Washer/dryer

(X) Furnished bedroom(s)   ( ) Dishwasher

( ) On bus line   ( ) Pets allowed

( ) Wheelchair accessible   ( ) Children allowed

AVAILABLE OFF-CAMPUS HOUSING FORM   007

1. Rental Address:

50 Yankee Drive

Street Address

Narragansett   RI   02882

City   State   Zip

2. Indicate name and phone numbers of owner of rental property

Mason   Jake

Last Name   First Name

(401)555-1983

Home Phone #   Work Phone #

3. Type of rental unit available (check one)

(X) House   ( ) Apartment

4. # of bedrooms: 1

5. How many miles is unit from campus? 7

6. Length of lease required (in months)? 9

7. Rent per month? 475

8. Date Available? 9/01/96

9. Please check all amenities that your rental unit features:

(X) Utilities included   ( ) Washer/dryer

( ) Furnished bedroom(s)   ( ) Dishwasher

( ) On bus line   ( ) Pets allowed

( ) Wheelchair accessible   ( ) Children allowed

AVAILABLE OFF-CAMPUS HOUSING FORM   008

1. Rental Address:

92 Worden Pond Road

Street Address

Kingston   RI   02881

City   State   Zip

2. Indicate name and phone numbers of owner of rental property

Kinyo   Janine

Last Name   First Name

(401)555-1195   (401)555-5367

Home Phone #   Work Phone #

3. Type of rental unit available (check one)

( ) House   (X) Apartment

4. # of bedrooms: 2

5. How many miles is unit from campus? 2

6. Length of lease required (in months)? 9

7. Rent per month? 425

8. Date Available? 9/01/96

9. Please check all amenities that your rental unit features:

(X) Utilities included   (X) Washer/dryer

(X) Furnished bedroom(s)   ( ) Dishwasher

(X) On bus line   (X) Pets allowed

( ) Wheelchair accessible   ( ) Children allowed

Figure 3-49 cont.

009

AVAILABLE OFF-CAMPUS HOUSING FORM

1. Rental Address:
100 Point Judith Road
Street Address
Narragansett   RI   02882
City   State   Zip

2. Indicate name and phone numbers of owner of rental property
Franconi   Joe
Last Name   First Name
(401)555-9921   (401)555-1239
Home Phone #   Work Phone #

3. Type of rental unit available (check one)
( ) House   (X) Apartment

4. # of bedrooms: _2_

5. How many miles is unit from campus? _8_

6. Length of lease required (in months)? _9_

7. Rent per month? _400_

8. Date Available? _01/01/97_

9. Please check all amenities that your rental unit features:
( ) Utilities included   ( ) Washer/dryer
(X) Furnished bedroom(s)   ( ) Dishwasher
(X) On bus line   ( ) Pets allowed
( ) Wheelchair accessible   ( ) Children allowed

010

AVAILABLE OFF-CAMPUS HOUSING FORM

1. Rental Address:
968 Ocean Drive
Street Address
Narragansett   RI   02882
City   State   Zip

2. Indicate name and phone numbers of owner of rental property
Marks   Heather
Last Name   First Name
(401)555-9973
Home Phone #   Work Phone #

3. Type of rental unit available (check one)
(X) House   ( ) Apartment

4. # of bedrooms: _3_

5. How many miles is unit from campus? _10_

6. Length of lease required (in months)? _9_

7. Rent per month? _650_

8. Date Available? _9/10/96_

9. Please check all amenities that your rental unit features:
( ) Utilities included   (X) Washer/dryer
( ) Furnished bedroom(s)   ( ) Dishwasher
(X) On bus line   ( ) Pets allowed
( ) Wheelchair accessible   (X) Children allowed

011

AVAILABLE OFF-CAMPUS HOUSING FORM

1. Rental Address:
1 Goat Island Circle
Street Address
Narragansett   RI   02882
City   State   Zip

2. Indicate name and phone numbers of owner of rental property
Razor   Charles
Last Name   First Name
(401)555-9357   (401)555-9111
Home Phone #   Work Phone #

3. Type of rental unit available (check one)
(X) House   ( ) Apartment

4. # of bedrooms: _4_

5. How many miles is unit from campus? _8_

6. Length of lease required (in months)? _9_

7. Rent per month? _700_

8. Date Available? _09/01/96_

9. Please check all amenities that your rental unit features:
( ) Utilities included   (X) Washer/dryer
( ) Furnished bedroom(s)   ( ) Dishwasher
( ) On bus line   ( ) Pets allowed
( ) Wheelchair accessible   (X) Children allowed

012

AVAILABLE OFF-CAMPUS HOUSING FORM

1. Rental Address:
12 Wooded Lane
Street Address
Kingston   RI   02881
City   State   Zip

2. Indicate name and phone numbers of owner of rental property
Johnston   Evan
Last Name   First Name
(401)555-1357   (401)555-4131
Home Phone #   Work Phone #

3. Type of rental unit available (check one)
( ) House   (X) Apartment

4. # of bedrooms: _1_

5. How many miles is unit from campus? _1_

6. Length of lease required (in months)? _12_

7. Rent per month? _425_

8. Date Available? _01/01/97_

9. Please check all amenities that your rental unit features:
(X) Utilities included   ( ) Washer/dryer
(X) Furnished bedroom(s)   ( ) Dishwasher
( ) On bus line   ( ) Pets allowed
(X) Wheelchair accessible   ( ) Children allowed

Figure 3-49 cont.

Querying a Database

Retrieving Information from the W&M Database

CASE

Wells & Martinez Advertising Agency One morning you find a note on your desk. The note is from Nancy requesting a list of all jobs in the JOBS table. She wants the list to show only the JOB_NO, CLIENT_ID, MEDIA, DUE_DATE, and QUOTE values for each job. As you read Nancy's note, Martin stops by and asks for a list of all jobs with a quoted amount above $5,000. He also wants to see a list of all the jobs—both completed and in progress—for the Santa Fe Tourist Center and for Alexander's Insurance. After Martin leaves, Nancy calls to inform you that she'll need additional information from both the JOBS and CLIENTS tables, and that she'll stop by later to give you the details.

To give Nancy and Martin the information they requested, you need to query the W&M database.

Introduction to Queries

Querying a database is simply the process of retrieving information from one or more tables in the database and displaying it either on the screen or in a printout. A **query** is the question you ask the database to get the results you want.

Database systems are developed to provide information to help solve business problems. As database developers create these systems, they try to anticipate the questions business people might want answered from the data in a database. They also try to develop reports that can be produced on a regular basis. Despite their efforts, however, developers cannot anticipate all the questions business people will ask. In such instances, database users rely on the query facility of a DBMS.

In dBASE, you create a query by filling in a query form that resembles a table. In this form, called the query skeleton, you specify the fields to be included in the resulting display, and you determine the selection criteria for retrieving the records. This method of specifying a query is known as **Query by Example** (QBE). dBASE interprets the information in the query form and places the answer to your query in a separate window, the Query Results window.

In this tutorial you will use dBASE's query facility to develop the queries you need to answer Nancy's and Martin's requests for information.

Understanding the Query Designer Window

To create a query in dBASE, you work in the Query Designer window. You use this window to choose the fields you want displayed in the query results and to specify any search conditions, or criteria, for the query. The Query Designer window contains an image of the database table you want to query. This image is called a **query skeleton**, or simply a **skeleton**. The skeleton displays the same fields in the same order as the table it represents. The major difference is that the skeleton does not display any of the data contained in the table.

Figure 4-1 shows the skeleton of the JOBS table as it initially appears in the Query Designer window.

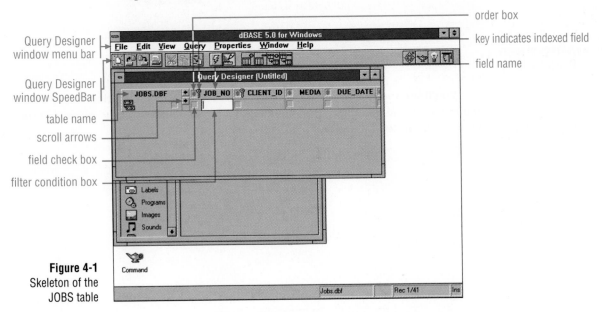

Figure 4-1
Skeleton of the JOBS table

The name of the table appears in the first column of the skeleton, followed by left and right scroll arrows, and then a column for each field in the table. Next to each field name is a box with a double-headed arrow. This box allows you to specify the order in which the records will be displayed in the Query Results window. A key next to a field name indicates that the field is indexed.

Each column contains an empty check box. You use the check boxes to select the fields you want to see in the query results. For example, to create a query that shows the JOB_NO, CLIENT_ID, and DUE_DATE for each job in the table, you would click the check boxes below each of those fields.

The space next to each check box, called the **filter condition box**, is used to specify the filter conditions (criteria) the data must satisfy in order for a record to be displayed. For example, to create a query that shows the JOB_NO, CLIENT_ID, and DUE_DATE for only those jobs in the table with a QUOTE value of $5,000 or more, you would click the check boxes for JOB_NO, CLIENT_ID, and DUE_DATE, and you would specify a filter condition of ">5000" in the QUOTE field. (Note that the resulting display would not include the QUOTE values because the QUOTE field's check box was not selected.)

If all the columns of the skeleton cannot fit on the screen at one time, you can use the left and right scroll arrows to move to any fields that are not visible.

Like other windows in dBASE, the Query Designer window includes a menu bar at the top of the screen and a SpeedBar immediately below the menu bar. (The SpeedBar contains buttons for working with queries.)

You can use the keyboard to move around the skeleton. Figure 4-2 describes keystrokes and their actions in the Query Designer window.

Keystroke	Result in Query Designer Window
[Tab]	Move to next field
[Shift][Tab]	Move to previous field
[Ctrl][Home]	Move to first field in skeleton
[Ctrl][End]	Move to last field in skeleton
[F3]	Move to previous skeleton (in a multi-table query)
[F4]	Move to next skeleton (in a multi-table query)

Figure 4-2
Keystrokes in Query
Designer window

You'll use the Query Designer window to retrieve the information Nancy and Martin requested. In the first query, you will display certain fields for all the records in the JOBS table, as requested by Nancy.

Creating a Query to View All the Records in a Table

Creating a query involves placing checkmarks in the boxes for the fields you want to include in the display and specifying any filter conditions that the data must meet. The first step in creating a query is to open the Query Designer window.

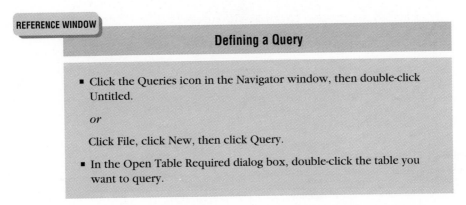

REFERENCE WINDOW

Defining a Query

- Click the Queries icon in the Navigator window, then double-click Untitled.

  or

  Click File, click New, then click Query.

- In the Open Table Required dialog box, double-click the table you want to query.

Let's start dBASE and use its Query Designer to answer Nancy's request for a list of all the jobs in the JOBS table, showing only the values for certain fields.

To start dBASE and open the Query Designer window:

❶ Place your Student Disk in the disk drive.

❷ Start dBASE.

❸ Make sure the current directory is A:\WM.

❹ Click the **Queries icon** in the Navigator window, then double-click **Untitled** (or click **File**, click **New**, then click **Query**). The Query Designer window opens and the Open Table Required dialog box appears. See Figure 4-3.

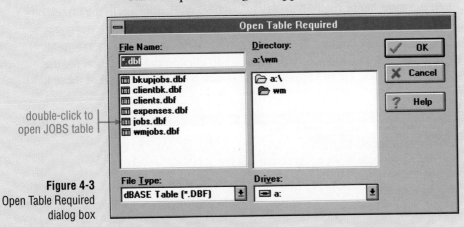

double-click to open JOBS table

Figure 4-3
Open Table Required
dialog box

Next, you select the table you want to use for the query.

❺ Double-click **jobs.dbf**. The Query Designer window displays a skeleton of the JOBS table.

❻ Click the **Maximize button** on the Query Designer window to see more of the skeleton. See Figure 4-4.

menu bar options
have changed

SpeedBar buttons
have changed

skeleton of
JOBS table

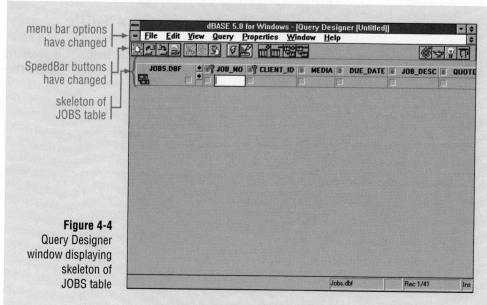

Figure 4-4
Query Designer
window displaying
skeleton of
JOBS table

Notice that the menu bar and the SpeedBar changed when you opened the Query Designer window.

When you first open a new skeleton, all the check boxes are empty. To include a field in the display of the query results, you need to place a checkmark in the field's check box. To place a checkmark, you click the field's empty check box.

Nancy wants to see the JOB_NO, CLIENT_ID, MEDIA, DUE_DATE, and QUOTE values for each job in the JOBS table. Let's select these fields.

To select the fields to be included in the query results:
❶ Click the **check box** in the JOB_NO field. A checkmark appears in the check box. (Refer to Figure 4-1 for the location of the check box.)

❷ Click the **check box** in the CLIENT_ID, MEDIA, DUE_DATE and QUOTE fields. Notice that the skeleton scrolls left when you click in the check box for the QUOTE field. Checkmarks appear in the check boxes under each of these fields. See Figure 4-5.

Figure 4-5
Query skeleton with
checkmarks in
check boxes

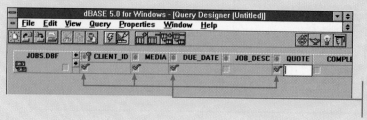

checkmarks indicate
fields to be included in
query results

When using check boxes, keep in mind the following:
- If you change your mind and don't want to include a field you've checked, click the check box to remove the checkmark.
- A quick way to select all the fields in a table is to click the check box below the table name. A checkmark appears in this check box and in all the other check boxes in the skeleton. Clicking this check box again clears all the check marks in the skeleton.

Now that you've defined the query in the skeleton, you can run the query to see the results.

Running a Query

You must **run**, or execute, a query in order for dBASE to display the results. When you run a query, dBASE selects the records from the queried table(s) that meet the conditions specified (if any) and displays the results of your query in a new window called the Query Results window. The Query Results window will contain only the fields you checked when you created the query.

REFERENCE WINDOW

Creating and Running a Query

- Open the Query Designer window to display the skeleton of the table you want to query.

- Place checkmarks in all the check boxes of the fields you want to include in the Query Results window.

- Type in any filter conditions.

- Click the Run Query button on the SpeedBar.

Now you can run the query you created and show the results to Nancy on the screen.

To run the query:
❶ Click the **Run Query button** 🔲 on the SpeedBar. The Query Results window appears. See Figure 4-6.

fields selected for
query results

dBASE 5.0 for Windows - [Query Results [Untitled]]				
File **Edit** **View** **Table** **Properties** **Window** **Help**				

Rec	JOB_NO	CLIENT_ID	MEDIA	DUE_DATE	QUOTE
1	1001	S03	Print	08/15/96	2500.00
2	1002	V01	Broadcast	08/10/96	32500.00
3	1003	M01	Print	06/01/96	3000.00
4	1004	A01	Print	06/05/96	3500.00
5	1005	S01	Print	06/10/96	22500.00
6	1006	S03	Print	08/01/96	2200.00
7	1007	S01	Direct	08/02/96	3000.00
8	1008	V01	Broadcast	11/05/96	12000.00
9	1009	R01	Print	08/05/96	2500.00
10	1010	A01	Direct	10/10/96	1250.00
11	1011	S03	Direct	08/22/96	8450.00
12	1012	A01	Broadcast	09/01/96	3425.00
13	1013	S01	Direct	10/15/96	8900.00
14	1014	R01	Direct	11/20/96	2200.00
15	1015	S01	Direct	09/15/96	4400.00
16	1016	S03	Print	10/15/96	10000.00
17	1017	C01	Other	09/20/96	850.00
18	1018	V01	Broadcast	12/05/96	35700.00
19	1019	S01	Print	09/12/96	8900.00
20	1020	R01	Direct	10/10/96	9400.00
21	1021	R01	Broadcast	09/03/96	23000.00

query results →

Jobs.dbf   Rec 1/41   Ins

Figure 4-6
Query Results
window after
running query

Notice that the Query Results window is maximized, just as the Query Designer
window was.

The Query Results window displays all the records in the JOBS table, showing only those
fields you checked in the skeleton. The order of the fields in the Query Results window
matches the order of the fields in the source table. The left-most field checked in the skeleton
is the left-most field in the Query Results window; the second field checked in the skeleton is
the second field in the Query Results window, and so on. You can change the order of the
fields by moving them in the query skeleton or by moving them in the Query Results window.
To move a field, place the pointer on the field name until the pointer changes to ☝, then
click and drag the field to its new position. Changing the order of fields in the Query Results
window affects only the display of these results; it does not affect the order of the fields in the
JOBS table structure. When you run the query again, the fields will be displayed in the order
they are shown in the skeleton.

The Query Results window represents a **view** of the JOBS table. You can add, delete,
or modify records in the Query Results window just as you can in the Table Records window. Any changes you make to records in the Query Results window are recorded in the
JOBS table. Notice that if you add or modify a record, you will be able to enter values only
in the fields visible in the Query Results window. Deleting a record in the Query Results
window marks the entire record for deletion from the table.

By default, the records in the Query Results window are sorted in natural order, that
is, the order in which they were entered in the table. To have records appear in a different sort order, you must specify the sort order in the Query Designer window.

Nancy asks if you can display the query results sorted by the values in the DUE_DATE
field.

Specifying the Sort Order in a Query

You can change the order in which records are displayed in the Query Results window. To do so, you specify the sort order in the Query Designer window.

Specifying the Sort Order in the Query Designer Window

- Click the Design button to display the Query Designer window.
- Click the order box for the field on which you want the records sorted, then select the sort order option you want.

Let's run the previous query again, this time sorting the records by DUE_DATE, as Nancy requested.

To specify a sort order for the query:

❶ Click the **Design button** 🖫 on the SpeedBar to return to the Query Designer window. Notice that the order box next to the field name for the DUE_DATE field shows a double-headed arrow. This indicates that no sort order has been specified for this field.

❷ Place the pointer on the **order box** next to the field name for the DUE_DATE field, then click and hold down the mouse button to display the sort options. See Figure 4-7.

Figure 4-7
Sort options list for
the DUE_DATE field

order options for
DUE_DATE field

There are three sort options for the DUE_DATE field. The up arrow specifies sorting in ascending order, from the earliest date to the latest. The down arrow specifies sorting in descending order, from the latest date to the earliest. The double arrow specifies no sorting (natural order).

Now choose the sort order.

❸ Drag the highlight until the up arrow is highlighted, then release the mouse button. The up arrow appears in the order box for the DUE_DATE field. See Figure 4-8.

ascending
order selected

Figure 4-8
Query Designer
window after
choosing field to
sort by

The records in the Query Results window will be sorted by DUE_DATE, earliest date first, when you run the query.

You can order records by more than one field. For example, you can order jobs by the CLIENT_ID field and within CLIENT_ID by the DUE_DATE field. To order by multiple fields, you select order options in the order boxes for the additional fields. The sort order is determined by the order of the fields in the query skeleton. From left to right, the primary sort key is the first ordered field in the skeleton, the secondary sort key is the second ordered field, and so on. You can change the sort order by changing the order of the fields in the skeleton. When you use multiple fields for ordering records, dBASE creates a "read only" view of the table; that is, you cannot add, delete, or modify records in the Query Results window, which you *can* do when sorting on only one field. Therefore, if you plan to make changes in the Query Results window, make sure you sort on only one field.

Now that you've specified the necessary sort order, you can run the query.

To run the query:

❶ Click the **Run Query button** 🔲 on the SpeedBar. The Query Results window now displays the records sorted in ascending order by DUE_DATE. See Figure 4-9.

query results listed
in order by
DUE_DATE

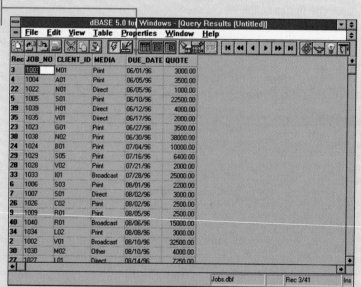

Figure 4-9
Results sorted by
DUE_DATE

The sort order does not affect the order in which fields appear in the Query Results window. The CLIENT_ID field appears before the DUE_DATE field even though the DUE_DATE field is the sort field. As mentioned above, to change the order of the *fields* (not the order of the *records*) appearing in the Query Results window, you can move the columns when viewing the skeleton in the Query Designer window.

The three sort options available for the DUE_DATE field are available for all field types except character fields. Character fields offer five options, which are described in Figure 4-10.

Order Options for Character Fields	
Option	**Description**
Ascending order (case-sensitive)	All uppercase letters are sorted alphabetically before lowercase letters. For example, "Zelig" will appear before "apple."
Descending order (case-sensitive)	All uppercase letters are sorted alphabetically after lowercase letters. For example, "zero" will appear before "Allen."
Ascending order (case-insensitive)	Ignores the distinction between uppercase and lowercase letters.
Descending order (case-insensitive)	Ignores the distinction between uppercase and lowercase letters.
Unordered	Uses natural order (the order in which the records were entered).

Figure 4-10
Order options for
character fields

Nancy has viewed the results of the queries you've done on your screen. Now she wants to see another listing. This time, she wants the same fields displayed in the query results, but she wants the query to show only those jobs that are assigned the Print media. How do you retrieve this information from the table? You need to create a query that contains a filter condition.

Filter Conditions in a Query

Until now, the queries in this tutorial have shown you how to display selected fields for all the records in the JOBS table. Typically, when you work with a database, you are more likely to create queries to select records that meet certain criteria, called filter conditions. As mentioned earlier in this tutorial, you use **filter conditions** in a query to specify which records will be displayed from the queried table.

To display the information Nancy requested—all jobs assigned the Print media—you need to ask dBASE to search the entire table and display only those records that meet this criterion. To search for specific records, you must enter a filter condition into a field in the skeleton.

Using Exact Match Criteria in a Filter Condition

The simplest queries containing filter conditions are those in which you specify a value for one or more fields. These queries are called **exact match queries**. You can define exact match criteria for character, date, numeric, and logical field types.

The query you need to create to display the information Nancy requested is an example of an exact match query. In this query you will display only those records in the JOBS table with the value "Print" in the MEDIA field. Let's create this query.

To enter the filter condition "Print" in the query:
❶ Click the **Design button** 🖾 on the SpeedBar.
❷ Click in the filter condition box below the MEDIA field name. A highlighted text box appears.

Now enter the exact match value.

❸ Type "**Print**" and make sure you type an uppercase "P" and include the quotation marks. When specifying a filter condition for a character field, you must enclose the string in quotation marks. See Figure 4-11.

instructs dBASE to select records containing "Print" in the MEDIA field

Figure 4-11
Exact match filter condition

The filter condition tells dBASE to select all records in which the value equals "Print" in the MEDIA field. Exact match queries display records with *exactly* the same spelling and case (uppercase or lowercase) as the filter condition you type in the query skeleton.

Now run the query.

❹ Click the **Run Query button** ⚡ on the SpeedBar. The Query Results window displays only the jobs that were placed with the Print media. Notice that the records are still listed in order by DUE_DATE because of the specified sort order. See Figure 4-12.

records listed in order by DUE_DATE

Rec	JOB_NO	CLIENT_ID	MEDIA	DUE_DATE	QUOTE
3	1003	M01	Print	06/01/96	3000.00
4	1004	A01	Print	06/05/96	3500.00
5	1005	S01	Print	06/10/96	22500.00
23	1023	G01	Print	06/27/96	3500.00
38	1038	N02	Print	06/30/96	38000.00
24	1024	B01	Print	07/04/96	10000.00
29	1029	S05	Print	07/16/96	6400.00
28	1028	V02	Print	07/21/96	2000.00
6	1006	S03	Print	08/01/96	2200.00
26	1026	C02	Print	08/02/96	2500.00
9	1009	R01	Print	08/05/96	2500.00
34	1034	L02	Print	08/08/96	3000.00
1	1001	S03	Print	08/15/96	2500.00
31	1031	F01	Print	09/09/96	7250.00
19	1019	S01	Print	09/12/96	8900.00
32	1032	V02	Print	09/26/96	10000.00
16	1016	S03	Print	10/15/96	10000.00
37	1037	G01	Print	11/11/96	17000.00
36	1036	S05	Print	12/25/96	3500.00

only records with MEDIA value of "Print" are selected

Figure 4-12
Query Results window displaying Print media jobs

TROUBLE? If dBASE displays the Alert box with the message "No records selected," you might have entered the filter condition incorrectly. Queries are case-sensitive; therefore, you must type the exact match filter condition exactly as the text appears in the table. Click OK, and make sure you entered the filter condition correctly. Then run the query again.

TROUBLE? If dBASE displays the Alert box with the message "Fix or remove errors before running query," you entered a filter condition that dBASE does not recognize. (For example, you might have omitted the quotation marks around "Print".) Click OK and edit the highlighted filter condition box. Then run the query again.

Martin calls to remind you that he'd like to see a list of all the jobs that have a quote above $5,000. To perform this type of query, you need to use a relational operator in the filter condition.

Using Relational Operators in Filter Conditions

Often you will want to find records that have some value that is less than or greater than some other value. An example of a search for a value greater than a certain amount is Martin's request for all jobs that have a quote above $5,000.

To create this type of query, you must include a relational operator in the filter condition. **Relational operators**, sometimes called comparison operators, let you retrieve records with field values that fall within a range of values. You can also use relational operators to retrieve records that are greater than or less than a value you specify. You can use any of the relational operators shown in Figure 4-13 to perform these types of queries.

Operator	Definition	Example
>	Greater than	>5000
<	Less than	<0
=	Equal to	="Paris"
<> or #	Not equal to	<>"Print"
>= or =>	Greater than or equal to	>=0
<= or =<	Less than or equal to	<=100
$	Contains (or "is contained in")	$"Tacoma" Matches records with "Tacoma" anywhere in the field
Like	Pattern match	Like "*Allen" Matches records with field that ends in "Allen." The * wildcard represents any number of characters (or none). Like "W???y" Matches records with five-character fields beginning with "W" and ending with "y." Matches "Woody" or "Wally" but not "Wily."

Figure 4-13
Relational operators
in queries

Let's create the query to answer Martin's request for a listing of the jobs with quotes above $5,000.

First you need to return to the Query Designer window and remove the current filter condition from the skeleton.

To remove the filter condition from the MEDIA field:
❶ Click the **Design button** 🖾 on the SpeedBar.
❷ Double-click the filter condition box below the MEDIA field name to highlight the filter condition.
❸ Press [Del]. The filter condition is removed from the MEDIA field.

Now you can enter the filter condition to display jobs with quotes above $5,000.

To enter the filter condition in the QUOTE field and run the query:
❶ Click in the filter condition box below the QUOTE field name.

Now enter the relational operator, followed by the value.

❷ Type **>5000**. See Figure 4-14.

Figure 4-14
Relational operator
included in
filter condition

">" relational operator

filter condition

Do not include dollar signs ($) or commas (,) when entering amounts for filter conditions or the query will not work properly. Also, because QUOTE is a numeric field, you do not need to include quotation marks around the filter condition.

❸ Click the **Run Query button** 🔧 on the SpeedBar. The Query Results window displays only the records with a quote above $5,000. Note that the records are still sorted by the values in the DUE_DATE field. See Figure 4-15.

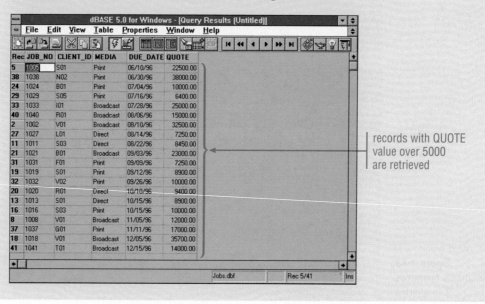

records with QUOTE
value over 5000
are retrieved

Figure 4-15
Query Results
window with quotes
over $5,000

After viewing the results of the query on your screen, Martin realizes that he'd prefer to see a list of only the *completed* jobs with quotes greater than $5,000. To perform this query, you must use a compound filter condition.

Using Compound Filter Conditions

When you created the query to retrieve *all* jobs with quotes greater than $5,000, you used only one filter condition in the query. For many situations, you need to enter only one filter condition to form the query. There are times, however, when you need to create a query based on two or more filter conditions. This is the case with Martin's request for a list of only the completed jobs quoted at more than $5,000.

If you place filter conditions in separate fields on the same line of the skeleton, all the filter conditions on that line must be met for a record to be included in the query results. This is a compound filter condition called the **AND condition**. With the AND condition, all filter conditions must be met. If you place two or more filter conditions in *different* lines of the skeleton, only one of the filter conditions must be met for a record to be included in the query results. This is a compound filter condition called the **OR condition**.

Creating an AND Query

Let's create Martin's query to list all the completed jobs with quotes over $5,000. To list these jobs, the skeleton must contain two filter conditions on the same line: the filter condition "Completed is True" finds completed jobs, and the condition "Quote greater than 5000" finds jobs with quotes above $5,000. Both conditions must be met in order for a record to be retrieved.

To enter the query with the AND condition:

❶ Click the **Design button** on the SpeedBar to return to the Query Designer window.

The skeleton still has the selection condition >5000. You do not have to reenter this filter condition. Just modify the skeleton so that it also includes the filter condition to retrieve completed jobs.

TROUBLE? If you accidentally added a row to the skeleton, which you could have done by inadvertently pressing [↓], you can remove the row by placing the highlight anywhere in it and pressing [↑].

❷ Click the **check box** in the COMPLETED field to include the field in the Query Results window.

Now enter the condition in the COMPLETED field.

❸ Click in the filter condition box below the COMPLETED field name, then type **.Y.** (making sure you type the periods before and after the letter Y). The COMPLETED field is a logical field. The periods around the Y indicate that you are searching for a logical value, not the letter Y. Notice that you could also enter.T.,.t., or.y. to indicate "Yes" for this field. "No" is indicated by.F.,.f.,.N., or.n.

There are now two filter conditions in the skeleton. Because both conditions are on the same line, you have formed an AND condition. See Figure 4-16.

Figure 4-16
AND condition
in the Query
Designer window

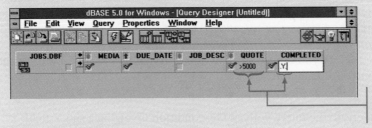

AND condition formed by
two filter conditions on
the same line

Now run the query.

❹ Click the **Run Query button** on the SpeedBar. dBASE processes the query and displays the records that meet both filter conditions—that is, with a value equal to Y in the COMPLETED field and a quote greater than 5000. See Figure 4-17.

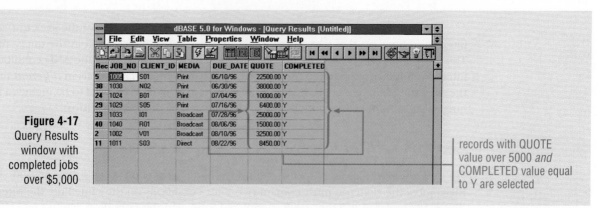

Figure 4-17
Query Results
window with
completed jobs
over $5,000

records with QUOTE
value over 5000 *and*
COMPLETED value equal
to Y are selected

The query you just created has two filter conditions entered in different fields. For some queries, you might need to enter more than one filter condition *in the same field* and require that all the filter conditions be met. To do this, you form the AND condition by separating the filter conditions in the field with a comma (,). The comma acts as an **AND operator,** telling dBASE that both filter conditions must be met for a record to be displayed. For example, suppose you wanted a list of jobs with quotes between $5,000 and $9,000. You would enter this AND condition in the QUOTE field as ">=5000,<=9000" (Figure 4-18).

Figure 4-18
AND condition
specifying two filter
conditions in the
same field

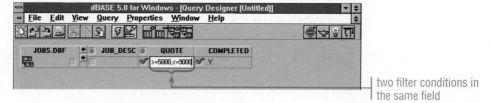

two filter conditions in
the same field

Martin reminds you that he also wants to see a list of all the jobs for the Santa Fe Tourist Center (S01) and Alexander's Insurance (A01). To create this type of query, you need to use the OR condition.

Creating an OR Query

The query that will display the information Martin requested requires a different type of logic from that of the previous query. Here you have a situation where *either one of two* filter conditions must be satisfied in order for a record to be retrieved—that is, *CLIENT_ID equals S01* or *CLIENT_ID equals A01*. This is an OR condition.

Before you enter this new query, remember that you must remove the current filter conditions from the skeleton.

To create the query with an OR condition involving a single field:
❶ Click the **Design button** 📇 on the SpeedBar to return to the Query Designer window.

First remove the filter conditions from the previous query.

❷ Click in the filter condition box for the QUOTE field to highlight it.

❸ Double-click in the filter condition box below the field name to select the text, then press **[Del]**.

❹ Repeat Steps 2 and 3 to remove the filter condition from the COMPLETED field.

❺ Scroll the skeleton until the CLIENT_ID field is visible, then click in the filter condition box below the CLIENT_ID field name.

❻ Type "**A01**" (making sure you include the quotation marks).

❼ Press [↓] to create a new line in the skeleton.

❽ Type "**S01**" (making sure you include the quotation marks). See Figure 4-19.

Figure 4-19
OR condition
in the Query
Designer window

Two filter conditions
on separate lines

TROUBLE? If you make a mistake while typing the filter condition, you can double-click the filter condition box and reenter the condition. If you add an extra blank line, you can remove it by pressing [↑]. Any blank lines in the skeleton are automatically removed when you run the query.

Now run the query.

❾ Click the **Run Query button** 🖩 on the SpeedBar. The Query Results window displays all records with a CLIENT_ID of either A01 or S01. Note that the records are still sorted by DUE_DATE. See Figure 4-20.

records with
CLIENT_ID value
A01 *or* S01
are selected

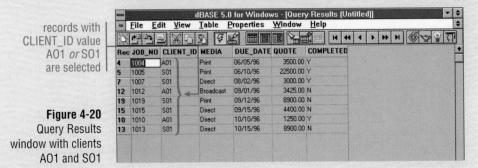

Figure 4-20
Query Results
window with clients
A01 and S01

As you've just seen, you use multiple lines in the skeleton to create queries in which you define two or more OR conditions for a *single* field. This works as well when the OR condition relates to *two or more* fields. For example, if you wanted a list of all jobs that either are placed with the Broadcast media or have a quote over $10,000, you would use two separate lines to enter "Broadcast" in the filter condition box below the MEDIA field name and >10000 in the filter condition box below the QUOTE field name. Let's try creating this query.

To define an OR condition involving two fields:

❶ Click the **Design button** 🖩 on the SpeedBar to return to the Query Designer window.

❷ Remove the filter conditions from both lines of the CLIENT_ID field.

❸ Click in the filter condition box below the MEDIA field name in the first line, then type "**Broadcast**" (making sure you include the quotation marks).

❹ In the second line, click in the filter condition box below the QUOTE field name, then type **>10000**. See Figure 4-21.

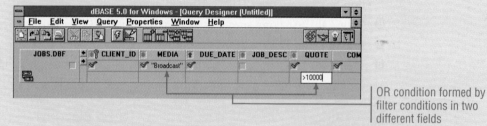

Figure 4-21
OR condition for
multiple fields

OR condition formed by
filter conditions in two
different fields

Now run the query.

❺ Click the **Run Query button** 🗲 on the SpeedBar. The Query Results window displays the results. See Figure 4-22.

records with MEDIA
value equal to
"Broadcast" or
QUOTE value over
10000 are selected

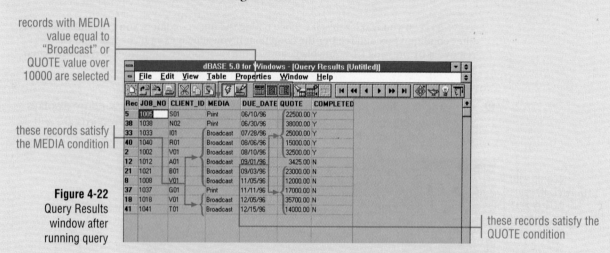

these records satisfy
the MEDIA condition

Figure 4-22
Query Results
window after
running query

these records satisfy the
QUOTE condition

When you place filter conditions on separate lines of the skeleton, dBASE retrieves records that match *either* condition. In this case all records that either are placed with the Broadcast media *or* have a quote over $10,000 appear in the results. Note that some records satisfy both filter conditions, but a record must satisfy only one in order to be included in the results.

Martin asks if he can have a printout of the query you just completed so that he can take it to a budget meeting later in the day.

Printing the Query Results

You can print the contents of the Query Results window in the same way you print the contents of the Table Records window. Let's print the current query results so that Martin can take the printout to his meeting.

To print the query results:

❶ Make sure the printer is turned on and contains paper.

❷ Make sure the Query Results window is displayed.

❸ Click the **Print button** 🖳 on the SpeedBar. The Print Records dialog box appears.

❹ Click **OK**. Figure 4-23 shows the printout of the Query Results window.

```
                       Query Results (Untitled)

JOB_NO      CLIENT_ID      MEDIA      DUE_DATE      QUOTE      COMPLETED
1005        S01            Print      06/10/96      22500.00   Y
1038        N02            Print      06/30/96      38000.00   Y
1033        I01            Broadcast  07/28/96      25000.00   Y
1040        R01            Broadcast  08/06/96      15000.00   Y
1002        V01            Broadcast  08/10/96      32500.00   Y
1012        A01            Broadcast  09/01/96       3425.00   N
1021        B01            Broadcast  09/03/96      23000.00   N
1008        V01            Broadcast  11/05/96      12000.00   N
1037        G01            Print      11/11/96      17000.00   N
1018        V01            Broadcast  12/05/96      35700.00   N
1041        T01            Broadcast  12/15/96      14000.00   N
```

Figure 4-23
Printout of
query results

You can now remove all filter conditions and the second line from the skeleton.

To remove the filter conditions and the second line:

❶ Click the **Design button** 🖾 on the SpeedBar to return to the Query Designer window.

❷ In the second line, click in the filter condition box below the QUOTE field to highlight it.

❸ Double-click the filter condition to select it, then press **[Del]**.

❹ Press [↑] to remove the blank line from the skeleton.

❺ Scroll the skeleton until the MEDIA field is visible.

❻ Click in the filter condition box below the MEDIA field to highlight it.

❼ Double-click the filter condition, then press **[Del]**.

If you want to take a break and resume the tutorial at a later time, close the Query Designer window *without saving*, click the Restore button on the Navigator window to restore it to its original size, then exit dBASE. When you resume the tutorial, place your Student Disk in the disk drive, start dBASE, then make sure the current directory is A:\WM. Click the Queries icon in the Navigator window, then double-click Untitled to open a new query. Select the jobs.dbf table and maximize the Query Designer window. Place checkmarks in the following fields: JOB_NO, CLIENT_ID, MEDIA, DUE_DATE, QUOTE, and COMPLETED. Specify DUE_DATE as the sort order by clicking its order box and selecting ascending order. Then continue with the tutorial.

■   ■   ■

Martin received a call from Sandy Alonso, director of Communications at the Santa Fe Tourist Center, asking if W&M could finish by next week each of the three projects they're currently working on for the Tourist Center. In return for putting a "rush" on these jobs, the Tourist Center would be willing to pay a five-percent premium on the quoted price.

Martin asks you to calculate a revised quote including the five-percent premium for each job being done for the Tourist Center.

Performing Calculations in a Query

A query can be used for more than just retrieving records from a database table; it can also be used to perform calculations. When you run the query, dBASE creates a new field in the Query Results window to contain the calculated results.

Creating a Calculated Field

In order to perform a calculation using a field in the table, you must define a new field, called a calculated field. A **calculated field** uses an expression to calculate a new value. An **expression** is a combination of field names, constants, functions, and operators that results in a single value.

Expressions can be very simple or quite complex. In complex expressions you can use parentheses ( ) to indicate which calculation should be performed first. In expressions without parentheses, dBASE calculates in the following order of precedence: multiplication and division, then addition and subtraction. dBASE calculates operations having equal precedence from left to right.

REFERENCE WINDOW

Creating a Calculated Field

- Activate the Query Designer window.

- Click Query then click Create Calculated Field.

- Double-click in the field name box and change the field name for the calculated field if you want a different name in the query results.

- Click in the expression box and enter a dBASE expression.

- Click in the filter condition box and enter a filter condition, if necessary.

Figure 4-24 shows several examples of dBASE expressions. For more information about creating expressions, explore the dBASE Help topic "About dBASE Expressions."

dBASE Expression	Description
PRICE*.10	Multiplies the value in the PRICE field by .10.
PAY_DATE-INV_DATE	Calculates the number of days between two dates.
PRICE+TAX	Adds the values of two fields.
MAX(BASE_PAY, HOURS*10)	MAX( ) is a function. A function calculates a single value. MAX( ) calculates the larger of the two values listed within the parentheses.
TRIM(LNAME)+",“+FNAME	TRIM( ) is a function that removes trailing blanks from a character field. This expression creates a new character field consisting of LNAME (with trailing blanks removed) followed by a comma, a blank, and then FNAME.
QUOTE>10000	Determines whether the field value is greater than 10000. The result is a logical value, .T. or .F.

Figure 4-24
Examples of dBASE expressions

To calculate the revised quote for the Santa Fe Tourist Center—which adds a five-percent premium to the existing quote amounts—you must create the new calculated field. Then you need to tell dBASE the type of calculation you want to perform. Let's define a new calculated field named REV_QUOTE to contain the revised QUOTE values.

To create the new calculated field:
❶ If necessary, scroll the skeleton until the JOB_NO field is visible.
❷ Click **Query** then click **Create Calculated Field**. A new skeleton appears showing a new calculated field. See Figure 4-25.

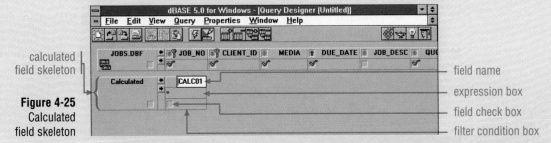

calculated field skeleton

Figure 4-25
Calculated field skeleton

field name
expression box
field check box
filter condition box

The new calculated field is named CALC01. (Subsequent calculated fields would be named CALC02, CALC03, and so on.) Below the field name is the expression box, where you can enter the dBASE expression. Below the expression box are the field check box and the filter condition box for this field.

Let's start by changing the name of the new field from CALC01 to REV_QUOTE, which is more descriptive.

❸ Double-click in the field name box for the new field to select CALC01, then type **REV_QUOTE**. Notice that the box expands to accommodate text as you type.

Now enter the expression for calculating the revised quote.

❹ Click in the expression box, then type **QUOTE*1.05**.

❺ Click the **field check box** to include this field in the Query Results window. The new calculated field has now been completely defined. See Figure 4-26.

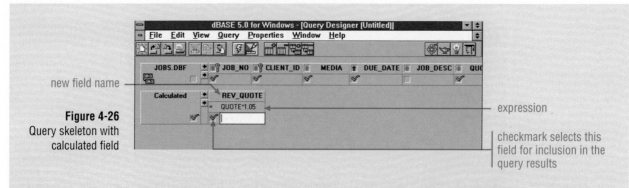

new field name ⎯

Figure 4-26
Query skeleton with
calculated field

expression

checkmark selects this
field for inclusion in the
query results

Notice that two checkmarks appear in the calculated field skeleton. The check-mark for REV_QUOTE selects the field for inclusion in the query results. The checkmark below Calculated indicates that all fields in the calculated field skeleton (in this case, only one field) are selected for inclusion in the query results.

The query is not yet complete. You need to restrict the calculation to uncompleted jobs for the Santa Fe Tourist Center (S01). If you don't include these filter conditions, you will calculate revised quotes for all the records in the JOBS table.

To enter the filter conditions and run the query:

❶ Click in the filter condition box for the COMPLETED field. You might need to scroll the skeleton to see the COMPLETED field.

❷ Type **.N.** (making sure you include the periods around the letter N).

❸ Click in the filter condition box for the CLIENT_ID field. You can move back to the CLIENT_ID field by scrolling.

❹ Type **"S01"** (making sure you include the quotation marks around S01). Also, make sure you type the number 0 and not the capital letter O.

❺ Click the **Run Query button** 🗲 on the SpeedBar. The Query Results window now contains a new field, the calculated field, as the result of the calculation. The calculated field appears at the end of the table. See Figure 4-27.

only records for
CLIENT_ID S01
are selected

new calculated field

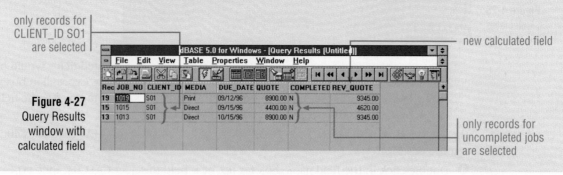

Figure 4-27
Query Results
window with
calculated field

only records for
uncompleted jobs
are selected

Using Summary Operators

You can calculate summary statistics, such as the total, average, and maximum value, on all or selected records in a database table. To do this you use the Table Utilities option of the Table menu. Figure 4-28 lists the summary statistics available.

Statistic	Description
Average	Calculates the average value for the field. Valid for numeric fields only.
Minimum	Calculates the minimum value for the field. Valid for numeric, date, or character fields.
Maximum	Calculates the maximum value for the field. Valid for numeric, date, or character fields.
Standard Deviation	Calculates the population standard deviation for values in the field. Valid for numeric fields only.
Sum	Calculates the sum of the values in the field. Valid for numeric fields only.
Variance	Calculates the population variance for values in the field. Valid for numeric fields only.

Figure 4-28
Summary statistics
in dBASE

For example, what if you wanted to calculate the average quote for uncompleted jobs for the Santa Fe Tourist Center? To do this, you must select the appropriate summary statistic from the list. Let's calculate this statistic.

To calculate the average quote for uncompleted jobs:
❶ Click **Table**, click **Table Utilities**, then click **Calculate Records...** to display the Calculate Records dialog box. See Figure 4-29.

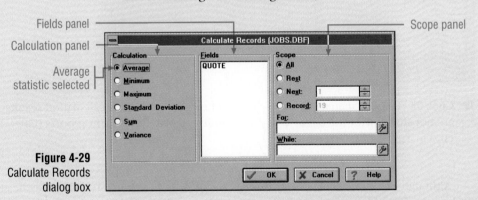

Fields panel

Calculation panel

Average
statistic selected

Figure 4-29
Calculate Records
dialog box

Scope panel

The Calculate Records dialog box contains three panels. The Calculation panel lets you select the statistic you want to calculate. The Fields panel lets you select the fields for which you want to calculate the statistic. This panel shows only those fields for which the selected statistic can be calculated. For example, the CLIENT_ID field does not appear in this list because you can't calculate the average of the values in this field. The Scope panel lets you restrict the calculation to a subset of the records in the table.

Let's calculate the average value of the QUOTE field for all records in the Query Results window.

❷ Make sure that the Average radio button in the Calculation panel is selected.

❸ Click the **QUOTE** field in the Fields panel (see Figure 4-29).

❹ Make sure that the All radio button in the Scope panel is selected. This specifies that all records in the Query Results window (in this case, three records) will be included in the calculation. See Figure 4-30.

Figure 4-30
Calculating the average of the QUOTE field

QUOTE field selected

❺ Click **OK**. dBASE calculates the average value in the QUOTE field for records in the Query Results window and displays the results in the Calculation Results window. See Figure 4-31.

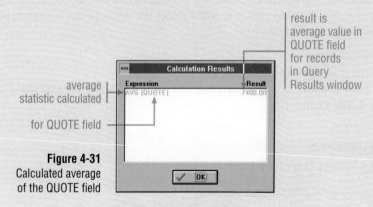

result is average value in QUOTE field for records in Query Results window

average statistic calculated

for QUOTE field

Figure 4-31
Calculated average of the QUOTE field

❻ Click **OK**. The Calculation Results window closes. Note that the calculation results are not stored with the table. You can include calculated results in reports (covered in Tutorial 6).

Although you can calculate only one statistic at a time, you can request that the statistic be calculated for several fields. You can select multiple fields in the Fields panel by holding the [Ctrl] key down while clicking the field names. The Calculation Results window displays the result for all selected fields.

You have now completed the steps to answer Martin's request for revised quotes for the Santa Fe Tourist Center. Let's close the Query Results window without saving the query skeleton and return to the Navigator window on the Desktop.

To close the Query Results window without saving and return to the Navigator window:

❶ Click the **Restore button** in the Query Results window to restore the window to its original size.

❷ Double-click the **Control menu box** for the Query Results window to close it and return to the Navigator window on the Desktop.

❸ Click **No** in the Changes Made—Query Designer dialog box to close the window without saving the query skeleton.

If you want to take a break and resume the tutorial at a later time, you can exit from dBASE now. When you resume the tutorial, place your Student Disk in the disk drive, start dBASE, make sure the current directory is A:\WM, then continue with the tutorial.

■   ■   ■

After returning from his budget meeting, Martin asks for your help in preparing a "Jobs Due" list for jobs in progress. He wants the list to provide all the information about each job and the associated client. Specifically, he wants the list to show the name of the client, the contact person, the job number, the media type, the due date, and the quoted amount. He knows that all the information is in the W&M database, but he also knows that no single table contains all this information. He asks what he should do.

If you examine the contents of the JOBS table, you see that this table contains the job number, media type, due date, and quote information Martin requested. If you examine the CLIENTS table, you see that the remaining information—client name and contact person—is in that table. You can gather the information Martin wants in one list by creating a **multi-table query**, a query based on two or more linked tables.

Introduction to Linking Tables

So far in this text, you have queried the database by retrieving data from only one database table. But what if answering a query or creating a report requires data from two or more tables? For example, to display the list that Martin needs, you must retrieve data from both the CLIENTS table and the JOBS table.

To retrieve data from two or more tables, you must link them. The process of linking tables is often called **defining a relation**. You can link two database tables if the tables have a common field. A **common field** is a field in each table that contains the same kind of information, that is, the same type and size. For example, because both the CLIENTS and the JOBS tables include the CLIENT_ID field, you can link them (Figure 4-32).

CLIENTS

CLIENT_ID	NAME	CONTACT	PHONE	FAX	STREET	CITY	STATE	ZIP
A01	Alexander Insurance	Paul Alexander	(505)883-9222	(505)883-9000	105 Canyon Road	Santa Fe	NM	87501
B01	Boatslip Inn	Victor Santos	(505)432-6590	(505)432-0560	32 Commercial Street	Taos	NM	87544
B02	Bullard Inc.	Gregory Bullard	(505)642-8674	(505)342-4789	4008 Washington Road	Albuquerque	NM	87434
C01	Celebrity Catering	Linda Randall	(505)833-9922	(505)833-9921	890 Third Avenue	Santa Fe	NM	87501
C02	Castro Bicycle Co-op	Mark Salgado	(505)628-9132		314 Castro Street	Santa Fe	NM	87501
F01	Fire Island Realtors	Jeffrey Stryker	(505)345-9234	(505)454-3478	434 West Evelyn Road	Santa Fe	NM	87501
G01	Gauntlet	Samuel Domingo	(505)234-7878	(505)897-3897	25 Market Street	Santa Fe	NM	87501
H01	Holistic Jewelry	Susan Glover	(505)432-9366		Rural Route 5	Taos	NM	87544
I01	Industrial Light & Sound	James Musil	(505)343-5278	(505)343-5277	549 North Halsted	Albuquerque	NM	87434
L01	Lambda Engineering	Jay Sharp	(505)437-1043	(505)437-1002	643 North Clark	Albuquerque	NM	87434
L02	Limelight	Juniaf Montingier	(505)523-2348	(505)234-5213	3243 Fifth Avenue	Albuquerque	NM	87434

JOBS

JOB_NO	CLIENT_ID	MEDIA	DUE_DATE	JOB_DESC	QUOTE	COMPLETED
1001	S03	Print	08/15/96	Best in Southwest	2500.00	Y
1002	V01	Broadcast	08/10/96	Fall TV ad	32500.00	Y
1003	M01	Print	06/01/96	Ski equipment sale	3000.00	Y
1004	A01	Print	06/05/96	B/W magazine ad	3500.00	Y
1005	S01	Print	06/10/96	4-page color ad in Southwest Magazine	22500.00	Y
1006	S03	Print	08/01/96	Fall promotion	2200.00	Y
1007	S01	Direct	08/02/96	Pamphlet	3000.00	Y
1008	V01	Broadcast	11/05/96	Thanksgiving sale	12000.00	N
1009	R01	Print	08/05/96	Bicycle magazine ad	2500.00	Y
1010	A01	Direct	10/10/96	Brochure	1250.00	Y
1011	S03	Direct	08/22/96	Fall catalog	8450.00	Y
1012	A01	Broadcast	09/01/96	Radio ad	3425.00	N

Query Results

NAME	CONTACT	JOB_NO	MEDIA	DUE_DATE	QUOTE
Alexander Insurance	Paul Alexander	1004	Print	06/05/96	3500.00
Alexander Insurance	Paul Alexander	1010	Direct	10/10/96	1250.00
Alexander Insurance	Paul Alexander	1012	Broadcast	09/01/96	3425.00
Boatslip Inn	Victor Santos	1021	Broadcast	09/03/96	23000.00
Boatslip Inn	Victor Santos	1024	Print	07/04/96	10000.00
Celebrity Catering	Linda Randall	1017	Other	09/20/96	850.00
Castro Bicycle Co-op	Mark Salgado	1026	Print	08/02/96	2500.00
Fire Island Realtors	Jeffrey Stryker	1031	Print	09/09/96	7250.00
Gauntlet	Samuel Domingo	1023	Print	06/27/96	3500.00
Gauntlet	Samuel Domingo	1037	Print	11/11/96	17000.00
Holistic Jewelry	Susan Glover	1039	Direct	06/12/96	4000.00
Industrial Light & Sound	James Musil	1033	Broadcast	07/28/96	25000.00
Lambda Engineering	Jay Sharp	1027	Direct	08/14/96	7250.00
Limelight	Juniaf Montingier	1034	Print	08/08/96	3000.00
Mountain Top Ski Resort	Victor Juarez	1003	Print	06/01/96	3000.00
Manana Outfitters	Daniel Gibbs	1030	Other	08/10/96	4000.00
Meteorological Survey	Sunil Jain	1025	Direct	10/04/96	5000.00
Nell's Rib Pit	Janelle May	1022	Direct	06/05/96	1000.00
Newsday	Esther Ling	1038	Print	06/30/96	38000.00
Rocky Mountain Tours	Helen Carson	1009	Print	08/05/96	2500.00
Rocky Mountain Tours	Helen Carson	1014	Direct	11/20/96	2200.00
Rocky Mountain Tours	Helen Carson	1020	Direct	10/10/96	9400.00
Rocky Mountain Tours	Helen Carson	1040	Broadcast	08/06/96	15000.00
Santa Fe Tourist Center	Liddy Posada	1005	Print	06/10/96	22500.00
Santa Fe Tourist Center	Liddy Posada	1007	Direct	08/02/96	3000.00
Santa Fe Tourist Center	Liddy Posada	1013	Direct	10/15/96	8900.00
Santa Fe Tourist Center	Liddy Posada	1015	Direct	09/15/96	4400.00
Santa Fe Tourist Center	Liddy Posada	1019	Print	09/12/96	8900.00
Southwest Styles	Gary Higgins	1001	Print	08/15/96	2500.00
Southwest Styles	Gary Higgins	1006	Print	08/01/96	2200.00
Southwest Styles	Gary Higgins	1011	Direct	08/22/96	8450.00
Southwest Styles	Gary Higgins	1016	Print	10/15/96	10000.00
Stonewall	Larry Kramer	1029	Print	07/16/96	6400.00
Stonewall	Larry Kramer	1036	Print	12/25/96	3500.00
Viking Auto Group	Jeff Serito	1002	Broadcast	08/10/96	32500.00
Viking Auto Group	Jeff Serito	1008	Broadcast	11/05/96	12000.00
Viking Auto Group	Jeff Serito	1018	Broadcast	12/05/96	35700.00
Viking Auto Group	Jeff Serito	1035	Direct	06/17/96	2000.00
Viola d'Amore	Julie Edwards	1028	Print	07/21/96	2000.00
Viola d'Amore	Julie Edwards	1032	Print	09/26/96	10000.00
Taco Heaven	Bert Clinton	1040	Broadcast	12/15/96	14000.00

Common field

Fields from CLIENTS table

Fields from JOBS table

Figure 4-32 Data from two linked tables

After you link the two tables, you can perform tasks, such as listing fields, using both tables as though they were one.

To create queries that require data from more than one table, you must place skeletons of all the necessary tables in the Query Designer window. You link tables by specifying the corresponding common fields of the skeletons.

How can you link the CLIENTS and JOBS tables?

In the Query Designer window, you can create a query that links the two database tables by their common field, CLIENT_ID. The Query Designer window will contain *two* skeletons: one for the CLIENTS table and one for the JOBS table. Once the skeletons are in the Query Designer window, you define the relation by clicking the Set Relation button on the SpeedBar or by choosing Set Relation from the Query menu. The Define Relation dialog box appears to allow you to specify the common field. When you link two tables, dBASE matches records in the two tables that have the same value in the common field.

Adding or Removing a Table

To add a table to the Query Designer window:

- Click the Add Table button on the SpeedBar.

  or

  Click Query then click Add Table....

- In the Open Table Required dialog box, double-click the table you want to add to the query.

To remove a table from the Query window:

- Click anywhere in the skeleton of the table you want to remove.

- Click the Remove Table button on the SpeedBar.

  or

  Click Query then click Remove Selected Table.

First, you need to open the Query Designer window, select the CLIENTS table, and then add the JOBS table to the window.

Let's create a query to link the two tables.

To open the Query Designer window with the CLIENTS table then add the JOBS table:
1. Click the **Queries icon** in the Navigator window, then double-click **Untitled**. The Open Table Required dialog box appears.
2. Double-click **clients.dbf** to select the CLIENTS table. The Query Designer window displays a skeleton of the CLIENTS table.
3. Maximize the Query Designer window to see more of the skeleton.
4. Click the **Add Table button** on the SpeedBar. The Open Table Required dialog box appears.
5. Double-click **jobs.dbf** to select the JOBS table. The JOBS skeleton appears in the Query Designer window, below the CLIENTS skeleton. See Figure 4-33.

skeletons for the
CLIENTS and
JOBS tables

Figure 4-33
Query Designer
window with
two skeletons

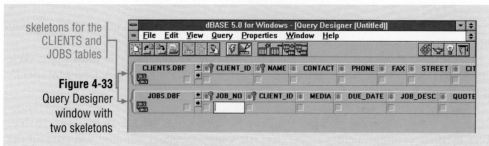

TROUBLE? If you add the wrong table to the Query Designer window, click anywhere in the skeleton for the incorrect table, then click the Delete Table button 🖿 on the SpeedBar. Then repeat Steps 4 and 5.

TROUBLE? If you want to start over, double-click the Control menu box for the Query Designer window, click No when dBASE asks if you want to save the changes, then repeat Steps 1 through 5.

Now you need to set up the link between the two database tables. CLIENT_ID is the common field between JOBS and CLIENTS, so you will use this field to link the two tables. Because each value in the CLIENT_ID field appears only once in the CLIENTS table, but potentially many times in the JOBS table—because a client can have multiple jobs, but each job is performed for only one client—you will make a link from the CLIENTS table to the JOBS table. The CLIENTS table is therefore known as the **parent table** in the relation, and the JOBS table is known as the **child table** in the relation. The child table must be indexed on the common field, because dBASE uses the index to locate matching records.

Because one record in the parent table can be linked to several records in the child table, this type of relation is a **one-to-many** relation. In other contexts, a relation can be **one-to-one** (for example, in a query relating concert ticket holders to seat reservations) or **many-to-many** (for example, in a query relating stock owners to companies). You specify the parent table, the child table, and the type of relation in the Define Relation dialog box.

Linking tables also allows you to specify that dBASE enforce rules of referential integrity. **Referential integrity** is a feature available in many relational databases that permits the DBMS to maintain consistency among records of two separate but related tables. Specifically, referential integrity is a set of rules that enables the DBMS to ensure that the value or values in one table match values in the key field or fields in another table. Thus, dBASE will not let you delete a record in the parent table if there is a matching record in the child table, nor will it let you add a record in the child table for which there is no matching record in the parent table. A record in the child table with no matching record in the parent table is known as an **orphan**. Enforcing referential integrity prevents the creation of orphan records. For example, you would not want a job record entered in the JOBS table if it had no corresponding parent record in the CLIENTS table. You can enforce referential integrity only when viewing records in the Query Results window.

Now you're ready to link the CLIENTS and JOBS tables so that you can retrieve the information Martin wants.

To link the two tables on their common field:
❶ Click the **Set Relation button** 🖳 on the SpeedBar. The Define Relation dialog box appears. See Figure 4-34.

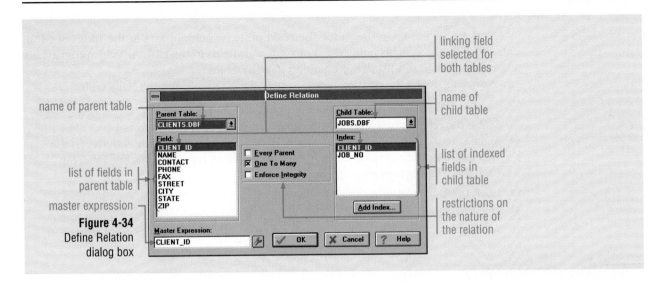

name of parent table

list of fields in
parent table

master expression

Figure 4-34
Define Relation
dialog box

linking field
selected for
both tables

name of
child table

list of indexed
fields in
child table

restrictions on
the nature of
the relation

The Define Relation dialog box contains three panels in which you specify the details of the relation. In the left panel, you specify the name of the parent table and the linking field in the parent table. In the right panel, you specify the name of the child table and the linking field in the child table. In the center panel, you can specify options that modify the nature of the relation. The Master Expression text box allows you to define the link between tables when a single field is not used as the link.

Figure 4-35 describes the three options for modifying the nature of the relation, specifically the relation between CLIENTS and JOBS.

Option	Status	Query Results
Every Parent	Checked	All CLIENTS records will be included whether or not there is a matching CLIENT_ID in JOBS.
	Unchecked	Only those records for which there is a matching CLIENT_ID in the JOBS table will be included.
One To Many	Checked	Every JOBS record that matches a CLIENT_ID in the CLIENTS table will be included.
	Unchecked	Only the first matching record in the JOBS table for each CLIENT_ID in the CLIENTS table will be included, thus creating a one-to-one relation.
Enforce Integrity	Checked	dBASE will not allow a record in the CLIENTS table to be deleted if a matching record exists in the JOBS table, nor will it allow a record to be added to the JOBS table for which there is not a matching record in CLIENTS.
	Unchecked	dBASE will not enforce the rules of referential integrity.

Figure 4-35
Options for
modifying relation

Because CLIENTS.DBF is the first skeleton in the Query Designer window, it is the default choice as the parent table, and JOBS.DBF is the default choice as the child table. CLIENT_ID is the default in both tables as the linking field. In this case, the defaults define the relation you want for the query. If the defaults were not correct, you could change them by clicking the appropriate table or field name.

Notice that the list of fields for the child table, which appears in the Index section, contains only those fields defined as key (indexed) fields in the table. dBASE automatically selects the field in this list that is common to both tables.

Now let's define the relation between the CLIENTS table and the JOBS table.

To define the relation between the two tables:

❶ Make sure that the One To Many check box is checked. The relation between the two tables is a one-to-many relation, because a client can have multiple jobs, but each job is performed for only one client.

❷ Click the **Enforce Integrity check box** to enforce referential integrity.

❸ Make sure that the Every Parent check box is not checked, so that the query results will display only CLIENTS records that match a CLIENT_ID in JOBS. See Figure 4-36.

tables are linked by
CLIENT_ID field

CLIENTS is the
parent table

JOBS is the
child table

integrity rules will
be enforced

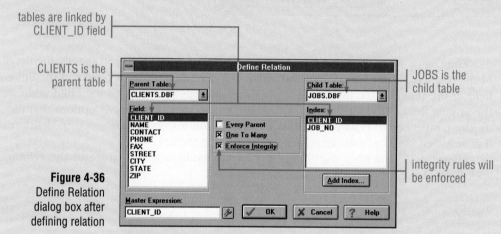

Figure 4-36
Define Relation
dialog box after
defining relation

❹ Click **OK** to close the Define Relation dialog box and return to the Query Designer window.

The Query Designer window now shows the relation between the CLIENTS table and the JOBS table. The arrow between the two skeletons indicates that CLIENTS is the parent table and JOBS is the child table in the relation. Child tables appear indented in the Query Designer window. See Figure 4-37.

link is from CLIENTS
(parent) table to
JOBS (child) table

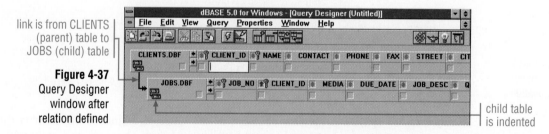

Figure 4-37
Query Designer
window after
relation defined

child table
is indented

In queries where you are linking more than two tables, you add each new table to the Query Designer window and define a relation between it and one of the other tables. Figure 4-38 shows the Query Designer window used to link the three tables in the W&M database.

CLIENTS is parent, JOBS is child in CLIENTS-JOBS relation

Figure 4-38
Linking the CLIENTS, JOBS, and EXPENSES tables

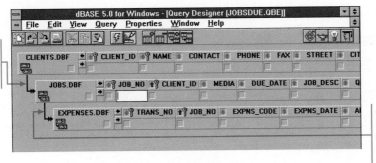

JOBS is parent, EXPENSES is child in JOBS-EXPENSES relation

As shown in Figure 4-38, the CLIENTS and JOBS tables are linked through the CLIENT_ID field, which is their common field. Similarly, the JOBS and EXPENSES tables are linked through the JOB_NO field. The only way to link the CLIENTS and EXPENSES tables is by linking all three tables, because the CLIENTS and EXPENSES tables do not share a common field.

Now that you have established the link between the CLIENTS and JOBS tables, the two tables will be treated as one for querying purposes. This means that you can place filter conditions in either of the linked tables to specify which records to retrieve, and you can place checkmarks in any of the fields in the linked tables.

To answer Martin's request—a listing of all jobs in progress showing data from both the CLIENTS and JOBS tables—you need to add a filter condition to the query to retrieve only the records of jobs that are not completed.

To enter the filter condition:

❶ In the JOBS skeleton, scroll right to see the COMPLETED field, then click in the filter condition box for the COMPLETED field.

❷ Type **.N.** (making sure you type the periods on either side of the N).

Next modify the skeletons to include the information that Martin wants to see. Martin is interested only in the client name and the contact name from the CLIENTS table, and the job number, media, due date, and quote amount from the JOBS table.

To select the fields to display in the query results, then run the query:

❶ In the CLIENTS skeleton, click the **check box** for the NAME and CONTACT fields. Checkmarks appear in these fields.

❷ In the JOBS skeleton, click the **order box** next to the DUE_DATE field name and select ascending order.

❸ In the JOBS skeleton, click the **check box** for the JOB_NO, MEDIA, DUE_DATE, and QUOTE fields, scrolling the skeleton if necessary. Checkmarks appear in these fields. See Figure 4-39.

Notice that the order box for the CLIENT_ID field (in the JOBS skeleton) is set to ascending order. dBASE does this by default because CLIENT_ID is the indexed field in the child table. Because you want the query results sorted by DUE_DATE, you need to set the ordered option to unordered for the CLIENT_ID field.

❹ In the JOBS skeleton, click the **order box** for the CLIENT_ID field and select unordered (the double arrow). See Figure 4-39.

selected fields

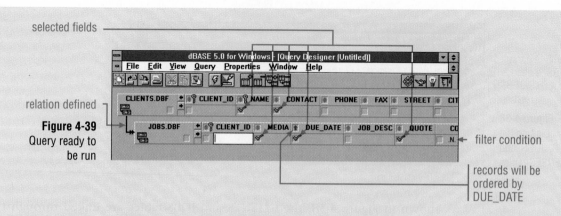

relation defined

Figure 4-39
Query ready to
be run

filter condition

records will be
ordered by
DUE_DATE

Now you are ready to run the query.

❺ Click the **Run Query button** 🗲 on the SpeedBar. A list of all jobs in progress appears
   in the Query Results window. See Figure 4-40.

fields from
CLIENTS table

fields from
JOBS table

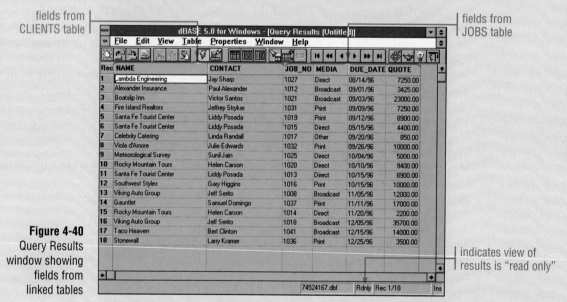

Figure 4-40
Query Results
window showing
fields from
linked tables

indicates view of
results is "read only"

Notice that the Query Results window includes information from two tables: the
CLIENTS table (NAME and CONTACT) and the JOBS table (JOB_NO, MEDIA,
DUE_DATE, and QUOTE). The message "Rdnly" in the status bar indicates that this
view of the CLIENTS and JOBS table is "read only," meaning that you cannot make
changes to records in the Query Results window. dBASE creates a read only view
whenever you ask for the records to be sorted by a field in the child table that is
not indexed (in this case, the DUE_DATE field). dBASE does this because the
records are not displayed in an order that it can easily process.

dBASE uses the relation definition to link the tables, matching the values in the common field in each table. If a match is found—that is, if the values are equal—the *joined*
record is included in the Query Results window. Figure 4-41 shows how joining works
for client S01.

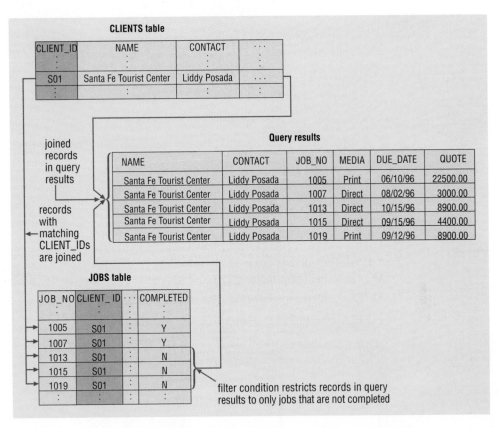

Figure 4-41
Joining two tables
on a common field

Now that you have defined the query, you can save it to avoid repeating these steps each time you want information about jobs in progress.

Saving the Query

As noted earlier, when you save a query it is added to your Student Disk as a query file. You can also build forms and reports directly from queries if they are saved. When you save a query, all information about relations, selected fields, and filter conditions is also saved.

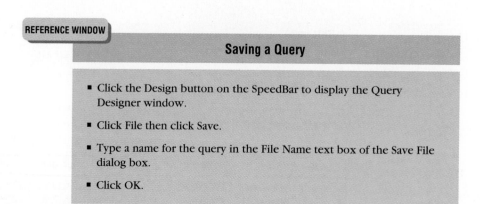

REFERENCE WINDOW

Saving a Query

- Click the Design button on the SpeedBar to display the Query Designer window.
- Click File then click Save.
- Type a name for the query in the File Name text box of the Save File dialog box.
- Click OK.

Let's save the query for finding jobs in progress and name it "jobsdue."

To save the current query as "jobsdue":

❶ Click the **Design button** 🖼 on the SpeedBar to return to the Query Designer window.

❷ Click **File** then click **Save**. The Save File dialog box appears. See Figure 4-42.

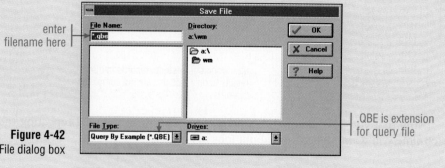

enter filename here →

.QBE is extension for query file

Figure 4-42
Save File dialog box

❸ Type **jobsdue** in the File Name text box.

The name you type must follow the rules for naming any DOS file.

❹ Click **OK**.

dBASE automatically adds a QBE extension to the file, and the file is stored on your Student Disk as JOBSDUE.QBE.

Opening a Saved Query

You can open a query that you previously saved if you want to modify or run the query. To do so, you click the Queries icon in the Navigator window, then double-click the name of the saved query in the current selection panel (or click File, click Open, then double-click the name of the query file).

Opening a Saved Query

- Click the Queries icon in the Navigator window.
- Double-click the name of the saved query in the current selection panel.

or

- Click File, click Open, then double-click the query you want.

You've given Nancy and Martin all the information they requested. You can now restore any open windows to their original size and exit dBASE.

To exit dBASE:
❶ Click the **Restore button** in the Query Designer window to restore it to its original size, then close the window.
❷ Exit dBASE.

■   ■   ■

By creating and executing different queries, you were able to retrieve information from the W&M database. You used many of the dBASE querying features—such as filter conditions, relational operators, AND and OR conditions, and relations—to give Nancy and Martin the exact results they requested.

Questions

1. Explain the purpose of each of the following components found in a query skeleton:
   a. check box
   b. filter condition
   c. order box
   d. scroll arrows
2. Explain the purpose of each of the following SpeedBar buttons:
   a.
   b.
   c.
   d.
   e.
3. Suppose you find a file on your Student Disk named COMPLTED.QBE. What type of file is this?
4. For each of the following situations, indicate if you would use an AND or an OR condition:
   a. married taxpayer with income above $125,000
   b. employees between the ages of 40 and 50
   c. students majoring in Finance or Accounting
   d. customers located in the following states: Texas, Virginia, and New York

5. Explain the difference between the following filter conditions:

— a. Quote _AND_   Quote
    >5000,<=6500   <=5000 _or_
                                  >6500

— b. Customer _ALL JONES_   Customer _start ī J_
    Jones   J???s   _3 Letter end with S 5 letter words_

Use Figures 4-43 and 4-44 to answer Questions 6 through 10. These figures present information about basketball teams (TEAM.DBF) and their players (PLAYERS.DBF).

Layout of TEAM table - one record per team

Field Name	Type	Width
TEAM_ID	C	3
TEAM_NAME	C	30
OWNER	C	25
LOCATION	C	2

Figure 4-43

Layout of PLAYER table - one record per player

Field Name	Type	Width
PLAYER_ID	C	4
PLAYR_NAME	C	30
POSITION	C	1
SALARY	N	10(0)
TEAM_ID	C	3

Figure 4-44

6. What table(s) must be displayed in the Query Designer window if you want to list the player name, position, and salary for the team with the Team ID NYK?

7. Describe the steps you would take to compute the total salary for the team with the Team ID NYK.

8. Each player will have two percent of his salary placed in a strike fund. Sketch what the query skeleton would look like if you want to display the player name, Team ID, and contribution of each player.

9. Sketch the query skeleton to display the team name and player name.

10. Sketch the query skeleton to display the team name, player name, and salary for all players earning more than $1,000,000, in order by player name.

E   11. Sketch the query skeleton to display the team ID, team name, team owner, player name, and position, sorted by team name, and within team by player name.

E   12. dBASE's Help system provides short, easy-to-understand lessons called Interactive Tutors. From the dBASE Desktop, click the icon for the Interactive Tutors. Try the Queries and Reports lesson. Complete the lessons on Creating a Single Table Query and Creating a Multi-table Query.

Tutorial Assignments

Place your Student Disk in the disk drive, start dBASE, and set the working directory to A:\WM. Create each query in the Tutorial Assignments. Remember to remove all filter conditions from the previous query before beginning each assignment. You'll use both the CLIENTS and JOBS tables in the Tutorial Assignments.

1. Create a query to display the fields NAME, CONTACT, and CITY for all clients. Print the query results.

2. Create a query to display all the fields for clients located in Albuquerque. Print the query results. (*Hint:* Use landscape orientation for printing.)

3. Rerun the query in Figure 4-11 with the MEDIA value entered as "print" instead of "Print." What message appears on the screen? Why?

4. Develop a query to list the different media used by W&M. (*Hint:* The Query Results should contain only one column.) Print the query results.

5. For all jobs still in progress (COMPLETED equals .N.) and with a QUOTE above $10,000, display the fields CLIENT_ID, JOB_DESC, and QUOTE. Sort the results in ascending order by QUOTE. Print the query results.

6. For all Viking Auto Group (V01) jobs, display the fields CLIENT_ID, JOB_DESC, QUOTE, and COMPLETED. Print the query results.

7. For all jobs that are not Broadcast MEDIA but have a QUOTE above $20,000, display the fields CLIENT_ID, MEDIA, and QUOTE. Print the query results.

8. For all jobs with a QUOTE below $10,000 or above $30,000, display the JOB_NO, DUE_DATE, JOB_DESC, and QUOTE. Print the query results.

9. You are trying to find all jobs placed in either Print or Direct media. Your query skeleton contains the condition *"Print", "Direct"* in the MEDIA field. Why does the screen display the No Records Selected Alert box after you run the query?

10. Use the JOBS table to determine the following:
    a. total value (quote) of all jobs
    b. total value (quote) of all completed jobs
    c. total value (quote) of all completed jobs with a QUOTE over $5,000.

11. For jobs due in October 1996, determine the total number of jobs and their total value.

12. The Calculation Results window in Figure 4-45 shows the average quote for jobs due in November 1996. Reproduce these results.

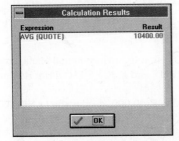

Figure 4-45

Link the CLIENTS (parent) table and the JOBS (child) table; then, for Assignments 13 through 15, include the following fields in your query display: NAME, JOB_NO, JOB_DESC, DUE_DATE, QUOTE.

13. Create a query to display all jobs. Sort the results by NAME. Print the query results.

14. Create a query to display all Print jobs with a quote between $10,000 and $15,000, inclusive. Sort the results by NAME. Print the query results.

E 15. Display all jobs in progress with a quote over $5,000. Sort the results by QUOTE, with the highest quote first. Print the query results.

E   16. Develop a query to display the JOB_NO, CLIENT_ID, NAME, MEDIA, and QUOTE for all uncompleted jobs with a quote above $15,000. Sort the results by MEDIA, and within media by QUOTE. Print the query results.

E   17. Figure 4-46 shows a query skeleton and query results based on the CLIENTS table. What was the question that resulted in the query skeleton displayed in Figure 4-46? Explain the entry in the CITYSTZIP calculated field. Look up "concatenation" and "concatenating strings" in the Help system.

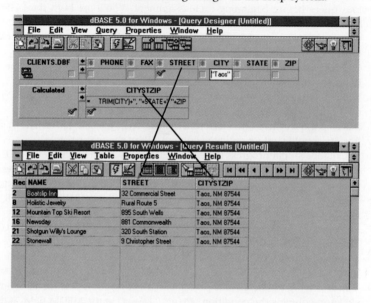

Figure 4-46

Case Problems

1. Inventory of State-owned Land

In this Case Problem you will use the tables LAND and LANDUSE instead of STATELND and LNDUSE, which you worked with in Tutorials 2 and 3. The tables have the same structure, but records have been added to the tables you will work with. For some problems, you need to work with only one of these tables; other problems require that you work with both.

Place your Student Disk in the disk drive, start dBASE, and set the working directory to A:\LAND.

1. For all parcels of land, display the LAND_ID, ACREAGE, VALUE, and LAND_DESC. Print the query results.

2. For all parcels of land owned by the Division of Environmental Management, display the LAND_ID, DIVISION, ACQUIRED, and LAND_DESC. Print the query results.

3. For all parcels of land with a value above $100,000, display the LAND_ID, LAND_DESC, ACREAGE, and VALUE. Sort the results by VALUE. Print the query results.

4. For all parcels of land with a land use code 04 (Offices) acquired in 1971, display the LAND_ID, DIVISION, LAND_DESC, and VALUE. Print the query results.

5. Calculate the total value of all properties and the number of parcels.

E   6. For all parcels of land, display the LAND_ID, USE_DESC (found in the LANDUSE table), ACQUIRED, and VALUE. Sort the results by USE_DESC. Change the column heading of the query results from USE_DESC to Land Use. (*Hint:* To change the column heading, use the Field Properties dialog box.) Print the query results.

E   7. Calculate the value per acre of each land parcel (VALUE divided by ACREAGE). Display the Land ID, Description (found in the LAND table), Land Use Description (found in the LANDUSE table), and the value per acre. The corresponding headings in the query results should be Land ID, Description of Land, Land Use, and Value per Acre. (*Hint:* To change the column headings, use the Field Properties dialog box.) Print the query results.

8. Display all parcels that have the word "State" anywhere in the LAND_DESC field. Include the LAND_ID, LAND_DESC, and DIVISION in the results. Print the query results.

E   9. Rank the parcels by VALUE (high to low). Include only those parcels acquired before 1975 or after 1985. Display the LAND_ID, ACQUIRED, DIVISION, and VALUE in the results. Print the query results.

2.   FINSTAT Inc.

In this Case Problem you will use the tables COMP and FIN instead of COMPANY and FINANCE, which you worked with in Tutorials 2 and 3. The tables have the same structure, but records have been added to the tables you will work with. For some problems, you need to work with only one of these tables; other problems require that you work with both. Note that values for sales, assets, and profits are in thousands of dollars. For example, the value $25,000 means $25,000,000. (The three final zeros have been omitted from the values in the FINANCE table.)

Place your Student Disk in the disk drive, start dBASE, and set the working directory to A:\FINANCE.

1. For all companies, display the fields COMP_NAME, INDUSTRY, and SYMBOL. Print the query results.

2. For all companies in the automobile industry (code CA), display the fields COMP_NAME and SYMBOL. Print the query results.

3. For all companies except those in the automobile industry (code CA), display the fields COMP_NAME, INDUSTRY, and SYMBOL. Print the query results.

4. For all companies with sales above $25,000,000, display the COMPANY_ID, YEAR, and SALES. (*Hint:* Remember that the values are defined without the final three zeros.) Print the query results.

5. For all companies with sales above $25,000,000 and profits above $500,000 in 1992, display the COMPANY_ID, YEAR, SALES, and PROFITS. Sort the results by SALES (low to high). Print the query results. (*Hint:* Remember that the values are defined without the final three zeros.)

6. For all companies, display the COMP_NAME, SALES, ASSETS, PROFITS, and rate of return for the year 1992. Rate of return is calculated by dividing profits by assets. Name the Rate of Return field RET_RATE. Print the query results.

7. Rank the companies by sales in 1992 (lowest to highest). Display the SALES, COMPANY_NAME, INDUSTRY, and RET_RATE. Print the query results.

8. Calculate the average sales and average profits for all companies for each year.

E   9. Rank the companies by SALES in 1992 (high to low). Only include companies that are in either the automobile industry (CA) or the chemical industry (CH). Display the Company Name, Industry, and Sales. Print the query results.

3.   Marine Diving Equipment, Inc.

In this Case Problem you will use the tables CUSTOMER and ORDERS instead of the tables CUST and ORD, which you worked with in Tutorials 2 and 3. The tables have the same structure, but records have been added to the tables you will work with. For some problems, you need to work with only one of these tables; other problems require that you work with both.

Place your Student Disk in the disk drive, start dBASE, and set the working directory to A:\MARINE.

1. For all customers located in the U.S.A., display the CUST_NAME, CITY, ST_OR_PROV, and PHONE. Print the query results.

2. For all orders that were shipped via Federal Express (FedEx), display the ORD_NO, CUST_NO, SALE_DATE, and INV_AMT. Print the query results.

3. For all orders with an INV_AMT value above $10,000 and a PAY_METHOD of Check, display the ORD_NO, CUST_NO, SALE_DATE, INV_AMT, and AMT_PAID. Sort the results by CUST_NO. Print the query results.

4. For all orders placed after October 31, 1994, display the ORD_NO, CUST_NO, SALE_DATE, INV_AMT, and AMT_PAID. Print the query results.

5. Calculate the total value and a count of the number of orders overall. Calculate the total value and a count of the number of orders for all orders in 1994.

6. Calculate the average total invoice and number of orders for orders from customers in the U.S.A.

7. For all orders with an AMT_PAID value of zero, display the CUST_NAME, PHONE, ORDER_NO, SALE_DATE, and INV_AMT. Print the query results.

8. Display all customers that have the word "Diver" anywhere in the CUST_NAME. Include the CUST_NO, CUST_NAME, and COUNTRY in the results. Sort the results by CUST_NAME. Print the query results.

9. What is the name of the customer with the largest unpaid invoice amount (invoice amount value minus amount paid)? What is the amount of that invoice? What is the total amount of the orders from this company? In what country is this company located?

E 10. Rank the orders by INV_AMT (highest to lowest). Include only those orders shipped by FedEx or UPS during 1994 or 1995. Display the ORDER_NO, CUST_NO, SALE_DATE, and SHIP_VIA in the results. (*Hint:* The Date criteria must appear in both lines of the query.) Print the query results.

E 11. Figure 4-47 shows a query skeleton and query results based on the ORDERS table. What was the question that resulted in the query skeleton in Figure 4-47? Explain the entry in the AMT_PAID column in the skeleton.

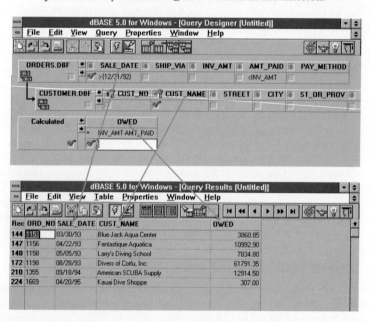

Figure 4-47

4. Teaching Activity

In this Case Problem you will use the tables FAC, CRS, and TCH instead of FACULTY, COURSE, and TEACHING, which you worked with in Tutorials 2 and 3. The tables have the same structure, but records have been added to the tables you will work with. For some problems, you need to work with only one of these tables; other problems require that you work with two or three tables.

Place your Student Disk in the disk drive, start dBASE, and set the working directory to A:\TEACH.

1. For all faculty in the Finance Department (FIN), display the FIRST_NAME, LAST_NAME, RANK, DEPT, and SALARY. Sort by LAST_NAME. Print the query results.
2. Display all courses in the CRS table that have a FIN prefix in the COURSE_NO. Include the COURSE_NO and TITLE. (*Hint:* Review the Like operator; see Figure 4-13.) Print the query results.
3. Use the TCH table to find the courses taught during the Fall 1992 term. Display the FAC_ID, COURSE_NO, SECTION, YEAR, TERM, and ENROLLMENT. Print the query results.
4. Use the TCH table to calculate the average class size and the number of classes for all courses taught in the Spring 1993 term.
5. All assistant professors in the Marketing (MKT) department will receive a two-percent salary increase. Display the FAC_ID, LAST_NAME, FIRST_NAME, and new salary. Sort the results by LAST_NAME. Print the query results.
6. List the courses taught by members of the Finance department (FIN). Display the faculty member's LAST_NAME, DEPT, COURSE_NO, SECTION, YEAR taught, and TERM. Sort the results by Last Name, and within Last Name by Year. Print the query results.
7. For all courses in which enrollment was under 5 or over 40, display the faculty member's LAST_NAME, FIRST_NAME, the COURSE_NO, and ENROLLMENT. Print the query results.
8. Calculate the average number of students in all sections. For your calculations, include only courses with an enrollment of 5 or more students.

E 9. For all courses in which enrollment was less than 5 or over 40, display the faculty member's LAST_NAME and FIRST_NAME, the COURSE_NO, course TITLE, and ENROLLMENT. Sort the results by COURSE_NO. Print the query results.

E 5. Student Enrollment Database

Place your Student Disk in the disk drive, start dBASE, and set the working directory to A:\PRACTICE. For each query you perform in this Case Problem, print the query results. Use some or all of the following tables to complete Problems 1 through 5.

- STUDENT.DBF (one record per student)
- COURSE.DBF (one record per course)
- CRSENRL.DBF (one record for each course a student is enrolled in)
- FACULTY.DBF (one record per faculty member)

1. Display all students (name, major, grade point average) who are either finance majors (FIN) or have a grade point average above 3.25.
2. Display all course numbers and titles (course names) with the letters "MAN" anywhere in the title.
3. Display the average faculty salary. (Note: You cannot print this summary statistic.)
4. Create a query that produces query results like those in Figure 4-48. (*Hint:* This query includes fields from all four tables.)

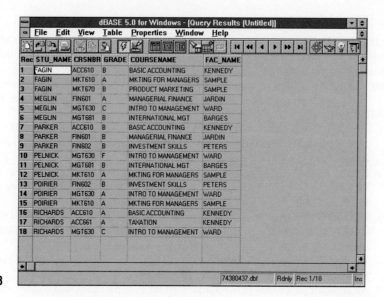

Figure 4-48

5. Display a list of all students and their courses. Include the student name, major, course number, title (course name), and grade. The output should include even students with no courses.

Customizing a Form

Designing a Job Authorization Form for Data Entry

CASE

Wells & Martinez Advertising Agency

Martin has been using Form layout to enter and edit data in the JOBS table. The data to be entered is listed on the Job Authorization Form that W&M completes for each job. Lately Martin has felt frustrated as he enters data. The flow of the information on the paper form does not match the order of the fields in the JOBS table. This slows the data entry process, as he is forced to keep looking back and forth between the document and the screen to match the correct location of the data.

Another frustration is the current screen design. It has no separations to highlight the various components of the data. With the use of colors, graphic elements, and fonts he could draw attention to the various components on the screen—display areas, data entry areas, and message areas.

To facilitate data entry into the JOBS table, Martin decides to design a new screen form based on the paper form. Figure 5-1 shows his sketch of the on-screen Job Authorization Form.

```
┌─────────────────────────────────────────────────────────────┐
│                                                               │
│              Job Authorization Form                           │
│                                                               │
│                                                               │
│        Job No        XXXX                 Client ID   XXX      │
│                                                               │
│        Media         XXXXXXXXXX                               │
│                                                               │
│                                                               │
│                                                               │
│                                                               │
│        Due Date      XX/XX/XX          ◯ Completed            │
│                                                               │
│        Quote         99999.99                                 │
│                                                               │
│        Job Description  X ─────────── X                       │
│                                                               │
│                                                               │
│                                                               │
│                                                               │
│                                                               │
└─────────────────────────────────────────────────────────────┘
```

Figure 5-1
Sketch of screen
layout for the Job
Authorization Form

Martin gives you his sketch and asks you to create a new form for entering data in the JOBS table.

Introduction to Form Design

In most database applications, forms play an important role in the data entry and data update processes. Properly designed forms can speed data entry and minimize mistakes. Thus, many users prefer to enter and view data using a well-designed form rather than enter data using the standard layouts you used in Tutorial 3.

In Tutorial 3 you used Browse layout, Columnar layout, and Form layout to view, add, edit, and delete records in a form. This approach is adequate for some situations; however, there are many situations where the data entry process can be made more efficient by the creation of a customized data entry form. The following are some guidelines to consider when you design a form:

- Arrange the fields on the screen in the same order as they appear on the printed form.
- Use attributes such as color, style, lines, and rectangles to emphasize important areas in a form. With customized forms you have more control over the appearance of the screen. You can change the order of fields; add descriptive text labels; highlight fields; and add design elements, such as lines, rectangles, and boxes to develop a more functional form.

- Arrange fields in groups based on the kind of information they show. Use lines and rectangles to separate groups.
- Keep the screen uncluttered. Use multiple screens rather than crowding all the information onto one screen. Leave empty space, if possible, for ease of reading.
- Make the screen self-documenting. Don't force the user to consult manuals to figure out how to use the screen. Display fields in different formats, such as check boxes, drop-down list boxes, and radio buttons to help document the screen.

In this tutorial you will see how important these guidelines are as you create three forms: one based on the JOBS table (single-table form), and two based on both the CLIENTS and JOBS tables (multi-table form).

First you need to start dBASE.

To start dBASE and get ready to create the forms:
❶ Place your Student Disk in the disk drive.

❷ Start dBASE.

❸ Make sure the current directory is A:\WM.

Now you're ready to begin designing the form Martin sketched in Figure 5-1. This form will be used at W&M to enter data in the JOBS table. When a form is based on fields from only one table, as is the case with the form for the JOBS table, it is called a **single-table form**.

In dBASE, there are two ways to create a new form: you can use the Form Expert to automate the form creation process, or you can design your own form. Martin suggests that you use dBASE's Form Expert to create the Job Authorization Form.

Using the Form Expert to Design a Single-Table Form

dBASE provides a number of **experts** that guide you through common tasks so that you can get results quickly and easily. In this tutorial you will use the **Form Expert**, which guides you through the process of creating a new form. The Form Expert allows you to begin designing a new form by using the Expert Assistance feature or by starting from a blank form. The Expert Assistance feature guides you in setting up a basic form, which you can then modify; a blank form lets you start a form from scratch. Generally, it is easier to let the Form Expert set up a basic form for you. At each step in the process, the Form Expert presents a dialog box in which you choose the tables, fields, and layout for the form. The Form Expert then creates the form based on your selections.

Creating a Form Using the Form Expert

- Click the Forms icon in the Navigator window, then double-click Untitled in the current selection panel (or click File, click New, then click Form).

- Click Expert Assistance in the Form Expert window, then click New.

- Make the appropriate choices in the Form Expert dialog boxes.

Let's use the Form Expert to create the Job Authorization Form.

To create a single-table form using the Form Expert:

❶ Click the **Forms icon** in the Navigator window.

❷ Double-click **Untitled** in the current selection panel to display the Form Expert dialog box. See Figure 5-2.

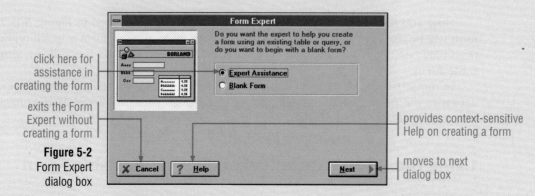

click here for assistance in creating the form

exits the Form Expert without creating a form

provides context-sensitive Help on creating a form

Figure 5-2
Form Expert dialog box

moves to next dialog box

Notice the Cancel and Help buttons at the bottom left of the dialog box. Every step in the Form Expert contains these two buttons. If you click Cancel, the Form Expert closes and you return to the Desktop. If you click Help, dBASE displays context-sensitive Help for the current step. The Next button brings you to the next step in the Form Expert. All Form Expert dialog boxes except the first also provide a Previous button, which you can click to return to the previous dialog box so that you can enter a new choice.

❸ Click the **Expert Assistance radio button** if it is not already selected.

❹ Click **Next** to display the next dialog box. See Figure 5-3.

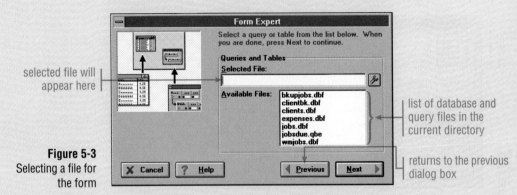

selected file will appear here

Figure 5-3
Selecting a file for the form

list of database and query files in the current directory

returns to the previous dialog box

In this dialog box you select the data upon which the form is based. Because a form can be based on a table or a query, the Available Files list displays the names of all .DBF and .QBE files in the current directory.

❺ Click **jobs.dbf** in the Available Files list box. The filename jobs.dbf appears in the Selected File text box.

❻ Click **Next** to move to the next dialog box. See Figure 5-4.

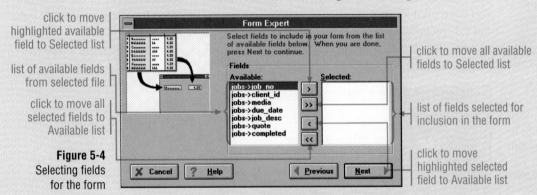

click to move highlighted available field to Selected list

list of available fields from selected file

click to move all selected fields to Available list

Figure 5-4
Selecting fields for the form

click to move all available fields to Selected list

list of fields selected for inclusion in the form

click to move highlighted selected field to Available list

This dialog box allows you to select the fields that will appear in the form. The Fields panel contains two list boxes: the Available list box shows all fields available for inclusion in the form; the Selected list box shows all fields selected for inclusion in the form. By clicking a field name in the Available list box, then clicking the right arrow button, you select the field for inclusion in the form. The field name moves to the Selected list box. By clicking a field name in the Selected list box and clicking the left arrow button, you remove the field from the form. (The field name then returns to the Available list box.) The double arrow buttons move all fields at once.

As shown in Figure 5-1, Martin wants all of the fields in the JOBS table to appear in the form.

❼ Click the **double right arrow button** ⟫ to select all fields for inclusion in the form, then click **Next** to move to the next dialog box. See Figure 5-5.

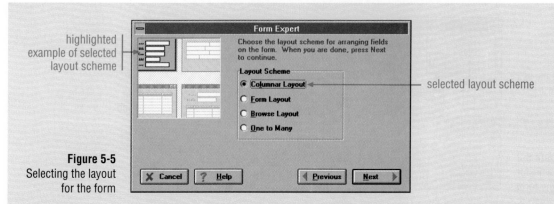

highlighted
example of selected
layout scheme

selected layout scheme

Figure 5-5
Selecting the layout
for the form

The Form Expert offers four different layouts for the basic form. You are already familiar with Columnar layout, Form layout, and Browse layout. The One to Many layout is used to display two linked tables in a single form. Notice that the left side of this dialog box provides a sample of the form layout for the selected layout scheme.

The design for this form, as shown in Figure 5-1, is not identical to any of the layouts you have used already, but it is closest to Columnar layout, so let's begin with this layout for the form.

❽ Click the **Columnar Layout radio button** if it is not already selected, then click **Next** to move to the next dialog box. See Figure 5-6.

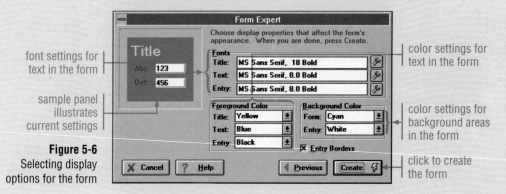

font settings for
text in the form

color settings for
text in the form

sample panel
illustrates
current settings

color settings for
background areas
in the form

Figure 5-6
Selecting display
options for the form

click to create
the form

This dialog box allows you to specify the display characteristics of the form. You can specify background and foreground colors, text colors, sizes, and fonts in this dialog box. The Fonts panel allows you to specify the fonts for the title, entry fields (areas where you can enter data in the form), and other text that appears in the form. The Foreground Color panel allows you to select the colors for text that appears in the form. The Background Color panel allows you to select the background color for the form itself and the background color for entry fields. A sample form using the current specifications is shown in the panel in the upper-left corner of the dialog box.

For now, you'll accept the default settings in this dialog box. Later you'll make modifications using the Form Designer.

❾ Click **Create** to have the Form Expert create the basic form. dBASE displays the form design in the Form Designer window. See Figure 5-7.

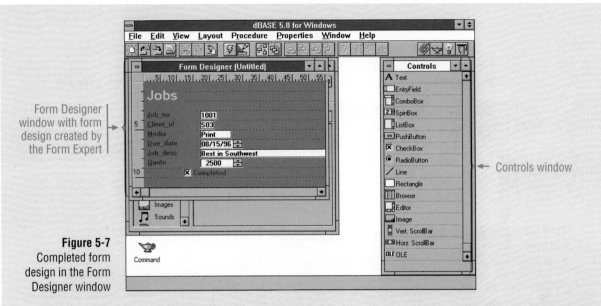

Form Designer
window with form
design created by
the Form Expert

Controls window

Figure 5-7
Completed form
design in the Form
Designer window

TROUBLE? If you selected an incorrect option while creating the form and have completed the final Form Expert dialog box, you must start the Form Expert from the beginning. Double-click the Control menu box in the Form Designer window. Click No when dBASE asks if you want to save the form. Then repeat Steps 1 through 9. If the Controls window does not appear on your screen, click View, then click Controls.

Notice that dBASE displays two new windows. The Form Designer window displays the current layout of the form. The Controls window contains a list of control objects that you can place on the form. Other windows (not visible now) are available in the Form Designer. You will use these windows to modify the Job Authorization Form later in this tutorial.

Although the form design provided by the Form Expert is not exactly like the sketch shown in Figure 5-1, it contains the basic elements you need for the final form. Martin reviews the form design you created using the Form Expert and decides that some enhancements are needed before the form is ready to be used to enter and view job-related data. First, he suggests that you save the form design.

Saving a Form Design

It's a good idea to save the form design, even though you know you're going to make several changes to it. If you don't save the form design now and you make changes you're not satisfied with, you might have to start the form creation process all over again.

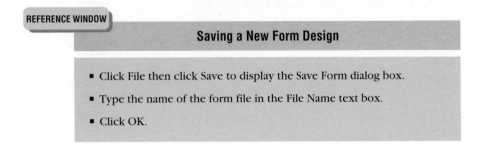

REFERENCE WINDOW

Saving a New Form Design

- Click File then click Save to display the Save Form dialog box.
- Type the name of the form file in the File Name text box.
- Click OK.

Let's save the form and close the Form Designer window.

To save the Job Authorization Form and close the Form Designer:

❶ Click **File** then click **Save** to display the Save Form dialog box. See Figure 5-8.

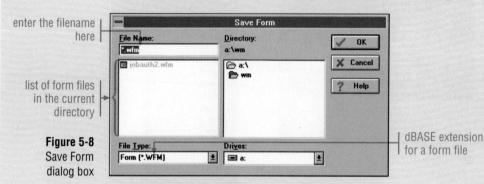

enter the filename here

list of form files in the current directory

Figure 5-8
Save Form dialog box

dBASE extension for a form file

❷ Type **jobauth** in the File Name text box.

❸ Click **OK**. dBASE saves the form to your Student Disk as JOBAUTH.WFM. dBASE automatically assigns the .WFM file extension to all saved forms.

❹ Double-click the **Control menu box** on the Form Designer window. The Form Designer and Controls windows close, and you are returned to the Desktop.

The first time you save a form using the Save command, dBASE asks for a filename. Thereafter, dBASE automatically saves the current version of the form, overwriting the previous version of the form without asking for confirmation to do so. If you want to keep the old version of the form and also save the modified version, use the Save As command on the File menu instead of the Save command.

Because there are many ways to customize a form, you should save frequently as you design a form. In fact, each time you add an element you want to keep, save the form. Then if you make a change you don't want, you can close the Form Designer window by double-clicking its Control menu box. dBASE will ask you if you want to save changes. You can respond No and then open the previously saved form.

If you want to take a break and resume the tutorial at a later time, exit dBASE. When you resume the tutorial, place your Student Disk in the disk drive, start dBASE, and make sure the current directory is A:\WM. Then continue with the tutorial.

■   ■   ■

Let's open the form design again and make the changes Martin wants.

Opening a Saved Form Design

You can open a form design that you previously saved using either the Navigator window or the Open option on the File menu.

Opening a Saved Form Design

- Click the Forms icon in the Navigator window.
- Click the name of the form you want to open, then click the Design button on the SpeedBar.

  or

  Click File then click Open... to display the Open File dialog box.

  Click the name of the form in the File Name list box.

  Click OK.

Let's open the saved JOBAUTH form design so that you can modify it.

To open the JOBAUTH form design:
❶ Click the **Forms icon** in the Navigator window.
❷ Click **Jobauth.wfm** in the current selection panel.
❸ Click the **Design button** on the SpeedBar.

dBASE displays the saved form in the Form Designer window. The Controls window appears also. Before looking at these windows in detail, let's run the form to see how it will appear when you use it to enter data.

Viewing Data in the Form

While you are designing a form, you can run it to see how the form will look to someone using it for viewing or editing records in a table.

To run the form:
❶ Click the **Run button** on the SpeedBar.

dBASE displays the Form window, which shows the JOBAUTH form design containing the data for the first record in the JOBS table.
❷ Click the **Maximize button** on the Form window to view the entire form. See Figure 5-9.

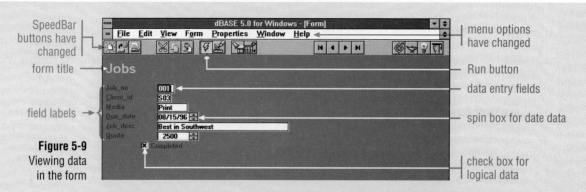

SpeedBar buttons have changed

form title

field labels

menu options have changed

Run button

data entry fields

spin box for date data

check box for logical data

Figure 5-9
Viewing data
in the form

The form contains a title at the top and field labels and data entry fields for each field in a JOBS record. The Form Expert used the table name, JOBS, for the title, and field names as labels for the data entry fields. Notice that the field labels display the field names differently from the way they appear in the actual table, which displays field names in all uppercase letters. The form also contains different types of data entry fields for different types of data (entry boxes for character data, a spin box for date data, a check box for logical data, and so on). The data entry field for Job_no is highlighted and the current value is selected, waiting for you to enter new data. Because the current entry, 1001, fills the data entry field, the left-most character is not visible when the entire value is selected. Later in this tutorial, you will change the size of this data entry field so that the entire value is visible. Also, notice that the menu options and the SpeedBar buttons have changed.

Viewing a record in a form is similar to viewing a record in the Table Records window using Form layout or Columnar layout. You can add, delete, or edit records in the Form window and the changes are recorded in the JOBS table. To make additional changes to the form's design, you must return to the Form Designer window.

To make this form look like Figure 5-1, you must make several changes. For example, the form in Figure 5-1 has the title "Job Authorization Form," a different arrangement of data entry fields, and so on. Let's return to the Form Designer window and make these changes.

❸ Click the **Design button** 🖋 on the SpeedBar to return to the Form Designer window. See Figure 5-10.

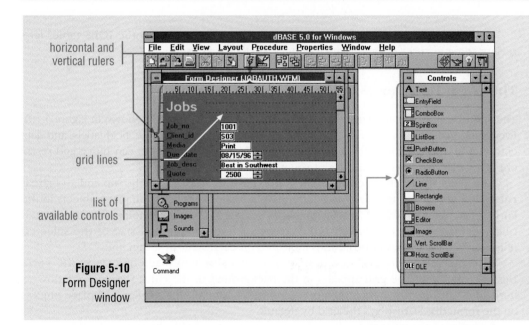

horizontal and
vertical rulers

grid lines

list of
available controls

Figure 5-10
Form Designer
window

Overview of the Form Designer

If the form you created using the Form Expert isn't exactly what you want, you can change it in the Form Designer window. The Form Designer window provides several tools to allow you to modify the form. Each tool has its own window that you can open and close as needed. Using the Form Designer tools, you can add, delete, move, and modify all objects on the form. You can also add design elements—such as rectangles, lines, and graphic images—to enhance the form. You can change the appearance of any object by inspecting the object and changing properties such as color, font, and style. Figure 5-11 summarizes the Form Designer tools and their functions.

Tool	Function
Form Designer window	Displays the current design of the form and allows placement and alignment of form objects
Controls window	Allows selection of control objects for placement on the form
Object Inspector	Allows modification of properties of objects on the form
Procedure Editor	Allows definition of special procedures linked to objects on the form (not covered in this book)
Menu Designer	Allows construction of custom-designed menus (not covered in this book)

Figure 5-11
Form Designer tools

Before you begin to customize the form for entering data in the JOBS table, let's review some features of the Form Designer tools you will use.

The Form Designer Window

The Form Designer window displays the current layout of the form (as shown in Figure 5-10). Everything that appears in the Form Designer window, such as the title, field labels, and data entry fields (and the form itself), is an object. Using the pointer, you can move and resize objects in the form to create the layout you want.

The Form Designer window displays a **horizontal ruler** along the top and a **vertical ruler** along the left side. (Refer to Figure 5-10.) These rulers help you place objects in the Form Designer window. When an object is selected, a corresponding section of each ruler changes color (is highlighted) to indicate the location and size of the selected object. The mouse pointer position is indicated on each ruler by a thin line.

Like the ruler, the **grid** is a design aid that helps you place objects in the Form Designer window. The grid appears in the background of the Form Designer window as horizontal lines of dots. When the grid is displayed, it helps you to align and place objects on the form. dBASE displays the grid by default.

Sometimes it is difficult to align objects visually, even with the rulers and the grid displayed. To assist you in aligning objects, you can activate the Snap To Grid feature, which automatically aligns objects on the grid lines and dots when you move, resize, or place objects on the grid. The Snap To Grid feature "pulls" objects to the nearest grid line or dot. Sometimes it is easier to work with this feature off if you want to move objects in very small increments and position them precisely. The Snap To Grid option is available in the Form Designer Properties dialog box, which you access by selecting Form Designer from the Properties menu.

All forms consist of one or more pages. Initially a form consists of one page. For tables with many fields, you can design multi-page forms. Each page can contain graphics, text, and/or field objects.

The Controls Window

For the form you are creating, the page initially consists of a title, field labels, and areas for entering data. Each of these objects is known as a control. A **control** is an object that appears on a form and provides a way to access data and initiate actions. The title and the field labels are examples of a **Text control**. The data entry area for JOB_NO is an **EntryField control**. The data entry areas for the DUE_DATE and QUOTE fields are examples of a **SpinBox control**. The COMPLETED field uses a **CheckBox control** for data entry. The Controls window displays a list of controls that you can place on a form. Figure 5-12 describes several of the controls available in this window.

Control	Description
Text	Displays literal text
EntryField	Data entry area for entering a single value
ComboBox	Data entry area for entering a single value or selecting a value from a list
SpinBox	Data entry area for entering a single numeric value
ListBox	Data entry area for selecting a single value from a list
CheckBox	Toggles between True and False for a logical value
RadioButton	Allows selection of a single value from a group of possible values
Line	Displays a line in the form
Rectangle	Displays a rectangle in the form

Figure 5-12
Some controls
available in the
Controls window

The Object Inspector

Each object in the form has certain properties that you can change. Properties include the position, size, and color of the object, the current value of the object, validity checks, and any links to data in tables. The Object Inspector allows you to change any of these properties for any objects in the form. When you change an object's properties, the changes will be reflected in the Form Designer window. The Object Inspector appears in its own window. You can open the Object Inspector window by clicking View, then clicking Object Properties on the menu bar.

Using the Form Designer Window

Designing a form involves moving existing objects and placing new ones in the Form Designer window. Before you can move, change, or inspect an object, you need to select it.

To select an object, you simply click it. A selected object appears with **handles** (small boxes) on each corner and each side.

Let's practice selecting objects before you begin modifying your form.

To practice selecting objects:

❶ Click the **Maximize button** on the Form Designer window to see the entire form.

❷ Move the pointer anywhere inside the field label for Job_no, then click the **left mouse button**. Handles appear around the object, indicating that the field label, which is a Text control object, is selected. The status bar indicates the position, name, and order of this object. See Figure 5-13.

handles appear around the selected object

shaded areas in rulers show object's size and position in the form

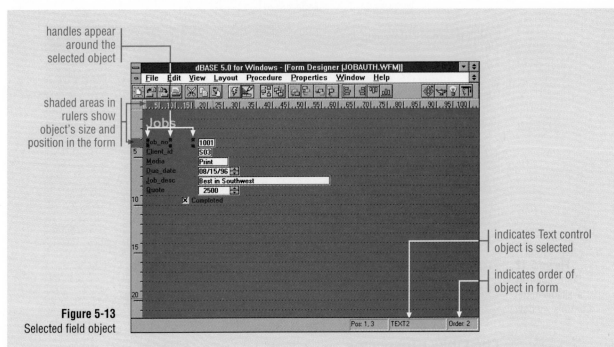

indicates Text control object is selected

indicates order of object in form

Figure 5-13
Selected field object

dBASE assigns a sequential number to every object in the Form window. The "2" in the object name "TEXT2" means that this object was the second text object included in the form. Similarly, the notation "Order: 2" in the status bar indicates that this object was the second object placed in the form (the title was the first). dBASE considers all elements—the form, the field objects, and so on—to be objects. As you include additional objects in your design, dBASE assigns them the next available number.

When an object is selected, a portion of the vertical ruler is highlighted to reflect the object's height, and a portion of the horizontal ruler is highlighted to reflect the object's width.

When you position the pointer on a handle, the pointer changes shape to show the direction in which you can resize the selected object. To move a selected object, move the pointer to the center of the object, then click and drag the object to the location you want.

Now select a different object.

❸ Click the **Due_date spin box**. Handles appear around the Due_date spin box, and the handles disappear from the Job_no field label. The status bar indicates that this is the first spin box object in the form and the ninth object in the form.

Now deselect all objects.

❹ Click outside any object. The form itself is selected. When the form is selected, handles do not appear around it. The handles around the Due_date spin box disappear and the status bar is cleared.

Now that you are familiar with the Form Designer window, you can begin to customize the form you are designing for Martin. Look again at Figure 5-1, the sketch of Martin's customized Job Authorization Form, and compare it to the present layout in the Form Designer window. Notice that you need to change the location of the fields and the title at the top of the form, and change the text in the field labels.

Let's start by moving the objects away from the upper-left corner of the form so they are more centered.

Selecting and Moving Objects

For many tasks you complete when designing a form, you need to select and work with only one object at a time. There are times, however, when you will find that selecting more than one object at a time enables you to work more efficiently. For example, to move several objects in the Form Designer window to a different location, you could move them one at a time. However, it is much easier to move them as a group. To do so you need to select the objects first.

REFERENCE WINDOW

Selecting Multiple Objects

- Press and hold [Shift], then click each object.

or

- Press the left mouse button, then drag the mouse to draw a rectangle around the objects you want to select. Release the mouse button.

or

- To select all objects inside the currently selected object at once, click Edit then click Select All.

Let's select and move all objects in the form as a group to a more central location in the form.

To select and move all objects:

❶ Click **Edit** then click **Select All**. Handles appear around all objects in the form. See Figure 5-14.

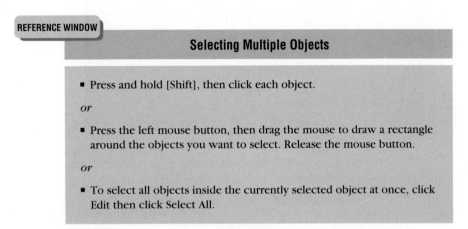

Figure 5-14
Selected objects

❷ Point to any selected field object, then click and drag the mouse down and to the right to move the group of selected objects. Drag the group down until the lower edge of the shaded region in the vertical ruler is at 14. Drag the group right until the left edge of the shaded region in the horizontal ruler is at 20. Release the **mouse button** when the objects are in position. See Figure 5-15.

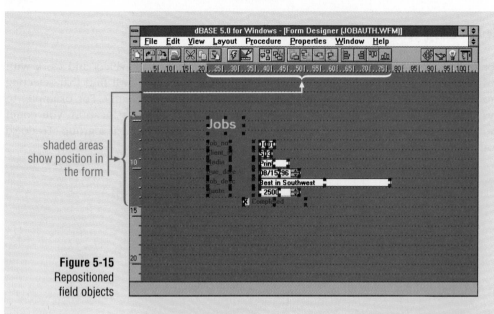

shaded areas
show position in
the form

Figure 5-15
Repositioned
field objects

Note that the ruler coordinates are given here as guidelines only; the placement of objects in your form does not need to match these exactly.

TROUBLE? If you released the mouse button too soon, simply repeat Steps 1 and 2 until the objects are in the correct position, or use the arrow keys to move the selected objects in small increments up, down, right, or left.

TROUBLE? If all the objects didn't move as expected, you can undo these steps and start over. Click Edit then click Undo Move. Click outside any of the objects, then repeat Steps 1 and 2.

❸ Click anywhere in the background of the Form Designer window to deselect the objects.

Now let's arrange the field label and data entry field for Client_id.

To move the field label and data entry field for Client_id:
❶ Click the field label **Client_id** in the form. Handles appear around the text object.
❷ Press and hold **[Shift]**, then click in the **data entry field** for Client_id. Handles appear around the data entry field for Client_id.
❸ Release the **[Shift]** key. Both the field label and the data entry field for Client_id are selected. See Figure 5-16.

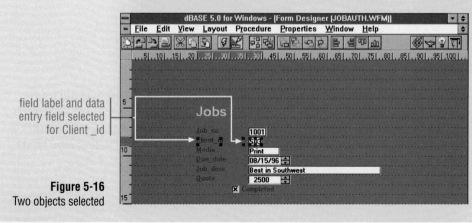

field label and data
entry field selected
for Client _id

Figure 5-16
Two objects selected

❹ Click anywhere in the selected objects and drag them up and to the right. Align the upper edge of the selected objects with 7 in the vertical ruler, and align the left edge of the selected objects with 67 in the horizontal ruler.

❺ Release the **mouse button**.

Now let's resize the data entry fields for Job_no and Client_id so that the entire field is visible in the box.

To resize the data entry fields for Job_no and Client_id:
❶ Click in the **Job_no data entry field** to select it.
❷ Position the pointer on the right edge of the data entry field. The pointer changes to ⤡. Click and drag the right edge to the right to align it with 45 on the horizontal ruler.
❸ Click in the **Client_id data entry field** to select it.
❹ Position the pointer on the right edge of the data entry field and drag the right edge to the right to align it with 90 on the horizontal ruler.

Now let's move the title to the top of the form and arrange the other objects in the form. The procedure for moving the title is similar to moving the text and data entry field objects for Client_id. However, the title text object is a single object.

To move the title text object to the top of the form and arrange the other objects:
❶ Click anywhere in the **title text object (Jobs)**. Handles appear around the object.
❷ Click and drag the **title text object** up and to the right. Align the selected object so that the shaded region is centered around lines 3 and 4 in the vertical ruler. Align the left edge of the selected object with 29 in the horizontal ruler.
❸ Release the **mouse button.**
❹ Move the rest of the objects in the form so that the form appears as shown in Figure 5-1.

Now that you've moved the objects, you can change the title from "Jobs" to "Job Authorization Form."

Using the Object Inspector

Each object on a form has a set of characteristics, or **properties**. Some properties determine the appearance of an object in the form; others determine its behavior when an event (such as a mouse click) occurs. You can change some properties, such as an object's position in the form, directly in the form, as you did when you repositioned objects in the previous steps. To change other properties, you must use the Object Inspector.

To make your form look like Figure 5-1, you need to change the appearance of the title, which is a text object. When you inspect a text object, you can change the text it contains, its size, its color, and other properties.

Let's open the Object Inspector to change the properties of the title text object.

To open the Object Inspector:

❶ Click the **Jobs text object** to select it.

❷ Click **View** then click **Object Properties** (or right-click the **Jobs text object**, then click **Object Properties**) to open the Properties window. Notice that the Form Designer window is restored to its original size. See Figure 5-17.

name of the
selected object

bullet (•) indicates
the name of an
individual property

plus sign (+)
indicates a list of
properties

Figure 5-17
Properties window

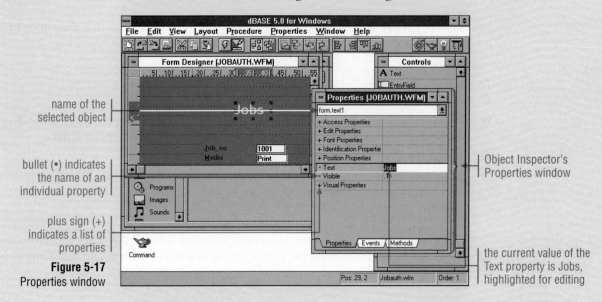

Object Inspector's
Properties window

the current value of the
Text property is Jobs,
highlighted for editing

The Object Inspector allows you to inspect and modify the properties associated with the selected object. These properties are displayed in the Properties window. The specific properties shown will vary depending on the type of object selected. The text box at the top of the window displays the name of the selected object. Below the object name is a list of property types and individual properties. A plus sign (+) next to an item in the list indicates a property type. Double-clicking a property type opens a list of individual properties for you to view or modify. A bullet (•) next to an item in the list indicates an individual property name. Next to the name is the current value for that property. The individual property called "Text" has the current value "Jobs." This property is highlighted, indicating dBASE is ready for you to edit it.

Let's change the title from "Jobs" to "Job Authorization Form."

To enter the new title:

❶ Type **Job Authorization Form**. The Form Designer window reflects the change in the title as you type it.

TROUBLE? If you make a typing error, you can correct it as you do any typing error (using [Backspace], [Del], and so on).

❷ Click the **Maximize button** in the Form Designer window to view the modified form.

Although you have entered the new title, the text object in the form is not big enough to display the title entirely. Let's change the width so that the entire title is visible. You can do this directly in the Form Designer window.

To change the width of the title text object:

❶ Place the pointer on the middle right handle of the title text object. The pointer changes to ⟨H⟩.

❷ Click the **mouse button** and drag the right edge of the object until the right edge of the shaded region in the horizontal ruler is at 76.

❸ Release the **mouse button**. The complete title now appears in the text object. See Figure 5-18.

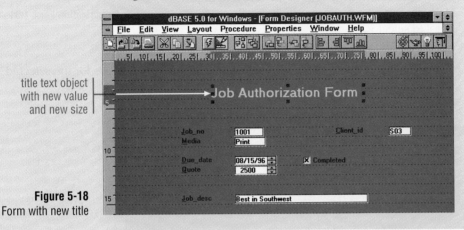

title text object with new value and new size

Figure 5-18
Form with new title

The procedure for changing the field labels for the data entry fields is very similar. Let's change them now.

To change the field labels for the data entry fields:

❶ Click the field label **Job_no** on the form. Handles appear around the text object.

❷ Click **Window** then click **Properties** to display the Properties window. The Properties window is maximized just as the Form Designer window was. The Text property is highlighted. Notice that the value for the Text property is "&Job_no". The ampersand (&) indicates that the letter "J" should be underlined in the text object. The letter "J" is a *mnemonic* for the object and can be used to navigate in the form using the keyboard. You will not use mnemonics in this text.

❸ Type **Job No** to enter the new text value.

❹ Click **Window** then click **Form Designer** to return to the Form Designer window. The new field label appears in the form.

❺ Repeat Steps 1 through 4 to modify the labels for the other fields in the form: **Client ID**, **Media**, **Due Date**, **Quote**, and **Job Description**. Notice that for the Media and Quote labels, the only change you need to make is to remove the underscore from the letter for the mnemonic. The Completed label needs no modification.

Martin stops by to see the form. He decides that he would like the color of the title to be black. Let's make this change.

Changing Colors

Color is another property you can change for objects in the form. It is a visual property of a text object. Let's change the color of the text in the title text object to black. To change the color, you must select the title text object and return to the Properties window.

To change the color of the text in the title text object:

❶ Make sure the Form Designer window is open. Click the **Job Authorization Form text object** to select it.

❷ Click **Window** then click **Properties** to display the Properties window.

❸ Double-click **Visual Properties** to display the list of visual properties for the selected object.

❹ Click **ColorNormal** to select this property. See Figure 5-19.

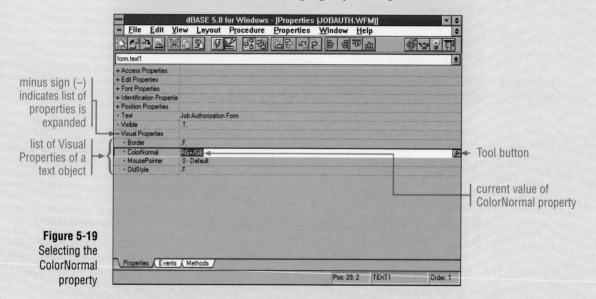

minus sign (−) indicates list of properties is expanded

list of Visual Properties of a text object

Tool button

current value of ColorNormal property

Figure 5-19
Selecting the ColorNormal property

The current value of the ColorNormal property is a code indicating the foreground and background colors for this object. The foreground color determines the color of the text. The background color determines the color of the background on which the text is displayed in the object. If you know the codes for the different colors, you can enter them here. If you prefer, you can select colors from the Choose Color dialog box and let dBASE enter the necessary codes.

Let's change the foreground color of the text to black using the Choose Color dialog box.

❺ Click the **Tool button** 🔧 to display the Choose Color dialog box. See Figure 5-20.

Changing Colors   **dB 179**

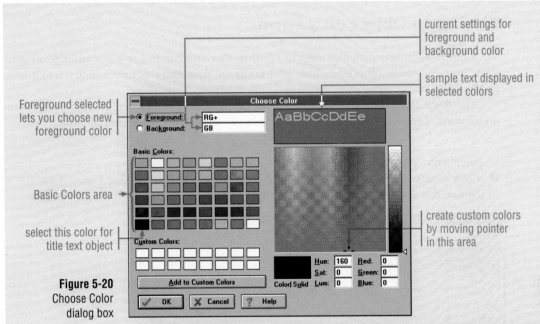

current settings for
foreground and
background color

sample text displayed in
selected colors

Foreground selected
lets you choose new
foreground color

Basic Colors area →

select this color for
title text object

Figure 5-20
Choose Color
dialog box

create custom colors
by moving pointer
in this area

The Choose Color dialog box lets you select foreground and background colors for
the selected object. The top of the dialog box displays the current foreground and
background color codes and an example of text displayed in these colors. A palette
of Basic Colors appears at the left of the box. You can choose any of these colors as
a foreground or background color or create a custom color using the color panel
on the right.

Let's select black as the foreground color.

❻ Make sure the Foreground radio button is selected, then click the **black color box** at
the lower left of the Basic Colors area. The code for the Foreground appears as N
and the sample text shows black letters.

❼ Click **OK** to close the Choose Color dialog box and return to the Properties window.

The new foreground color code appears in the value for the ColorNormal property.
Let's look at this change in the form.

❽ Click **Window** then click **Form Designer** to switch to the Form Designer window. The
title now appears in black.

The form now looks like Figure 5-1. Martin stops by to take a look at the form. After
viewing it, he asks if you can make the title stand out from the rest of the form so that it is
easier to identify the form. You decide to add a rectangle around the title and use shadows to make it stand out. To do this, you must place a new object on the form using the
Controls window.

Placing an Object on a Form

The Controls window provides a list of controls that you can use to place objects on your form. Some of these objects include text controls, data entry controls, lines, rectangles, and buttons.

The Rectangle control in the Controls window allows you to place a rectangle object on the form. Let's use the Rectangle control to place a rectangle around the title.

To place a rectangle on the form:
❶ Click **Window** then click **Controls** to display the Controls window. See Figure 5-21. Notice that the Controls window is maximized as was the Form Designer window.

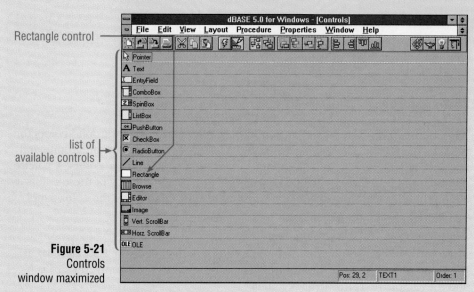

Rectangle control

list of available controls

Figure 5-21
Controls
window maximized

❷ Click the **Rectangle tool** in the Controls window. The Rectangle tool is now selected.

To place a new rectangle on the form, you need to switch to the Form Designer window.

❸ Click **Window** then click **Form Designer** to display the Form Designer window.

When you move the mouse into the Form Designer window, the pointer changes to $+$ and thin indicator lines on the rulers show the position of the pointer in the form.

Next, move the pointer to where you want to place the upper-left corner of the rectangle.

❹ Position the pointer so that the indicator lines are at 1 on the vertical ruler and 25 on the horizontal ruler.

❺ Click the **mouse button** and drag the pointer to vertical position 6 and horizontal position 79, then release the mouse button to place the rectangle. See Figure 5-22.

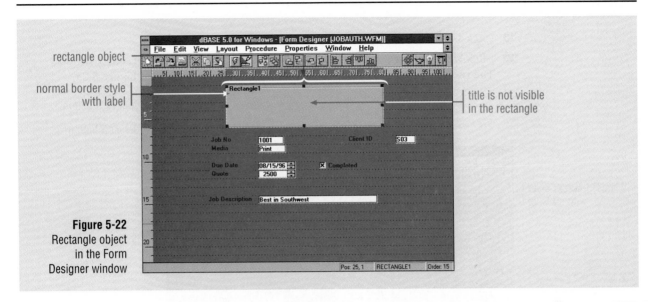

rectangle object

normal border style with label

title is not visible in the rectangle

Figure 5-22
Rectangle object in the Form Designer window

The new rectangle object has a normal border style, with a label on the upper edge and no shadowing. It also obscures the title it frames. Let's change the border style to a style that has shadows and no label, then make the title visible in the rectangle.

To change the border style of the rectangle:
❶ Make sure the rectangle is selected.
❷ Click **Window** then click **Properties** to display the Properties window.

To change the border style, you must change one of the visual properties of the rectangle.

❸ Click **BorderStyle** to select the BorderStyle property.

The current value of BorderStyle is 0-normal, that is, a simple line and a label. To make the rectangle stand out, you'll add shadowing to make it appear raised.

❹ Click the **list arrow** at the right edge of the BorderStyle value box to display the list of BorderStyle options. See Figure 5-23.

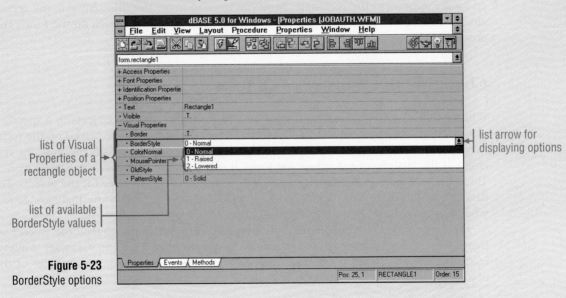

list of Visual Properties of a rectangle object

list of available BorderStyle values

list arrow for displaying options

Figure 5-23
BorderStyle options

❺ Click **1-Raised** to add shadowing to the rectangle.

❻ Click **Window** then click **Form Designer** to return to the Form Designer window. The rectangle object now has a shadow and no visible label. See Figure 5-24.

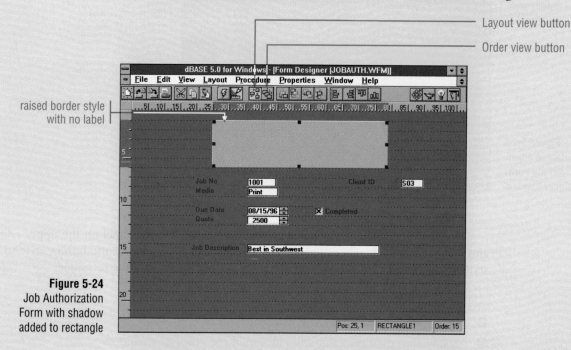

Layout view button

Order view button

raised border style
with no label

Figure 5-24
Job Authorization
Form with shadow
added to rectangle

It is difficult to see the shadow in the Form Designer window. The shadow is displayed more noticeably in the Form window, where you use the form to enter and edit data.

TROUBLE? If you don't like the way the rectangle appears, you can delete it and replace it. To delete the rectangle, you must first select the rectangle, then press [Del]. Then repeat Steps 1 through 6.

The rectangle now has a border that makes it stand out from the form, and the label no longer appears in the rectangle. Now you need to make the title visible in the rectangle. To do this, you must change the order in which objects are drawn on the form. This order is known as the z-order.

Changing the Z-order of Objects

When dBASE displays a form on the screen, it displays, or **draws**, objects in a specified order. By default, objects are drawn in the order in which they were placed on the form. An object obscures any part of a previously drawn object that it covers. Because the rectangle is the last object placed on the form, it obscures the title that was placed earlier. The order in which dBASE draws the objects is known as the **z-order** for the objects. For data entry objects, the z-order also determines the order in which the highlight moves when you move from field to field entering data.

To prevent the rectangle from obscuring the title, you must change the z-order so that the rectangle is drawn before the title. You do this in the Form Designer window using Order view rather than the default Layout view. Let's change the z-order of the objects now.

To change the z-order of the objects:

❶ Click the **Order view button** 🔲 on the SpeedBar. The Form Designer window now displays the objects in the form in Order view. See Figure 5-25.

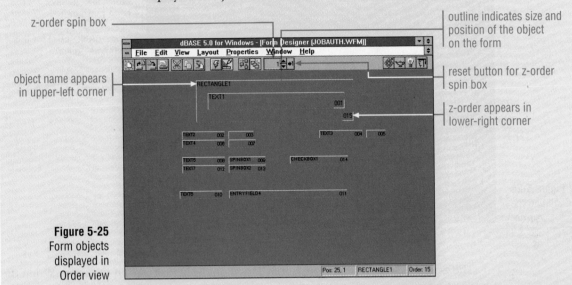

z-order spin box

outline indicates size and position of the object on the form

object name appears in upper-left corner

reset button for z-order spin box

z-order appears in lower-right corner

Figure 5-25
Form objects displayed in Order view

In Order view, each object in the form is shown as a box identified with the object's name. In the lower-right corner of each box is the z-order for that object. The first object placed on the form by the Form Expert was the title. It has the name TEXT1 and has z-order 1. The rectangle object, named RECTANGLE1, was the last object placed on the form and has z-order 15. To change the z-order of an object, use the spin box on the SpeedBar to set the z-order value and then click the object. dBASE automatically changes the z-orders of other objects if necessary.

Let's set the z-order of the rectangle object to 1.

❷ Use the spin box arrows on the SpeedBar to set the spin box value to 1, if necessary (or click the **reset button** immediately to the right of the spin box).

❸ Click anywhere in the **RECTANGLE1 object** (but outside of the TEXT1 object) in the form. The z-order for the RECTANGLE1 object is set to 001 and the other objects in the form are automatically renumbered. The spin box value automatically increments to 2. See Figure 5-26.

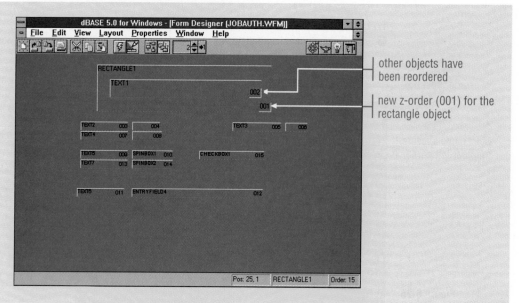

other objects have been reordered

new z-order (001) for the rectangle object

Figure 5-26
Changing the
z-order

The z-order also determines the order in which data is entered in the form. When the form is first displayed, dBASE highlights the data entry field with the lowest z-order. When you enter data in that field and move to the next field, the highlight moves to the field with the next lowest z-order. (Objects that are not data entry fields, such as text objects, are skipped.) If you were to enter a Due Date (z-order 10) for a job in this form, the highlight would move to the Job Description data entry field (z-order 12), and then to the Quote data entry field (z-order 14), and last to the Completed data entry field (z-order 15). This would be inconvenient and possibly confusing. Let's change these z-orders so that after the Due Date is entered, the order of data entry is Completed, Quote, and then Job Description.

To change the z-order of the Completed, Quote, and Job Description data entry fields:

❶ Use the spin box arrows on the SpeedBar to set the z-order to 11.

❷ Click the **CHECKBOX1 object** on the form (the data entry field for Completed). The z-order for the check box object changes to 11 and the other, higher numbered, objects have been renumbered. The z-order spin box value increments to 12.

❸ Click the **SPINBOX2 object** on the form (the data entry field for Quote). The z-order for the spin box object changes to 12. The z-order spin box value increments to 13.

The z-order for the ENTRYFIELD4 object on the form (the data entry field for the Job Description) has been automatically renumbered to 14. There is no need to change it.

❹ Click the **Layout view button** 🔲 on the SpeedBar to view the layout of the form.

❺ Click the **Maximize button** on the Form Designer window to view the entire form. The title is now visible in the rectangle. The changed z-orders of the data entry fields do not affect their appearance in the form. See Figure 5-27.

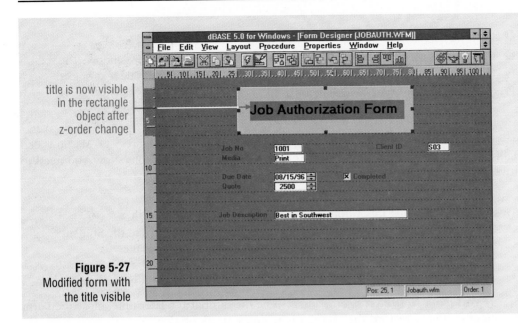

title is now visible
in the rectangle
object after
z-order change

Figure 5-27
Modified form with
the title visible

Notice that the background color of the rectangle is gray. Let's change it to match the background color of the title text object and the background color for the form. This will enhance the appearance of the form.

To change the background color of the rectangle object:
❶ Make sure the rectangle object is selected.
❷ Click **Window** then click **Properties** to display the Properties window.
❸ Click **ColorNormal** in the Visual Properties section to select the ColorNormal property.
❹ Click the **Tool button** 🖉 to display the Choose Color dialog box. See Figure 5-28.

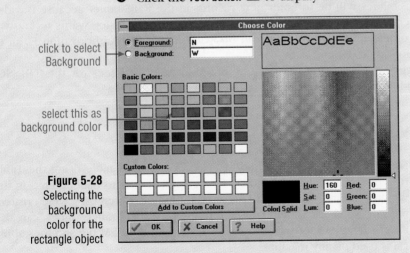

click to select
Background

select this as
background color

Figure 5-28
Selecting the
background
color for the
rectangle object

❺ Click the **Background radio button** to select this option.
❻ Click the **cyan color block** (see Figure 5-28) for the background color. (The cyan color block is in row 3, column 4 of the basic color blocks.)

The Background color code, GB, appears next to the Background radio button, and the sample text appears with the selected background color.

❼ Click **OK** to close the Choose Color dialog box.

❽ Click **Window** then click **Form Designer** to return to the Form Designer window. The rectangle object now appears with the same background color as the title text object.

❾ Click outside the object to deselect it and to view the modifications.

You have completed the form design as Martin sketched it (Figure 5-1). Martin is certain that the form will make it easier to enter data in the JOBS table. Now you need to save your modified form.

To save the customized Job Authorization Form:

❶ Click **File** then click **Save** to save the form. dBASE saves this form to the Student Disk as JOBAUTH.WFM, overwriting the previous version of this file.

If you want to take a break and resume the tutorial at a later time, close the Form Designer window, restore the Navigator window to its original size, then exit dBASE. When you resume the tutorial, place your Student Disk in the disk drive, start dBASE, and make sure the current directory is A:\WM. Click the Forms icon in the Navigator window, click Jobauth.wfm, then click the Design button on the SpeedBar. Click the View menu, and if the Object Properties option is not checked, click Object Properties to make the Properties window visible. Click the Maximize button on the Form Designer window to display the entire form, then continue with the tutorial.

■   ■   ■

Nancy reminds Martin that a new employee, David Liu, is starting today. One of David's responsibilities will be to enter new records in the JOBS table. Because David is new to the agency and not familiar with its business activities, Nancy wants to know if there are any other enhancements that can be made to the Job Authorization Form to make it easier for David to enter data.

Martin suggests customizing the form by entering validity checks for the JOB_NO, CLIENT_ID, and DUE_DATE fields in the form.

Entering Validity Checks

Recall that in Tutorial 3 you entered validity checks for the JOBS table using the Table Records Properties dialog box. Those validity checks applied only to data entered in the Table Records window and only for the particular computer on which they were created. Many of the same validity checks, including picture templates and range values, can also be attached to a form. These validity checks are recorded in the .WFM file and thus apply any time the form is used on any machine.

Recall that the validity check for the JOB_NO field requires a four-digit value with a minimum of 1000. The validity check for the CLIENT_ID field specifies that the first character must be an uppercase letter followed by two digits. And the validity check for the DUE_DATE field requires a date of 01/01/96 or later. Martin wants you to add these validity checks to the Job Authorization Form so that it will be easier for employees to enter data using the form. Let's start by adding the validity checks for the JOB_NO field.

To enter the validity checks for the JOB_NO field:

❶ Click in the **data entry field** for the JOB_NO field to select it. The status bar indicates that an entry field object is selected.

❷ Click **Window** then click **Properties** to display the Properties window.

Validity checks are edit properties of an object in the form.

❸ Double-click **Edit Properties** to display the list of edit properties for the selected object. See Figure 5-29.

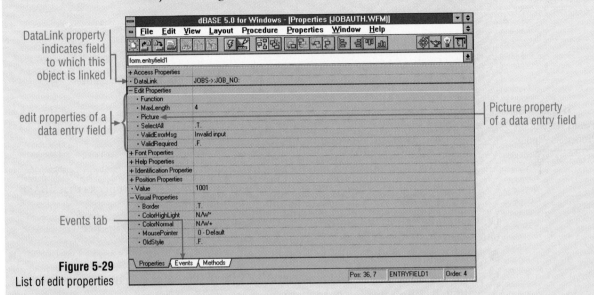

DataLink property indicates field to which this object is linked

edit properties of a data entry field

Picture property of a data entry field

Events tab

Figure 5-29
List of edit properties

Notice that the DataLink property indicates that this object is linked to the JOB_NO field of the JOBS table.

❹ Click **Picture** to select the Picture property.

Recall that the picture template character "9" indicates a numeric character. Because the allowed JOB_NO values have four digits, the picture template is "9999."

❺ Type **9999** then press **[Enter]** to enter the picture template for the JOB_NO field.

To enter the validity check specifying a minimum value for a job number, you must define an expression that dBASE can check when the user moves to another field in the form. Moving to another field is an event; therefore, you need to enter this expression on the Events page of the Properties window.

❻ Click the **Events tab** to display the Events page. See Figure 5-30.

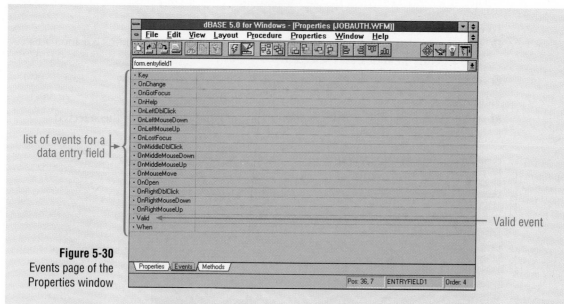

list of events for a
data entry field

Valid event

Figure 5-30
Events page of the
Properties window

The Events page allows you to define what dBASE should do when an event occurs while the user is using the form. The Valid event defines validity checks that dBASE should enforce when the user attempts to leave the field.

Let's enter the expression to tell dBASE to check the minimum value for a number entered in the JOB_NO field.

❼ Click **Valid** to select the Valid event.

❽ Type **JOB_NO>="1000"** then press **[Enter]**. Be sure to enter the quotation marks, indicating that this value is a character type, not numeric. Also, you must type the field name exactly as it appears in the table (in this case, "JOB_NO"). dBASE automatically encloses the expression in braces ({}). See Figure 5-31.

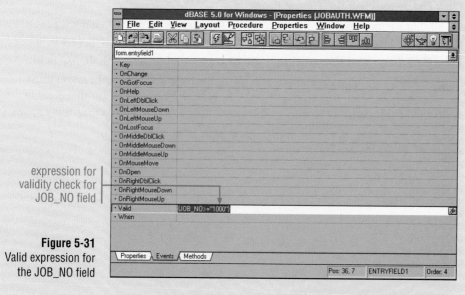

expression for
validity check for
JOB_NO field

Figure 5-31
Valid expression for
the JOB_NO field

TROUBLE? If dBASE displays an Alert box with the message "Error: syntax error," you have entered the expression incorrectly. Click OK then repeat Steps 7 and 8.

Although you have entered all the necessary validity checks for the JOB_NO field, dBASE does not automatically enforce them unless you explicitly ask it to do so. You do this by setting the edit property ValidRequired to .T. (True) on the Properties page of the Properties dialog box.

To specify that dBASE enforce the validity checks for the JOB_NO field:

❶ Click the **Properties tab** to display the Properties page.

❷ Click **ValidRequired** to select the ValidRequired property.

❸ Click the **list arrow** to display the list of values for the ValidRequired property.

❹ Click **.T.** to set the ValidRequired property to True.

You have completed the validity checks for the JOB_NO field. Let's return to the Form Designer window.

❺ Click **Window** then click **Form Designer** to return to the Form Designer window.

The picture template you used in Tutorial 3 for the CLIENT_ID field was @! A99. This template specifies that the first character is an uppercase letter, followed by two digits. Let's add this validity check to the data entry field for CLIENT_ID.

To add the picture template for the CLIENT_ID field:

❶ Click the **data entry field** for CLIENT_ID to select it.

❷ Click **Window** then click **Properties** to display the Properties window. Notice that the Edit Properties list is still displayed.

❸ Click **Picture** to select the Picture edit property.

❹ Type **@! A99** then press **[Enter]**. Be sure to include the space after the exclamation point. Recall that the @ specifies a function applied to the entire field. dBASE automatically enters the function symbol code (!) as the Function property and enters the picture template (A99) as the Picture property. See Figure 5-32.

dBASE automatically places the function code (!) here

value of Picture property is A99

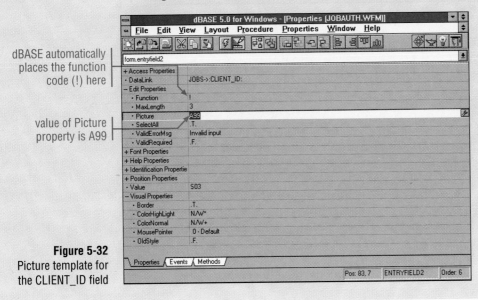

Figure 5-32
Picture template for the CLIENT_ID field

TROUBLE? If the Function and Picture property entries on your screen do not match Figure 5-32, you can remove them and reenter the correct values. Double-click the Function property entry then press [Delete] to remove it. Double-click the Picture property entry then press [Delete] to remove it. Then repeat Steps 3 and 4.

❺ Click **ValidRequired** to select the ValidRequired property.

❻ Click the **list arrow** to display the list of values for the ValidRequired property.

❼ Click **.T.** to set the ValidRequired property to True.

You have completed the validity check for the CLIENT_ID field. It is not necessary to enter a validity check on the Events page, because dBASE checks each character as it is entered, not when the user moves to a new field.

❽ Click **Window** then click **Form Designer** to return to the Form Designer window.

Finally, let's add the validity check for the DUE_DATE field. This validity check specifies that dBASE should not accept a value earlier than 01/01/96. dBASE will check this when the user attempts to move to a new field, so you will define this validity check on the Events page of the Properties window.

To add the validity check for the DUE_DATE field:

❶ Click the **spin box object** for the DUE_DATE field. The status bar indicates that a spin box object is selected.

❷ Click **Window** then click **Properties** to display the Properties window.

❸ Click the **Events tab** to display the Events page.

❹ Click **Valid** to select the Valid event.

❺ Type **DUE_DATE>={01/01/96}** then press [Enter]. dBASE automatically encloses the expression in braces ({}). See Figure 5-33.

valid expression for the DUE_DATE spin box object

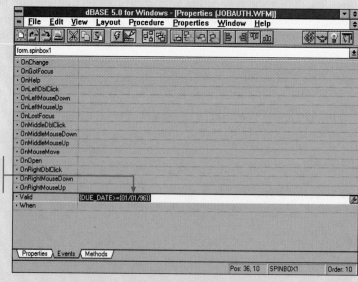

Figure 5-33
Valid expression for the DUE_DATE field

❻ Click the **Properties tab** to display the Properties page.

❼ Click **ValidRequired** to select the ValidRequired property.

❽ Click the **list arrow** to display the list of values for the ValidRequired property, then click **.T.** to set the ValidRequired property to True.

dBASE allows you to define an error message that is displayed when the user enters an illegal value. Recall that in Tutorial 3, you specified the message "Date must be 01/01/96 or later." Let's define this message to appear when a user enters an invalid date in the form.

❾ Click **ValidErrorMsg** to select the error message property, type **Date must be 01/01/96 or later** then press **[Enter]**. See Figure 5-34.

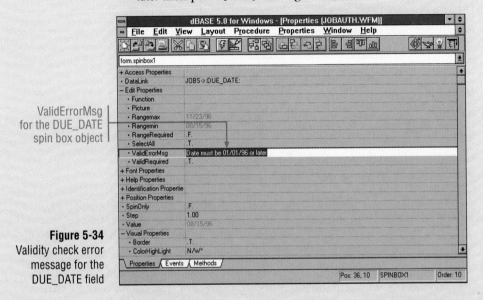

ValidErrorMsg for the DUE_DATE spin box object

Figure 5-34
Validity check error message for the DUE_DATE field

You have entered the validity check for the DUE_DATE field. Let's return to the Form Designer window.

❿ Click **Window** then click **Form Designer** to return to the Form Designer window.

You have made many changes to the Job Authorization Form. Let's save it now.

To save the modified Job Authorization Form:

❶ Click **File** then click **Save** to save the form. dBASE saves this form to the Student Disk as JOBAUTH.WFM, overwriting the previous version of this file.

Nancy wants David Liu, the new employee at W&M, to begin entering data in the JOBS table. She asks if you can "walk him through" adding a record, and she suggests that you use the revised Job Authorization Form to do so.

Using the Form to Add a Record

To add a new record to the JOBS table using the form, you must open the form and switch to Append mode. Figure 5-35 shows a new Job Authorization Form that Martin received recently. As Nancy suggested, you'll use the customized Job Authorization Form to add this new job to the JOBS table.

Wells & Martinez Ad Agency
Job Authorization Form

Job No: 1042

Client ID: S03

Client: Southwest Styles

Address: 632 Highland Street

Albuquerque, NM 87434

Media: Other

Due Date: 12/03/96   Quote: $4,200

Description: Flyer

Accepted: *Gary Higgins* Date: *Sept. 9, 1996*

Figure 5-35
Job Authorization
Form for new job

To add the new record to the table using the form:

❶ Click the **Run button** 🗲 on the SpeedBar. The Form window appears and displays the Job Authorization Form.

❷ Click the **Add Record button** 🖾 on the SpeedBar to switch to Append mode. dBASE displays a blank record in the Job Authorization Form. The cursor is in the data entry field for Job No, ready for you to enter data. See Figure 5-36.

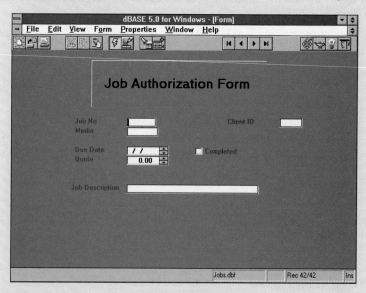

Figure 5-36
Blank record in form

Now enter the data.

❸ Type **1042**. dBASE beeps and the highlight moves to the Client ID entry field.

TROUBLE? If nothing appears in the Job No field as you type, you might be typing characters that conflict with the validity checks for the field. For example, if you enter the letter l (ell) instead of the digit 1, or the letter O instead of the digit 0, dBASE will not accept the entry. Type the correct job number.

❹ Type **S03** in the Client ID data entry field. dBASE beeps and the highlight moves to the Media entry field. *Make sure you type the number 0 and not the capital letter O when typing the Client ID.* The validity check for this field prevents dBASE from accepting any input other than a letter followed by two digits.

❺ Type **Other** then press **[Tab]**. The highlight moves to the data entry field for Due Date.

The correct due date for this job is 12/03/96. Let's enter an incorrect due date to test the validity check for the Due Date field. The minimum value for the field is 01/01/96. Let's enter an earlier date, 12/03/93, to test this.

❻ Type **120393**. dBASE beeps and displays an Alert box with the message "Date must be 01/01/96 or later." See Figure 5-37.

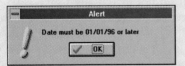

Figure 5-37
Error message
displayed for
incorrect date

❼ Click **OK**, then press **[Backspace]** to erase the 3 and type **6**. dBASE beeps and the highlight moves to the Completed check box (because you changed the z-order earlier).

When you use the check box to enter a value for Completed, you don't type the value Y or N. To place a checkmark in the box, place the pointer in the check box and click. By placing a checkmark in the check box, you are telling dBASE to store "Y" in the COMPLETED field. If the check box is checked, you can remove the checkmark, resulting in the value "N" being stored in the Completed field. Leave the check box for Completed unchecked because this is a newly authorized job. Recall that dBASE provides the default value "N" for a logical field. Therefore, dBASE will store "N" in this field automatically when you leave it unchecked.

❽ Press **[Tab]** to move the highlight to the Quote spin box.

❾ Enter the remaining values (Quote and Job Description), as shown in Figure 5-35. The finished record should look like Figure 5-38.

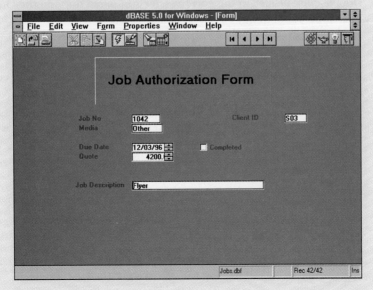

Figure 5-38
New record in the Job
Authorization Form

ⓠ Click the **Restore button** on the Form window to restore it to its original size. Close the form by double-clicking the **Control menu box** for the Form window. The new record is saved and you return to the dBASE Desktop.

If you want to take a break and resume the tutorial at a later time, exit dBASE. When you resume the tutorial, place the Student Disk in the disk drive, start dBASE, and make sure the current directory is A:\WM. Then continue with the tutorial.

■   ■   ■

Even though you have defined validity checks for the Job Authorization Form, Nancy and Martin have still encountered errors in the JOBS records. In particular, they have JOBS records with CLIENT_ID values that do not match any CLIENT_ID in the CLIENTS table. Martin asks whether you can modify the Job Authorization Form so that a CLIENT_ID in the JOBS table must match a CLIENT_ID in the CLIENTS table. To do this, you must modify the Job Authorization Form so that it can access data in two tables, CLIENTS and JOBS. A form that uses data from more than one table is called a **multi-table form**.

Multi-Table Forms[*]

All the information needed for the modified form comes from two tables—CLIENTS and JOBS. In order to create a multi-table form, you must first link the tables. You do this by creating a query that defines a relation between the tables. Then you must modify the original form so that it is based on the query rather than on the JOBS table. Because you want to access the records by JOB_NO (the primary key for the JOBS table), the JOBS table will be the parent table for the query. Let's create the query now.

To create the query:
❶ Click the **Queries icon** in the Navigator window.
❷ Double-click **Untitled** in the current selection panel to open the Query Designer. The Open Table Required dialog box appears.
❸ Double-click **jobs.dbf** to select the JOBS table and close the Open Table Required dialog box. The JOBS skeleton appears in the Query Designer window.
❹ Click the **Add Table button** ▦ on the SpeedBar. The Open Table Required dialog box appears.
❺ Double-click **clients.dbf** to select the CLIENTS table and close the Open Table Required dialog box. The CLIENTS skeleton is added to the Query Designer window. See Figure 5-39.

---

*For shorter courses, this section can be omitted without loss of continuity.

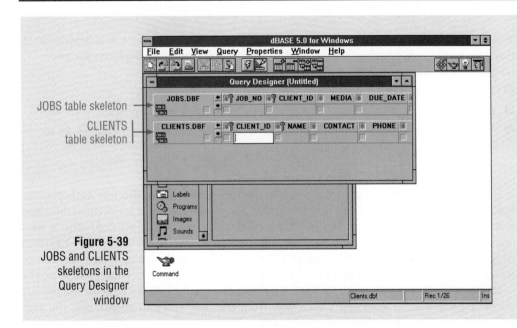

Figure 5-39
JOBS and CLIENTS
skeletons in the
Query Designer
window

In this relation, the JOBS table is the parent table and the CLIENTS table is the child table.

To set the relation between the two tables:
❶ Click **Query** then click **Set Relation...** to open the Define Relation dialog box.

❷ Make sure that JOBS.DBF is the parent table in the relation.

❸ Click **CLIENT_ID** in the Field panel for the parent table to select it as the common field.

❹ Make sure that CLIENTS.DBF is the child table in the relation.

❺ Click **CLIENT_ID** in the Index panel for the child table to select it as the common field.

The link in this relation is from the JOBS table to the CLIENTS table. Because there is only one record in the CLIENTS table for each record in the JOBS table, this relation is "one-to-one."

❻ Click the **One To Many check box** to remove the checkmark. The Define Relation dialog box should look like Figure 5-40.

remove checkmark
for one-to-one
relation

common field in
parent table

Figure 5-40
Definition of
JOBS-CLIENTS
relation

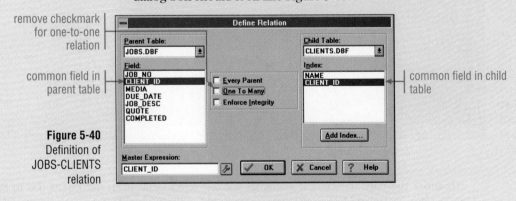

common field in child
table

❼ Click **OK** to close the Define Relation dialog box.

You have completed the definition of the query. It is not necessary to select fields or to run the query; the purpose of the query is simply to define the link between the two tables and thus make the fields in both tables available to the form.

❽ Double-click the **Control menu box** on the Query Designer window.

❾ Click **Yes** when the Changes Made-Query Designer dialog box appears.

❿ Type **jobauth** in the File Name text box of the Save File dialog box, then click **OK** to save this query as JOBAUTH.QBE.

Now that you have created the necessary query, let's modify the Job Authorization Form so that it is based on the JOBAUTH.QBE query rather than the JOBS.DBF table. You will start by replacing the data entry field object for the CLIENT_ID field with a new object, called a combo box, that can be linked to the CLIENT_ID field in the CLIENTS table. A **combo box** is a combination of a data entry field and a list of values that can be selected for the field. The values in the list can come from another table, such as the CLIENTS table. By including the CLIENT_ID values from the CLIENTS table in the list and restricting the user to selecting values only from that list, you can ensure that the user will enter matching client IDs in the JOBS table.

To replace the data entry field object for the CLIENT_ID field:

❶ Click the **Forms icon** in the Navigator window.

❷ Click **Jobauth.wfm** in the current selection panel, then click the **Design button** 📝 on the SpeedBar to open the Form Designer window.

❸ Click the **Maximize button** on the Form Designer window to see the entire form. See Figure 5-41.

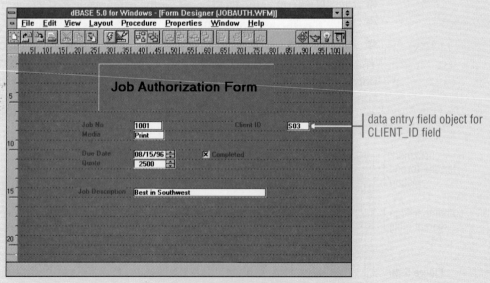

Figure 5-41
Job
Authorization Form

To allow the user to select a client ID for the JOBS table from the client IDs in the CLIENTS table, you can change the data entry field for the Client ID field in the JOBS table to a combo box.

Let's delete the data entry field object for the Client ID field and replace it with a combo box object. It will be easier to align the combo box object if you first turn off the Snap To Grid property of the Form Designer window.

To turn off the Snap To Grid property of the Form Designer window:
❶ Click **Properties** then click **Form Designer** to display the Form Designer Properties dialog box. See Figure 5-42.

click to clear
check box

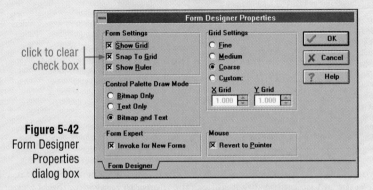

Figure 5-42
Form Designer
Properties
dialog box

❷ Click the **Snap To Grid check box** to clear it.
❸ Click **OK** to close the Form Designer Properties dialog box.

Now you can replace the data entry field object for the Client ID field.

To replace the data entry field object with a combo box object:
❶ Click the **data entry field object** for the Client ID field to select it.
❷ Press **[Del]** to delete the object from the form.
❸ Click **Window** then click **Controls** to display the Controls window.
❹ Click the **ComboBox control** to select it.
❺ Click **Window** then click **Form Designer** to return to the Form Designer window. Notice that when you move the pointer into the Form Designer window, the pointer changes to ✛ and thin indicator lines on the rulers show the position of the pointer in the form.

Move the pointer to where you want to place the upper-left corner of the new combo box object. When creating a combo box object, you don't have to draw the object; simply clicking the mouse button will place and create the object.
❻ Position the pointer so that the indicator lines are at 7 on the vertical ruler and 80 on the horizontal ruler, then click the mouse button to place the combo box object. See Figure 5-43.

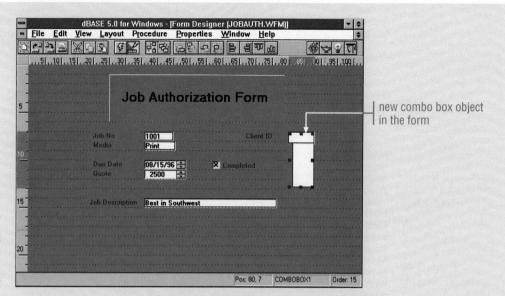

Figure 5-43
Job Authorization
Form with combo
box object

TROUBLE? If you did not get the combo box object placed exactly where you want it, click it to select it. Hold the mouse button down and use the mouse to reposition the object. Release the mouse button to place the object in its new position.

Notice that the combo box object has two areas. The upper area is the entry area. This is where the user will view or enter the client ID for the current record in the JOBS table. The lower area is the list area, where dBASE will display the list of current Client ID values stored in the CLIENTS table. If the list of Client ID values is too long to appear in the box all at once, then dBASE will automatically provide a scroll bar on the right side of the combo box object. You will define the combo box object properties so that the user can select only from Client ID values that appear in the list area.

Because you placed the combo box object on the form yourself (rather than having the Form Expert do it when the form was designed), it does not refer to any fields in either of the tables. To define these references, you must modify some of the properties for the combo box object. First, let's define the reference to the CLIENT_ID field in the JOBS table, which will appear in the entry area.

To define the data reference for the entry area:
❶ Make sure the combo box object is selected.
❷ Click **Window** then click **Properties** to display the Properties window.
❸ Double-click **Data Linkage Properties** to display the list of data linkage properties. See Figure 5-44.

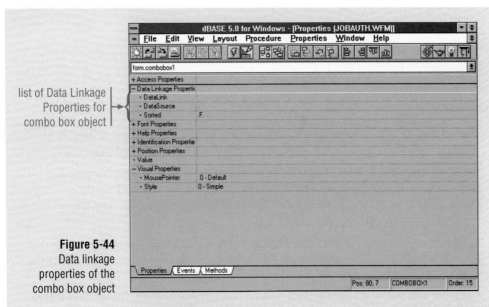

list of Data Linkage
Properties for
combo box object

Figure 5-44
Data linkage
properties of the
combo box object

❹ Click **DataLink** to select the DataLink property. The DataLink property defines the reference to the field that appears in the entry area. This is the field that the user can modify. In your form, that is the CLIENT_ID field of the JOBS table.

❺ Click the **Tool button** 🖉 to display the Choose Field dialog box. Notice that the JOBS table name is already highlighted, because it is the only table available in this form. The CLIENT_ID field name is already highlighted, because it happens to be the first field (alphabetically) in the field list. See Figure 5-45.

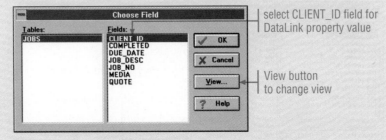

select CLIENT_ID field for
DataLink property value

View button
to change view

Figure 5-45
Choose Field
dialog box

❻ Click **OK** to select the CLIENT_ID field in the JOBS table. JOBS-> CLIENT_ID appears as the value for the DataLink property.

Now let's specify the CLIENT_ID values from the CLIENTS table as the values that will appear in the list area.

To define the data reference for the list area:

❶ Click **DataSource** to select the DataSource property. The DataSource property defines the source of the data that will appear in the list area. Values that appear in the list area are displayed for selection only; they cannot be edited. These values can come from several possible sources, including field values, field names, file names, and others.

❷ Click the **Tool button** 🖉 to display the Choose Data Source dialog box. See Figure 5-46.

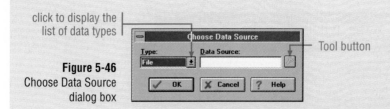

click to display the
list of data types

Figure 5-46
Choose Data Source
dialog box

Tool button

The Choose Data Source dialog box allows you to specify the type of data that appears in the list area of the combo box object and the source of that data.

❸ Click the **list arrow** in the Type box to display the list of data types. Because the values you want in the list area of the combo box object are values from the CLIENT_ID field of the CLIENTS table, you will select Field as the data type.

❹ Click **Field** to select the Field type.

The source of the data is the CLIENT_ID field in the CLIENTS table. To access this data, you must specify that the form is to be based on a view (query) that links the JOBS and CLIENTS tables.

❺ Click the **Tool button** 📝 on the Data Source box to display the Choose Field dialog box. Notice that the CLIENTS table does not appear in the Tables panel in the Choose Field dialog box. Up to this point, the form has been based only on the JOBS table. You will change that now so that the form will be based on the JOBAUTH.QBE query file you created earlier.

❻ Click **View...** to display the Choose View dialog box. The file list contains the names of all the tables and queries (.DBF,.DB, and.QBE files) in the current directory. See Figure 5-47.

name of
current directory

list of tables and
queries in the
current directory

Figure 5-47
Choose View
dialog box

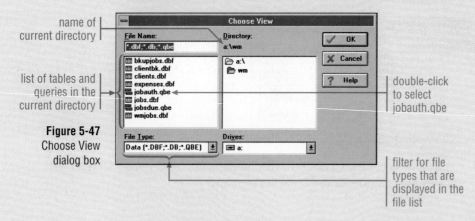

double-click
to select
jobauth.qbe

filter for file
types that are
displayed in the
file list

❼ Double-click **jobauth.qbe** to select the new query. The Choose View dialog box closes, and the Choose Field dialog box reappears with the CLIENTS table in the Tables panel.

❽ Click **CLIENTS** in the Tables panel to display the list of fields in the CLIENTS table. See Figure 5-48.

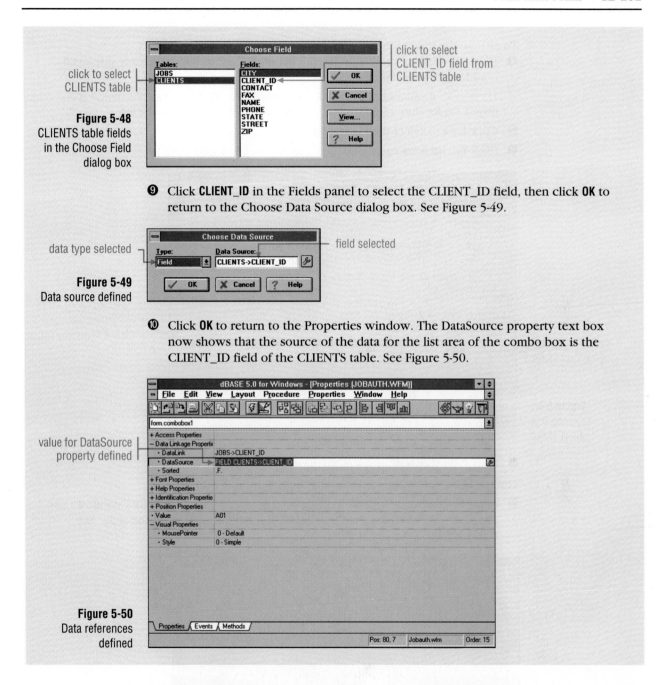

click to select
CLIENTS table

Figure 5-48
CLIENTS table fields
in the Choose Field
dialog box

click to select
CLIENT_ID field from
CLIENTS table

❾ Click **CLIENT_ID** in the Fields panel to select the CLIENT_ID field, then click **OK** to return to the Choose Data Source dialog box. See Figure 5-49.

data type selected

field selected

Figure 5-49
Data source defined

❿ Click **OK** to return to the Properties window. The DataSource property text box now shows that the source of the data for the list area of the combo box is the CLIENT_ID field of the CLIENTS table. See Figure 5-50.

value for DataSource
property defined

Figure 5-50
Data references
defined

The modified Job Authorization Form is now almost ready. The combo box object you have defined so far is the simplest style of combo box dBASE allows. It contains an entry area and a list area that is always displayed. Data values for the entry area can be selected from the list, but dBASE does not prevent the user from entering a value that does not appear on the list. Another style of combo box, the drop-down list combo box, displays the list area when the user clicks an arrow button next to the entry area and prevents the user from entering any value that is not in the list area. The combo box style is a visual property of the combo box object. Let's change the style of the combo box object to a drop-down list style.

To change the style of the combo box:

❶ If the list of visual properties for the combo box object is not already displayed, double-click **Visual Properties**.

TROUBLE? If you double-click Visual Properties when the list of visual properties is displayed, the list closes. Double-click Visual Properties again to display the list.

❷ Click **Style** to select the Style property.

❸ Click the **list arrow** to display the list of styles. See Figure 5-51.

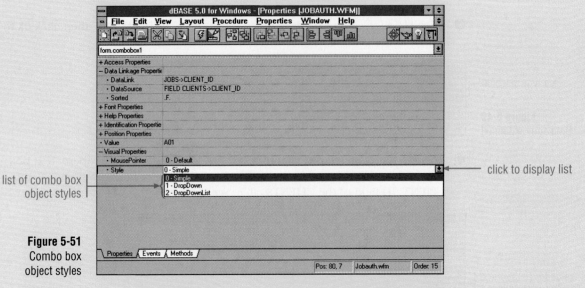

Figure 5-51
Combo box
object styles

❹ Click **2-DropDownList** to select the drop-down list style.

The modifications to the form are now complete.

❺ Click **Window** then click **Form Designer** to return to the Form Designer window. The combo box now appears with an entry area and a list arrow on the right. See Figure 5-52.

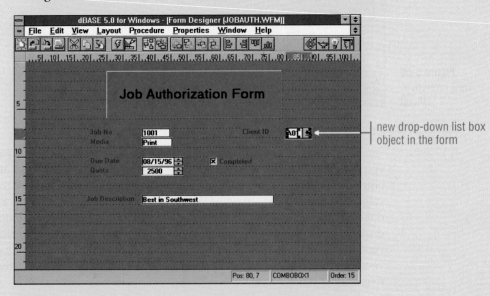

Figure 5-52
Job Authorization
Form with
combo box

Martin recently visited a client, the Boatslip Inn, and completed a Job Authorization Form for the client. He gives you the form (Figure 5-53) and asks you to enter the record in the JOBS table. You decide to use the modified Job Authorization Form you defined to enter the Client ID value when adding this new record.

Figure 5-53
Job Authorization
Form for
Boatslip Inn job

```
                        Wells & Martinez
                      Job Authorization Form


        Job No:      1043
        Client ID:   BO1


        Client:      Boatslip Inn

        Address:     32 Commercial Street

                     Taos, NM 87544



        Media:       Print

        Due Date:    12/20/96         Quote:   $5,500

        Description: Magazine ad

        Accepted:    Wendy Falchetti   Date: Oct. 1, 1996
```

Using the Combo Box to Add a Record

Let's enter the new job into the JOBS table using the modified Job Authorization Form. You need to run the form to add new data.

To add the new record using the modified form:
❶ Click the **Run button** ⚡ on the SpeedBar. dBASE automatically saves the changes you made to the form before it runs the form. The new Job Authorization Form appears. Notice that the entry area of the combo box for the Client ID field displays the CLIENT_ID value for the current job. See Figure 5-54.

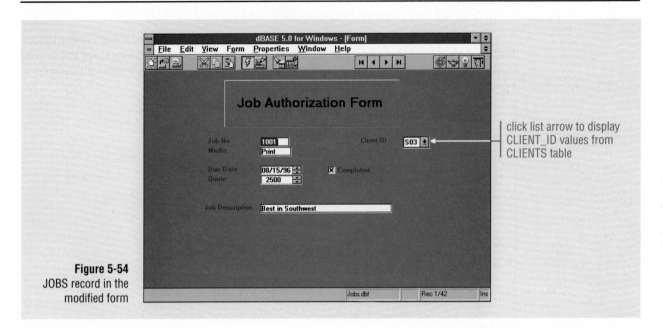

click list arrow to display
CLIENT_ID values from
CLIENTS table

Figure 5-54
JOBS record in the
modified form

Now enter the data for the new job using the Job Authorization Form Martin gave
you (Figure 5-53).

To enter the data into the form:

❶ Click the **Add Record button** 🔲 on the SpeedBar. A Job Authorization Form appears
that is blank except for an entry in the Client ID field. The cursor is in the data
entry field for Job No.

❷ Type **1043** in the Job No field. dBASE beeps and the highlight moves to the data
entry field for Media. Because you just added the combo box for the Client ID field,
its z-order is higher than any other object in the form.

❸ Refer to Figure 5-53 and enter the data for the Media and Due Date fields. Press
[Tab] to leave the Completed field blank and move to the Quote field. Enter the data
for Quote and Job Description. The combo box for the Client ID field contains S03,
the CLIENT_ID of the most recently accessed record.

❹ Click the **list arrow button** for the combo box to display the list of CLIENT_ID values
from the CLIENTS table. See Figure 5-55.

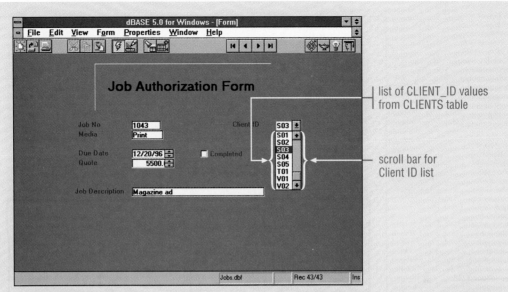

Figure 5-55
List of CLIENT_ID
values in the combo
box list area

❺ Use the scroll bar in the list area to scroll the list until B01 appears in the Client ID list, then click **B01** to select this CLIENT_ID. B01 appears in the entry area of the combo box and is entered as the Client ID for this JOBS record. The list box closes.

You can also enter a CLIENT_ID by typing the first character of the CLIENT_ID, in this case B, in the entry area. The entry area and the list area immediately display the first CLIENT_ID from the CLIENTS table that begins with the letter B. Typing B a second time would display the second CLIENT_ID that begins with B. If you continue to type B, the entry area and list area cycle through all the CLIENT_ID values that begin with B.

Whether you select the CLIENT_ID from the list or type it in, dBASE will not let you enter a CLIENT_ID that does not appear in the CLIENTS table.

You have completed entering the data for the new record.

❻ Click the **Restore button** on the Form window to restore it to its original size.

❼ Double-click the **Control menu box** for the Form window. dBASE saves the new record, closes the Form window, and returns to the Desktop.

If you want to take a break and resume the tutorial at a later time, exit dBASE. When you resume the tutorial, place your Student Disk in the disk drive, start dBASE, and make sure the current directory is A:\WM. Then continue with the tutorial.

■   ■   ■

Martin asks if you can create a new form, one that lists information about each client while also displaying information about the client's jobs. Figure 5-56 is a sketch of the screen layout he would like you to create.

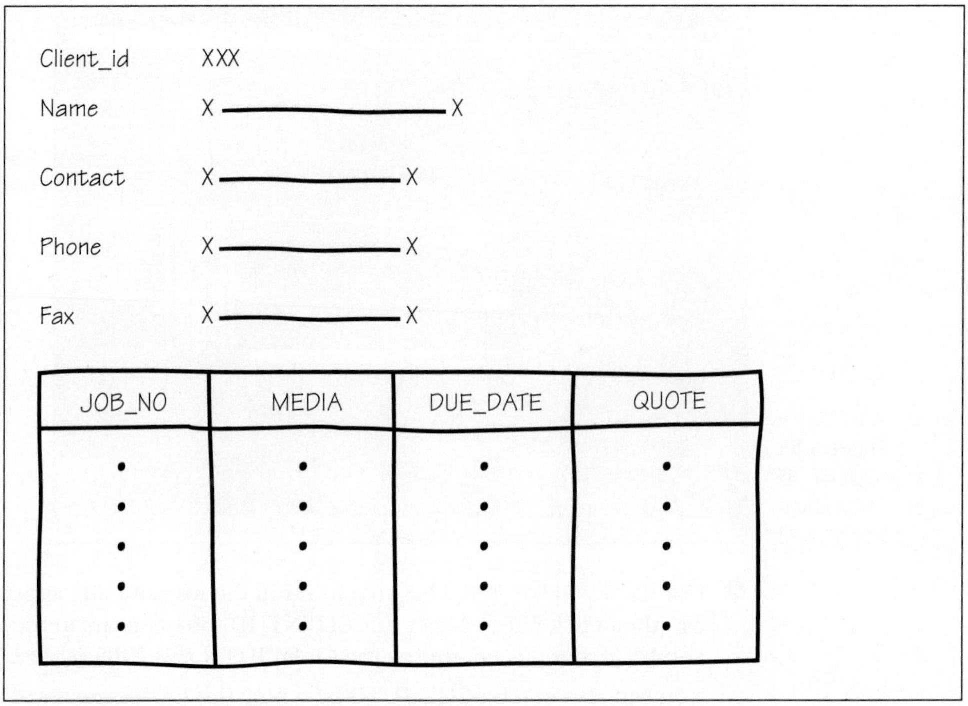

Figure 5-56
Sketch of new form
for Martin

The form Martin sketched is a multi-table form that uses data from both the CLIENTS and JOBS tables. Like the Job Authorization Form, this form must be based on a query that defines the link between the CLIENTS table and the JOBS table. But, unlike the Job Authorization Form, this form displays information from a single CLIENTS record together with information from all JOBS records for that client. The query on which this form is based must define a one-to-many relation from the CLIENTS table to the JOBS table. Let's start by creating the query.

To create the query:

❶ Click the **Queries icon** in the Navigator window.

❷ Double-click **Untitled** in the current selection panel to open the Query Designer. The Open Table Required dialog box appears.

❸ Double-click **clients.dbf** to select the CLIENTS table and close the Open Table Required dialog box. The CLIENTS skeleton appears in the Query Designer window.

❹ Click the **Add Table button** on the SpeedBar. The Open Table Required dialog box appears.

❺ Double-click **jobs.dbf** to select the JOBS table and close the Open Table Required dialog box. The skeleton for the JOBS table appears in the Query Designer window. See Figure 5-57.

CLIENTS table skeleton

JOBS table skeleton

Figure 5-57
CLIENTS and JOBS skeletons in the Query Designer window

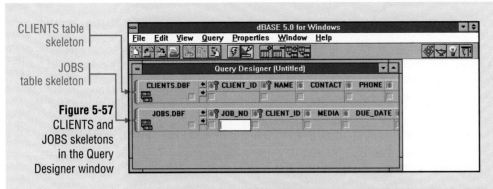

❻ Click **Query** then click **Set Relation...** to open the Define Relation dialog box.

❼ Make sure that CLIENTS is the parent table in the relation and that CLIENT_ID is selected in the Field panel.

❽ Make sure that JOBS is the child table in the relation and that CLIENT_ID is selected in the Index panel.

The link in this relation is from the CLIENTS table to the JOBS table. Because there are potentially many records in the JOBS table for each record in the CLIENTS table, this relation is "one-to-many."

To specify the relation between the two tables:
❶ Make sure the One To Many check box is selected. The Define Relation dialog box should look like Figure 5-58.

common field in parent table

One To Many check box selected

Figure 5-58
Definition of CLIENTS-JOBS relation

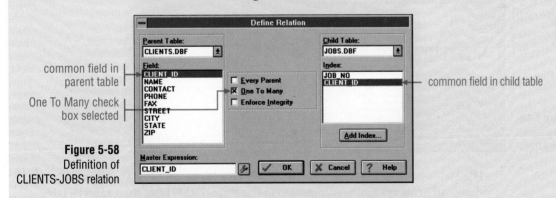

common field in child table

❷ Click **OK** to close the Define Relation dialog box.

You have completed the definition of the query. It is not necessary to select fields; the purpose of the query is simply to make the fields in both tables available to the form.

❸ Double-click the **Control menu box** on the Query Designer window.

❹ Click **Yes** when the Changes Made-Query Designer dialog box appears.

❺ Type **1tom** (for one-to-many) in the File Name text box of the Save File dialog box, then click **OK** to save this query as 1TOM.QBE.

Now you can use the Form Expert to create the multi-table form Martin sketched.

To create the multi-table form using the Form Expert:
❶ Click the **Forms icon** in the Navigator window.
❷ Double-click **Untitled** in the current selection panel to display the Form Expert dialog box.
❸ Click the **Expert Assistance radio button** if it is not already selected, then click **Next** to display the next dialog box, which allows you to select the data upon which the form will be based. See Figure 5-59.

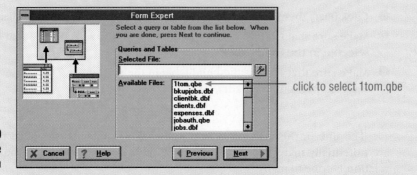

Figure 5-59
Selecting a file
for the form

click to select 1tom.qbe

❹ Click **1tom.qbe** in the Available Files box, then click **Next** to move to the next dialog box, which allows you to select the fields that will appear in the form. See Figure 5-60.

click to move
highlighted available
field to Selected list

click to move all
available fields to
Selected list

list of available fields
from selected file

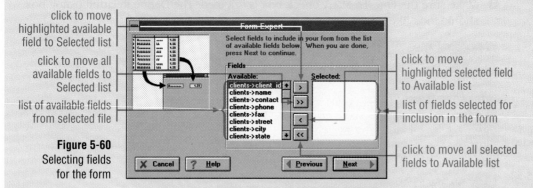

click to move
highlighted selected field
to Available list

list of fields selected for
inclusion in the form

click to move all selected
fields to Available list

Figure 5-60
Selecting fields
for the form

The Fields panel of this dialog box contains two list boxes. The Available list box shows all fields available for inclusion in the form. Fields from the CLIENTS table are preceded by clients->. Fields from the JOBS table are preceded by jobs->.

The sketch for Figure 5-56 shows that you need the CLIENT_ID, NAME, CONTACT, PHONE, and FAX fields from the CLIENTS table and the JOB_NO, MEDIA, DUE_DATE, and QUOTE fields from the JOBS table. Let's select these fields.

❺ Click **clients->client_id** to highlight the CLIENT_ID field from the CLIENTS table, then click the **right arrow button** ▷ to select this field for inclusion in the form.
❻ Use the same procedure to select the remaining fields for the form.
   TROUBLE? If you accidentally select the wrong field, click the field name in the list of selected fields to highlight it, then click the left arrow button to move it back to the list of available fields.
❼ Click **Next** to move to the next dialog box, which allows you to select the layout of the form. See Figure 5-61.

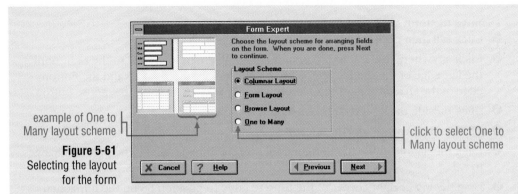

example of One to
Many layout scheme

Figure 5-61
Selecting the layout
for the form

click to select One to
Many layout scheme

For this form, you need the One to Many layout to display the records from the 1TOM query.

❽ Click the **One to Many radio button**, then click **Next** to move to the next dialog box, which allows you to select the display characteristics for the form.

❾ Click **Create** to have the Form Expert create the basic form. The Form Expert creates the form for you and displays it in the Form Designer window.

❿ Click the **Maximize button** on the Form Designer window to display the entire form. See Figure 5-62.

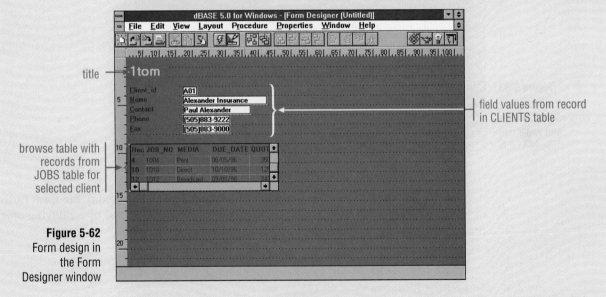

title

field values from record
in CLIENTS table

browse table with
records from
JOBS table for
selected client

Figure 5-62
Form design in
the Form
Designer window

TROUBLE? If your screen does not look like Figure 5-62, you can start over by double-clicking the Control menu box for the Form Designer window and answering No when dBASE asks if you want to save the form. Then repeat Steps 1 through 10.

In this form, the fields from the CLIENTS table are displayed in Columnar layout. The fields from the JOBS table are shown in Browse layout, listing all the selected fields from the JOBS table. The object that contains the JOBS records is known as a **browse table**. The design visible in the Form Designer window is not exactly like Figure 5-56. Let's move the form objects to a more central position and expand the browse table to make it look more like Figure 5-56.

To move the form objects and expand the browse table:

❶ Click **Edit** then click **Select All** to select all objects in the form.

❷ Click anywhere in the selected objects and drag them down and to the right until the left edge of the shaded region on the horizontal ruler is at 35 and the bottom edge of the shaded region on the vertical ruler is at 15. Release the mouse button.

❸ Click outside the selected objects to deselect them.

❹ Click in the browse table to select it.

❺ Click the handle in the lower-right corner of the browse table. The pointer changes to 🖱.

❻ Drag the lower-right corner of the browse table to position 85 on the horizontal ruler, position 21 on the vertical ruler. Release the mouse button. See Figure 5-63.

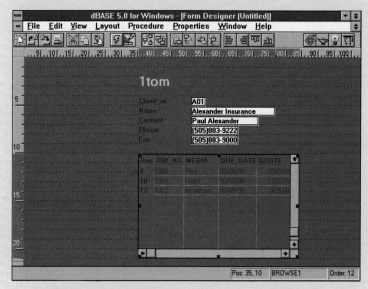

Figure 5-63
Form with repositioned objects and expanded browse table

The form now resembles Figure 5-56. Although you will not modify the form further in this tutorial, you can modify it by moving and resizing objects and by modifying object properties, just as you did for the Job Authorization Form.

Let's save the form and then use it to view data.

To save the form and view data:

❶ Click **File** then click **Save** to display the Save File dialog box.

❷ Type **1tom** (for one-to-many) in the File Name text box.

❸ Click **OK**. dBASE saves the form to your Student Disk as 1TOM.WFM.

❹ Click the **Run button** 🖅 on the SpeedBar. The first record in the CLIENTS table appears in the top of the form, and the associated jobs for the client appear in the bottom of the form. See Figure 5-64.

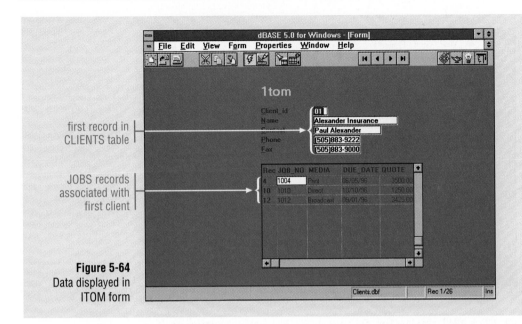

first record in
CLIENTS table

JOBS records
associated with
first client

Figure 5-64
Data displayed in
ITOM form

Martin would like to see the data for the Santa Fe Tourist Center displayed in the multi-table form. He'd also like to print this data to bring with him to a meeting he's having with this client later in the week. To display and print the data for the Santa Fe Tourist Center, you need to navigate through the form.

Navigating Through a Multi-Table Form

In this multi-table form, you see the client information at the top of the form and all the job information for this client below it. How can you use this form to navigate through the linked tables? With a multi-table form, all movement takes place through the parent table used to define the query on which the form is based. As each client record changes, the corresponding data from the JOBS table changes. For example, if you use the navigation buttons on the SpeedBar when the highlight is in the Client_id field, dBASE updates the data for the client record along with all the corresponding job information for that client. However, if you click a navigation button when the highlight is on a record in the JOBS table, dBASE moves to a record in the JOBS table for the current client.

First, let's practice moving through the CLIENTS table.

To practice moving through the multi-table form:
❶ With the cursor in the Client_id field, click the **Next Record button** on the SpeedBar. dBASE moves to the next client record in the CLIENTS table and displays all associated jobs for this client. See Figure 5-65.

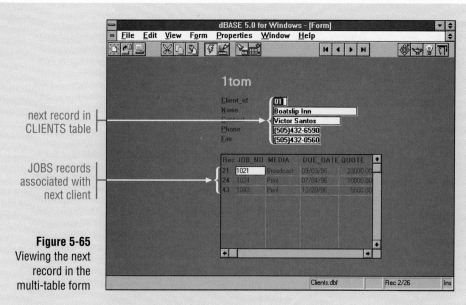

next record in
CLIENTS table

JOBS records
associated with
next client

Figure 5-65
Viewing the next
record in the
multi-table form

❷ Click **1043**, the last job number in the JOBS table portion of the form. The highlight moves to the data entry field for JOB_NO 1043.

❸ Click the **Top button** [≣] on the SpeedBar. The highlight moves to the first job record for the same client—JOB_NO 1021.

Rather than use the navigation buttons to find the Santa Fe Tourist Center record, it will be much quicker to use the Find button on the SpeedBar.

To find the Santa Fe Tourist Center record:
❶ Click the **data entry field** for Client_id. (If you leave the cursor in a field for the JOBS table, dBASE will search the JOBS table.)
❷ Click the **Find button** [≣] on the SpeedBar to display the Find Records dialog box. See Figure 5-66.

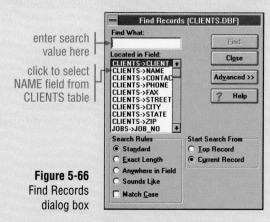

enter search
value here

click to select
NAME field from
CLIENTS table

Figure 5-66
Find Records
dialog box

❸ Click **CLIENTS->NAME** in the Located in Field list to select the NAME field.

Now enter the value you want to locate.

❹ Click in the **Find What text box**, type **San** then click **Find**. dBASE searches the CLIENTS table and finds the first record whose name begins with "San."

❺ Click **Close** to close the Find Records dialog box. The Santa Fe Tourist Center record appears in the top of the form, and its job data appears in the bottom of the form. See Figure 5-67.

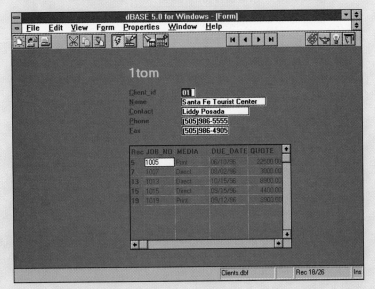

Figure 5-67
Data for Santa Fe
Tourist Center in
multi-table form

If this had not been the record you were looking for, you could continue the search by clicking the Find button and then clicking Find in the Find Records dialog box. dBASE would find the next record that begins with the letters "San."

Now you need to print the data so that Martin can bring it with him to his client meeting.

To print the data for the Santa Fe Tourist Center:
❶ Make sure your printer is on and contains paper.
❷ Click the **Print button** 🖬 on the SpeedBar. The Print dialog box appears.
❸ Click **OK** to print the current record. See Figure 5-68.

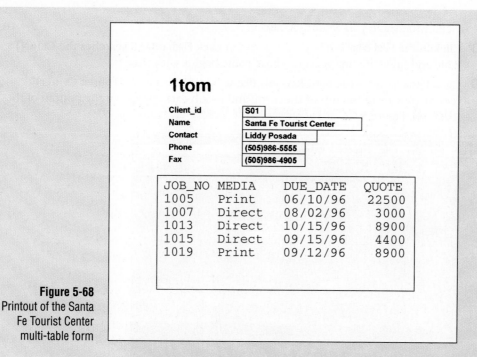

Figure 5-68
Printout of the Santa
Fe Tourist Center
multi-table form

TROUBLE? If your printer prints the form in landscape layout, you can change to portrait layout. Click File then click Printer Setup. Click the Portrait radio button in the Orientation panel, then click OK. Then repeat Steps 1 through 3.

Although you won't do so in this tutorial, you can use the multi-table form to add, edit, and delete records in both the CLIENTS and JOBS tables.

Now you can close the Form window and exit dBASE.

To close the Form window and exit dBASE:

❶ Click the **Restore button** on the Form window to restore it to its original size.

❷ Double-click the **Control menu box** for the Form window.

❸ Click **File** then click **Exit** to leave dBASE.

◼   ◼   ◼

Martin looks over his printout of the Santa Fe Tourist Center data. The 1TOM form provided him with exactly the information he needs. Nancy and Martin know that both the Job Authorization Form and the 1TOM form will enable them and their employees to enter and find information on W&M's jobs more easily.

Questions

1. Describe the function of the following:
   a. Form window
   b. Controls window
   c. Object Inspector
2. Define the following:
   a. object
   b. control
   c. property
   d. z-order

3. What menu commands would you select to do the following:
   a. open the Properties window
   b. switch from the Form window to the Controls window
   c. switch from Layout view in the Form window to Order view
4. Suppose that you just designed the form shown in Figure 5-69.

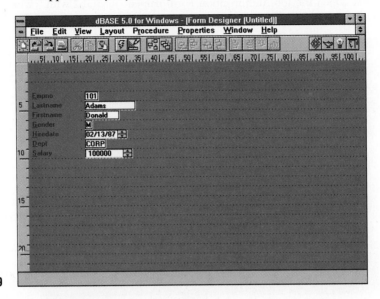

Figure 5-69

What fields might benefit from:
a. a combo box
b. a spin box
c. a minimum value validity check

5. Figure 5-70 shows the basic form for a Student Records database. Create a sketch of an improved form design. Consider the following:
   a. Group related fields together.
   b. Use rectangles and lines to organize the screen.
   c. Specify a z-order for each object so that no objects are obscured and data entry is orderly and logical.

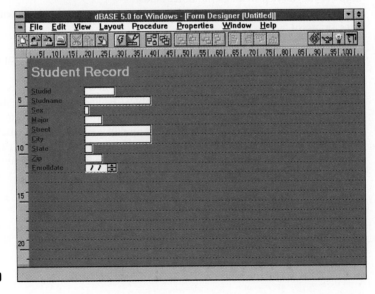

Figure 5-70

Tutorial Assignments

Place your Student Disk in the disk drive, start dBASE, and make sure the current directory is set to A:\WM. Open the Job Authorization Form named "jobauth2.wfm," which is provided on your Student Disk. Modify the form as shown in Figure 5-71.

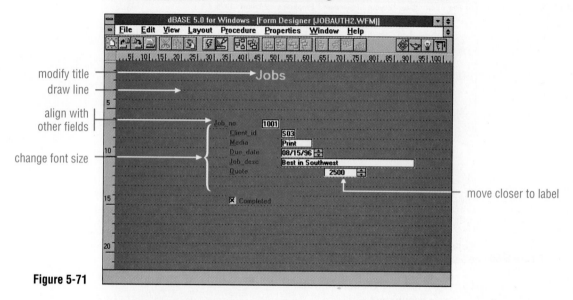

Figure 5-71

1. Change the title to "Job Authorization Form." Change the color of the title text to dark gray.
2. Draw a horizontal line to separate the title from the rest of the form. (*Hint:* Use the Line control on the Controls window.)
3. Change the font size for all the labels for all the fields on the form to 12 points. (*Hint:* Use the Font Size property in the Font Properties list of the Properties window. You might need to change the size of the boxes containing the labels.)
4. Move the data entry field for the Quote field closer to the label for the field.
5. Align the Job_no field with all the other fields.
6. Using the Save As command on the File menu, save the modified form with the name "jobform."
7. Print Job_no 1005 using the modified form. Close the form.
8. Use the Form Expert to design a form for the CLIENTS table. Select Form layout. Save the form as "clntform." Print one record using this form.

E   9. Open the multi-table form, "1tom.wfm," and modify it so that it includes a rectangle around the fields from the CLIENTS table. Change the title of the form to "Client Jobs." Save this form as "1toma." Print one record using this form.

E   10. Open the multi-table form, "1tom.wfm," and modify it so that all text labels look like those in Figure 5-56. Change the background color of all objects in the form to light gray. Change the background color of the form itself to light gray. Save this form as "1tomb." Print one record using this form.

Case Problems

1. Inventory of State-owned Land

Place your Student Disk in the disk drive, start dBASE, then set the current directory to A:\LAND.

1. Use the Form Expert to create a form based on the LAND table. Select Columnar layout. Name the form "lnd1form."
2. Print the record for the property with Land ID 0001 using the form lnd1form.

E

3. Use the Form Expert to create a new form based on the LANDUSE table, similar to the one shown in Figure 5-72. Save the form as "lnd2form." (*Hint:* Use Browse layout. To change the column headings, select the browse table object and change the ShowHeadings property to False. The ShowHeadings property is a visual property of the browse table object. Place new text objects above the table for the new headings.) Print the Land Use Code Table using the form lnd2form.

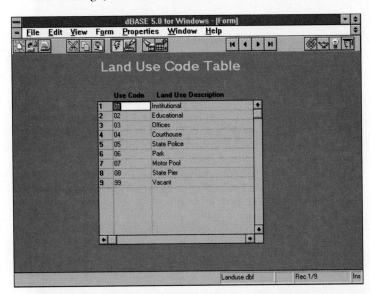

Figure 5-72

E

4. Use Figure 5-73 to create a form that displays the Land Use Code and Land Description. Save the form as "lnd3form." (*Hint:* Create a query using both the LAND and the LANDUSE tables. Save the query as "lnd3qry." Define a one-to-one relationship between the LAND and LANDUSE tables.) (*Note:* You must have completed the section "Multi-Table Forms" in the tutorial in order to complete Problems 4 and 5 for this case problem.)

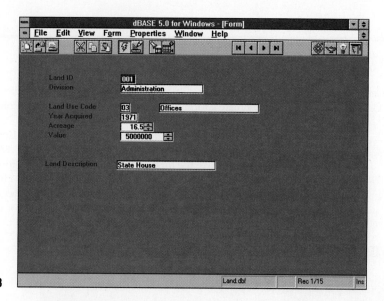

Figure 5-73

5. Print one record using the form lnd3form.

2.   FINSTAT Inc.

Place your Student Disk in the disk drive, start dBASE, then set the current directory to A:\FINANCE.

1. Use Figure 5-74 to create a form based on the COMP table. Save the form as "cmp1form." (*Hint:* Start with the Form Expert and Columnar layout. Then use the Form Designer to customize the form.)

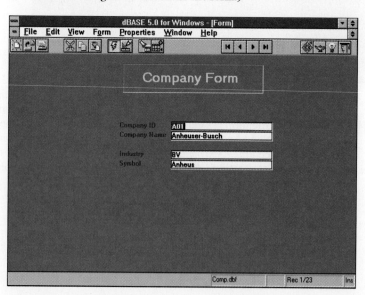

Figure 5-74

2. Print the record for the company "Avon Products" using the form cmp1form.
3. Create a multi-table form using the COMP table as the parent table and the FIN table as the child table (one-to-many relationship). You decide the layout of the form. Save the base query as "fin1qry" and save the form as "fin1frm." (*Note:* You must have completed the section "Multi-Table Forms" in the tutorial in order to complete Problems 3, 4, and 5 for this case problem.)
4. Print the record for the company "Anheuser-Busch" using the form fin1frm.

E   5. Create a multi-table form similar to Figure 5-75. The parent table is FIN and the child table is COMP (one-to-one relationship).

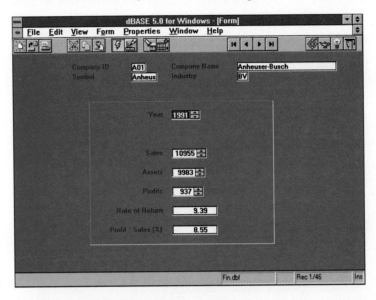

Figure 5-75

The formulas for the calculated fields are:

Rate of Return = (Profits/Assets)*100

Profit: Sales(%) = (Profits/Sales)*100

Save the base query as "fin2qry" and the form as "fin2frm." Print the data for the company "Fruit of the Loom" using this form. (*Hint:* To include calculated fields in a form, create the calculated fields in the query on which the form is based. Select all fields for inclusion in the query results—table fields and calculated fields—before saving the query.)

3. Marine Diving Equipment, Inc.

Place your Student Disk in the disk drive, start dBASE, then set the current directory to A:\MARINE.
1. Use Figure 5-76 to create a form based on the CUSTOMER table. Save the form as "mrn1form." (*Hint:* Start with the Form Expert and select Columnar layout. Then use the Form Designer to customize the form.)

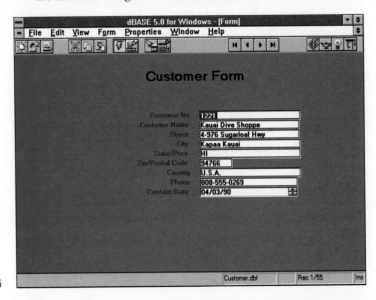

Figure 5-76

2. Print the record for the customer named "Kauai Dive Shoppe" using the form mrn1form.

3. Use Figure 5-77 to develop a form based on the ORDERS table for viewing and entering orders. Name the form "mrn2form."

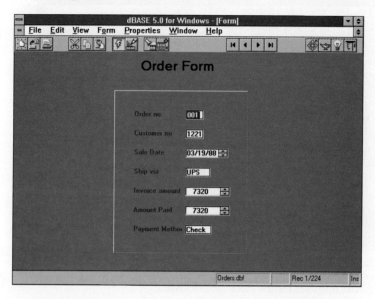

Figure 5-77

4. Print the record for Order no 1001 using the form mrn2form.

5. Modify the form mrn2form to include a drop-down list combo box for the Customer no field. Base the form on a query. Save the query as "mrn3qry." Save the modified form as "mrn3form." (*Note:* You must have completed the section "Multi-Table Forms" in the tutorial in order to complete Problems 5, 6, 7, and 8 for this case problem.)

6. Create a multi-table form based on a query using the CUSTOMER table as the parent table and the ORDERS table as the child table (one-to-many relationship). Save the query as "mrn4qry." You decide the layout of the form. Save the form as "mrn4form."

7. Print the record for the customer named "Kauai Dive Shoppe" using the form mrn4form.

E   8. You want to display the data on customers using the form mrn4form for customers located in Canada. List the steps you would take to accomplish this task.

4. Teaching Activity

Place your Student Disk in the disk drive, start dBASE, then set the current directory to A:\TEACH.

1. Use Figure 5-78 to create a form based on the FAC table. Save the form as "fac1frm." (*Hint:* Start with the Form Expert and select Columnar layout. Then use the Form Designer to customize the form.)

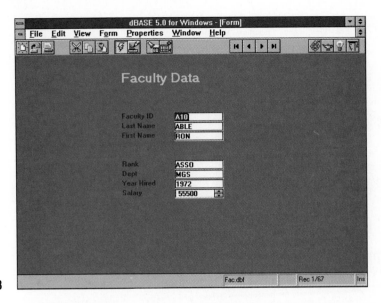

Figure 5-78

2. Print the faculty record for RON ABLE using the form fac1form.
3. Modify the form fac1frm to include validity checks for the Rank, Dept, Year Hired, and Salary fields. The values for the Rank and Dept fields must be uppercase. The Year Hired value must be greater than or equal to 1940. The Salary value must be greater than 0. Save the form as "fac2frm."
4. Create a multi-table form based on a query using the FAC table as the parent table and the TCH table as the child table (one-to-many relationship). You decide the layout of the form. Save the query as "fac3qry." Save the form as "fac3frm." (*Note:* You must have completed the section "Multi-Table Forms" in the tutorial in order to complete Problems 4, 5, and 6 for this case problem.)
5. Print the faculty record for RON ABLE using the form fac3frm.
6. Use Figure 5-79 to create a form based on the FAC, CRS, and TCH tables. Save the base query as "fac4qry." Save the form as "fac4frm." (*Hint:* When you create the query fac4qry, define a relation with CRS as the parent table and TCH as the child table. Define a second relation with TCH as the parent table and FAC as the child table. When you create the form, start with the Form Expert and select the one-to-many layout. Then use the Form Designer to customize the form.) Print one record using this form.

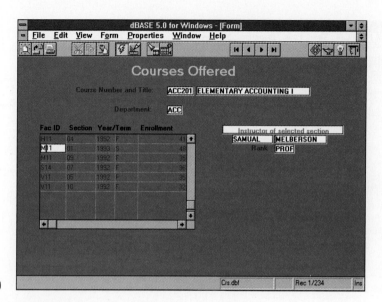

Figure 5-79

E **5. Software Registration System**

Place your Student Disk in the disk drive, start dBASE, then set the current directory to A:\PRAC-
TICE. Magic Software maintains a database of customers who have registered the purchase of their
software with the company. Use the document in Figure 5-80 to do the following:

1. Design and create a table that tracks Magic Software's registered users. Name the
   table REGUSERS. (*Hint:* Keep in mind that customers can check off more than
   one application area at the bottom of the form. Therefore, your table design
   must be able to provide Magic Software with information about whether or not
   its customers use their computers for each of these application areas.)
2. Design and create a customized form that you can use to enter data. Save this
   form as "userform."
3. Use the form you created in Problem 2 to add five records to the table.
4. Print one record using the "userform" you created in Problem 2.

Magic Software Registration Card

| C | h | a | r | l | e | s | | | | | | | | | | | | | | | | | |
First Name

| H | o | m | m | e | l | | | | | | | | | | | | | | | | | | |
Last Name

| U | n | i | v | e | r | s | i | t | y | | o | f | | P | u | g | e | t | | S | o | u | n | d |
Company Name (if company licenses product)

| M | a | t | h | e | m | a | t | i | c | s | / | C | o | m | p | u | t | e | r | | S | c | i |
Department/Address

| 1 | 5 | 0 | 0 | | N | | W | a | r | n | e | r | | | | | | | | | |
Additional Address Information

| T | a | c | o | m | a | | | | | | W | A | | | 9 | 8 | 4 | 1 | 6 |
City   State   Zip

| 2 | 0 | 6 | | 5 | 5 | 5 | | 3 | 5 | 5 | 9 | | 0 | 6 | 0 | 1 | 9 | 6 |
Daytime phone with area code   Purchase date (MMDDYY)

So that we may serve you better, please let us know how you currently use your computer:

_X_ Spreadsheet   ____ Project Scheduling   ____ Application Development

_X_ Word Processing   _X_ CD-ROM   ____ Accounting

_X_ Relational database ____ Basic Programming   ____ Recreation

_X_ Presentation graphics

Product Number _1956V20_

Figure 5-80

Designing Reports

Creating a Client List Report and a Media Summary Report

Wells & Martinez Advertising Agency

CASE

Nancy is close to landing a contract with a new client located in Taos, New Mexico. The client has asked Nancy for the names of clients in Taos that W&M has done business with. Up until now, Nancy has produced a client list manually by typing the necessary information. However, with the increase in W&M's client list, this is no longer feasible. Also, both Nancy and Martin think that the typed lists do not project a professional image for their agency.

Nancy decides that W&M needs to give the potential client a report that lists current W&M clients located in Taos in a clear, professional-looking format. She also wants to produce other reports—such as a report that summarizes jobs by media type—to analyze information about W&M's jobs. She asks you to use dBASE's report features to produce a client list report and a media summary report.

Introduction to Reports

When you developed queries in Tutorial 4, you gave little attention to the format of the resulting display. Your focus was on getting the information you needed quickly, without concern for its appearance. For instance, the headings were not as descriptive as they could have been, the printouts were not clearly titled, and so on.

To print information retrieved from a dBASE database in a more professional format, you need to use the dBASE report designer, a special program known as Crystal Reports. The reports you generate should provide information succinctly, clearly, and correctly. Before working at the computer, you should take a few minutes to plan your report and its format. Start by asking yourself the following questions:

- What information do I need?
- How much detail do I want to include?
- Do I need to display every record or only summary totals?
- How should I present the data—in columns, as a form, or as a graph?
- How often will I need to produce the report?

Next, as part of your planning process, you should think about how you want the report to look. A good approach is to use a report layout sheet. A **report layout sheet** is a sketch of your report that you can prepare on plain paper, graph paper, or special printer-spacing charts. Figure 6-1 shows the report layout sheet that Nancy prepared for the new client list report.

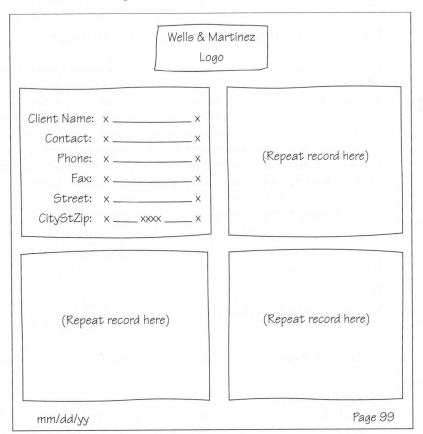

Figure 6-1
Report layout sheet for the client list report

As you design your report layout, you should address the following questions:
- Where on the report should each field be located?
- What column headings should be included?
- How should the records be sorted?
- Should records be subtotaled?
- Which fields should be totaled?

You will need a way to represent data on the report layout sheet. An effective method is to use a series of x's to represent alphanumeric fields (as shown in Figure 6-1), a series of 9's to represent numeric fields, and mm/dd/yy to represent date fields. If you have room, you can include the name of the field in parentheses under the symbols. You will typically put only one or two lines on the report layout sheet to represent repeated lines that will contain the same type of information in the actual report.

Many reports contain several types of lines: heading lines, detail lines, and summary lines. **Heading lines** usually are printed at the top of each page to describe the nature of the data in your report. **Detail lines** appear in the body of the report and provide detailed information about the results of processing the data in the report. Typically, you print one detail line for each record in the database. **Summary lines**, which usually appear at the end of a report, generally give the totals of numbers from the detail lines.

Now that you have seen how a report layout sheet helps you visualize a report's format, you will use dBASE's Crystal Reports to translate Nancy's report layout sheet (Figure 6-1) into a client list report.

Creating a Report Using Crystal Reports

To create a report in dBASE, you use a program called Crystal Reports. Crystal Reports starts automatically when you tell dBASE you want to design, view, or print a report. Like the Form Designer, Crystal Reports presents you with a Report Designer window in which you design the layout of the report you want. Unlike the Form Designer, there is no expert to guide you through designing a basic report. Instead, you begin with a blank design, place fields in position, then specify formats and fonts. You can easily preview the report in the Preview window. You can make changes directly in the Preview window or return to the Report Designer window to make changes. When you exit Crystal Reports, you return to the dBASE Desktop.

To design the report shown in Figure 6-1, you must first start dBASE.

To start dBASE in preparation for creating the client list report:
❶ Place your Student Disk in the disk drive.
❷ Start dBASE.
❸ Make sure the current directory is A:\WM.

Let's tell dBASE to start Crystal Reports in order to construct Nancy's report.

To start Crystal Reports:
❶ Click the **Reports icon** in the Navigator window, then double-click **Untitled**. dBASE displays the Open Table Required dialog box. Because a report can be based on a table or a query, the file list shows all .DBF and .QBE files in the current directory. See Figure 6-2.

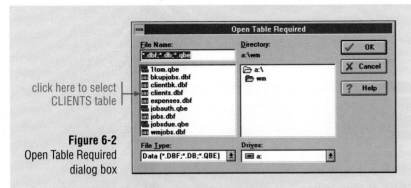

click here to select
CLIENTS table

Figure 6-2
Open Table Required
dialog box

For the client list report, you need to select the CLIENTS table.

❷ Double-click **clients.dbf** in the file list to select the CLIENTS table and start Crystal Reports.

dBASE starts Crystal Reports. After displaying a welcome message for a few seconds, the Crystal Reports For dBASE window opens. See Figure 6-3.

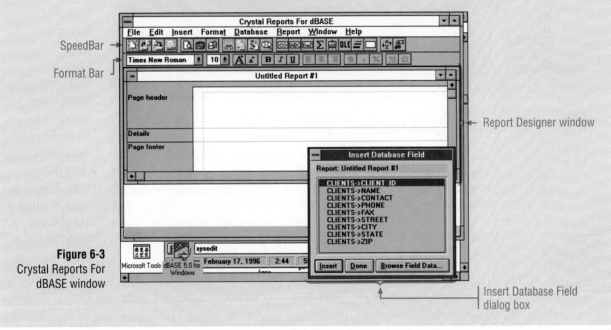

SpeedBar

Format Bar

Report Designer window

Figure 6-3
Crystal Reports For
dBASE window

Insert Database Field
dialog box

An Overview of the Crystal Reports For dBASE Window

The Crystal Reports For dBASE window provides you with tools for designing a report. The SpeedBar contains buttons that provide shortcuts for common report design steps. Below the SpeedBar is the Format Bar, which contains buttons that provide shortcuts for common formatting procedures. The Report Designer window, which currently is titled "Untitled Report #1," displays the current report design. The Insert Database Field dialog box displays the list of fields available for insertion into the report design.

Let's maximize the Report Designer window and look at it in more detail.

To maximize the Report Designer window:

❶ Click the **Maximize button** for the Crystal Reports For dBASE window.

❷ Click the **Maximize button** for the Report Designer window. See Figure 6-4.

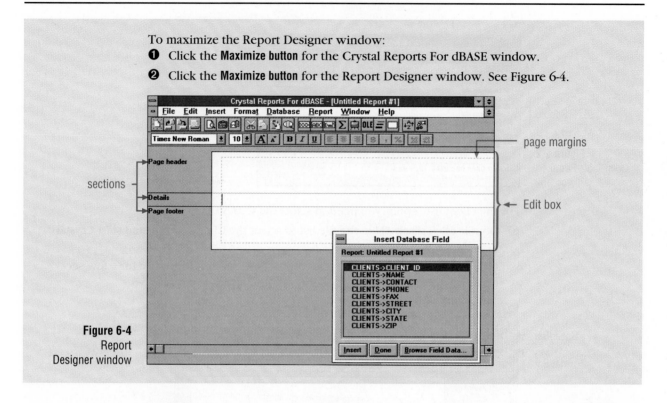

Figure 6-4
Report
Designer window

The Report Designer Window

Just as the Form Designer window displays the current form design, the Report Designer window displays the current report design. The large white area is the **Edit box**, the area in which you place the text and fields you want to appear in the report. The dotted lines near the edge of the Edit box mark the current margin settings. The horizontal scroll bar at the bottom of the window allows you to scroll to see the right edge of the Edit box. The horizontal lines in the Report Designer window divide the report into sections, with the section names appearing to the left of the Edit box.

dBASE uses sections to define where text, fields, and other objects appear in your report. A **section** is a horizontal area that represents the structure of your report (header lines, detail lines, and footer lines) and lets you control where and how information appears. When you begin designing a report, the Report Designer window contains three sections: Page header, Details, and Page footer. Two other sections, the Group header and Group footer, are optional. When included in the Report Designer window, the Group header and Group footer sections are used for grouping records together in a report.

The following paragraphs describe the Page header, Details, and Page footer sections. Group header and Group footer sections are covered later in this tutorial.

A simple report contains three sections: Page header, Details, and Page footer. The **Page header** section contains text or data that appears at the top of each page of a report. This area typically includes information such as the page title, current date, or page number.

The **Page footer** section contains text or data that appears at the bottom of each page of a report. This area is often empty, but can include the current date and/or page number if you decide to place this information at the bottom of the page instead of at the top.

The **Details section**, which appears between the Page header and Page footer sections, represents the body of the report. Any information placed in this area prints once per record. This section defines what information is printed for every record in the table. You can put field values, calculated values, summary values, and text labels in this section.

Figure 6-1 shows that the Page header section should contain W&M's logo, and the Page footer section should contain the page number and the report date. The Details section should contain the NAME, CONTACT, PHONE, FAX, STREET, CITY, STATE, and ZIP fields from each record, arranged in a multi-column layout. Designing this report will take several steps. Let's start by setting the page margins for the report and placing the fields in the Details section.

To set the page margins for the report:

❶ Click **File** then click **Page Margins...** to open the Printer Margins dialog box. See Figure 6-5.

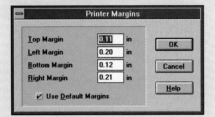

Figure 6-5
Printer Margins
dialog box

The Printer Margins dialog box displays the top, left, bottom, and right margins (measured in inches) for the report. The actual margin values on your screen might be different. The text box for the top margin is already highlighted, ready for you to enter a new value. By default, the page margins are relatively narrow. Most laser printers will not print within one quarter inch of the edge of a page; that is, most laser printers require a margin of at least one quarter inch. To make sure that the margins are wide enough, let's reset the printer margins to .5 inches.

❷ Type **.5** to set the top margin to .5 inches, then press **[Tab]** to move to the Left Margin text box.

❸ Type **.5** to set the left margin to .5 inches, then press **[Tab]** to move to the Bottom Margin text box.

❹ Type **.5** to set the bottom margin to .5 inches, then press **[Tab]** to move to the Right Margin text box.

❺ Type **.5** to set the right margin to .5 inches.

❻ Click **OK** to close the Printer Margins dialog box.

The Edit box now displays dotted lines indicating the new margin settings. Because the Edit box appears larger than its actual printed size, the margins appear to be larger than the actual .5 inches.

Now let's place the fields in the Details section of the report. The value for each field in this section will be printed for each record in the table. Let's start by placing the NAME field.

To place the NAME field in the Details section of the report:

❶ Click **CLIENTS->NAME** in the Insert Database Field dialog box.

❷ Hold the left mouse button down and drag the NAME field into the Details section of the Edit box. The position of the NAME field is indicated by a small rectangle.

❸ Place the rectangle approximately one and a half inches from the left margin line, then release the mouse button. See Figure 6-6.

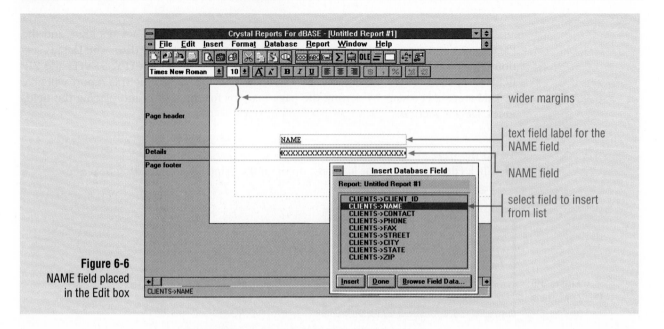

Figure 6-6
NAME field placed
in the Edit box

Crystal Reports displays a rectangle indicating the position and size of the field you placed in the Details section. The rectangle is filled with X's to indicate that this is a character field. The Page header section displays a label for the field. The label is a **text field** containing the underlined name of the field you placed in the Details section.

The NAME field in the Details section has handles at each end of the rectangle, indicating that this field is selected. Just as in the Form Designer, you can use the mouse to change the size and position of a selected field in a report. Let's change the size and position of the text field (the label for the NAME field) so it looks like Figure 6-1.

To resize and move the text field label for the NAME field:

❶ Click in the **text field** for the label to select it.

❷ Position the pointer on the right handle for the text field. The pointer changes to ↔.

❸ Click the **left mouse button** and move the right edge of the rectangle to the left until the rectangle is just big enough to hold the label. Release the mouse button. See Figure 6-7.

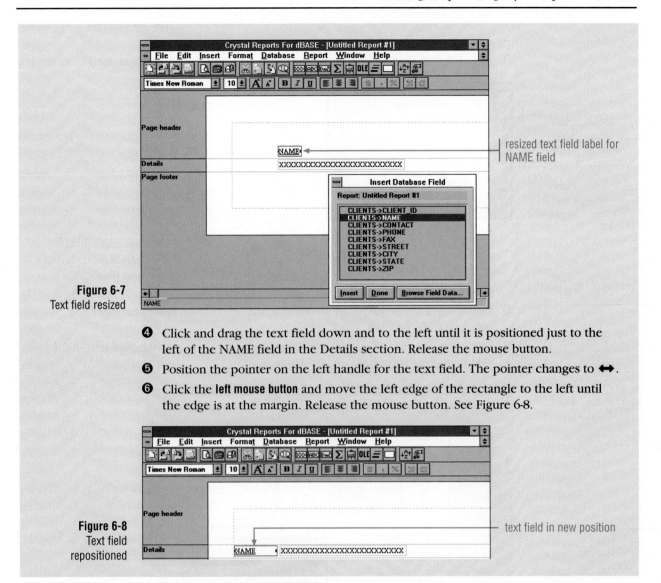

Figure 6-7
Text field resized

Figure 6-8
Text field
repositioned

❹ Click and drag the text field down and to the left until it is positioned just to the left of the NAME field in the Details section. Release the mouse button.

❺ Position the pointer on the left handle for the text field. The pointer changes to ↔.

❻ Click the **left mouse button** and move the left edge of the rectangle to the left until the edge is at the margin. Release the mouse button. See Figure 6-8.

The text field is now in the correct position. However, the label is left-justified (flush with the left edge) in the text field. Figure 6-1 indicates that the labels should be right-justified; you will fix this in later steps.

You must also change the contents of the text field to "Client Name:". Let's do that now.

To change the contents of the text field:

❶ Click **Edit** then click **Text Field...** to display the Edit Text Field dialog box. See Figure 6-9.

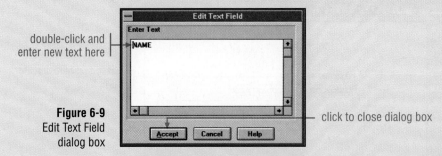

double-click and
enter new text here

click to close dialog box

Figure 6-9
Edit Text Field
dialog box

The Edit Text Field dialog box contains a small edit box where you can edit the contents of the text field. When you move the pointer into the edit box, it changes to an I-beam. The edit box displays the current contents of the text field. Let's replace the current contents with the new label.

❷ Double-click the word NAME to select it, then type **Client Name:**. Include the colon (:) after the label.

❸ Click **Accept** to close the Edit Text Field dialog box and place the new text in the text field. See Figure 6-10.

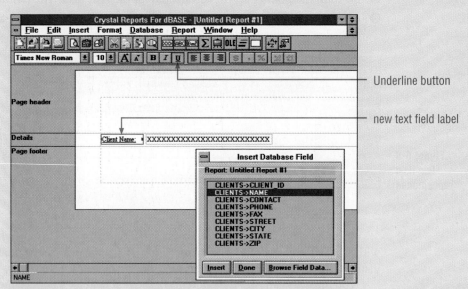

Underline button

new text field label

Figure 6-10
New text in text field

The text field now contains the correct label, but it is still underlined. Underlining is a formatting option, and the Underline button on the Format Bar makes it easy to change. Let's remove the underline.

❹ With the text field selected, click the **Underline button** 🅄 on the Format Bar. Because the selected text is already underlined, the Underline button removes the underline.

You are now ready to insert the remaining fields in the Details section. To do so, you must insert a blank line in the Details section to make room for each new field. Let's do that now.

To insert the remaining fields in the Details section:

❶ Click anywhere in the Details section (but not in a field). The blinking cursor appears at the left margin.

❷ Press **[Enter]** to insert a blank line. A blank line appears below the line with the blinking cursor.

❸ Insert the CONTACT field, then resize, reposition, and edit its label so that it agrees with Figure 6-1. Notice that when you place the CONTACT field, it will be partially obscured by the Insert Database Field dialog box.

❹ Repeat Steps 1 through 3 to insert the PHONE, FAX, and STREET fields. Note that to insert the PHONE, FAX, and STREET fields, you might need to move the Insert Database Field dialog box out of the way. To do so, click the title bar for the dialog box, then drag the box to the lower-left corner of the screen. Notice that moving the Insert Database Field dialog box exposes an area in the status bar that indicates the position of the selected field in the Edit box.

❺ Insert a blank line and then insert the CITY field below the STREET field. Resize and reposition the label for this field. Edit its contents to say **CityStZip:** (as shown in Figure 6-1).

❻ Insert the STATE field to the right of the CITY field. Notice that the STATE field is five characters wide because its field name (STATE) is five characters long. Resize the STATE field to contain two characters.

Crystal Reports has created a text field label (in the Page header section) for the STATE field. Because you are using a single text field to label CITY, STATE, and ZIP, you can delete the text field in the Page header section.

❼ Click in the text field in the Page header section to select it, then press **[Delete]** to remove the text field from the Report Designer window.

❽ Insert the ZIP field to the right of the STATE field. Delete the text field label that Crystal Reports created in the Page header.

❾ Click in the line containing the CITY, STATE, and ZIP fields (but not in any of the fields), then press **[Enter]** to insert a blank line at the bottom of the Details section.

You are now finished inserting database fields in the Report Designer window. Let's close the Insert Database Field dialog box to view the report design.

❿ Click **Done** in the Insert Database Field dialog box to close it. The Report Designer window should now look like Figure 6-11.

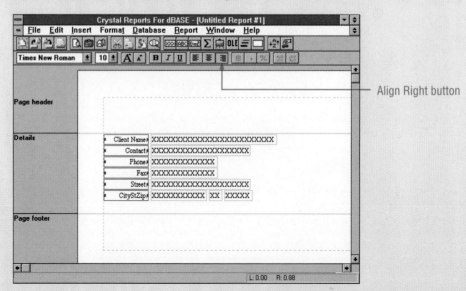

Figure 6-11
Report Designer
window with all
fields inserted

TROUBLE? If your Report Designer window does not look like Figure 6-11, insert or delete fields as necessary. To insert a field, click the Insert Database Field button 🔲 on the SpeedBar. Resize, reposition, or edit any text fields that are not correct. To remove an extra blank line, click in the line then press [Backspace].

Notice that the text labels are left-aligned in their fields. That is, the text in each text field begins at the left edge of the field. Nancy's sketch shows these labels right-aligned in their fields. Let's make that change now.

To right-align the text labels in their fields:
❶ Click the **Client Name: text field** to select it.

❷ Hold the **[Shift]** key down and click the remaining five text fields to select them.

❸ Click the **Align Right button** 🔲 on the Format Bar. Crystal Reports right-aligns each of the text labels in their fields. See Figure 6-12.

Figure 6-12
Text labels
right-aligned in fields

TROUBLE? After aligning the text labels, your screen might show some, but not all, of the text fields selected. However, all of the text fields that you selected before are still selected. Simply proceed with the tutorial.

Although you have not finished designing the report, you have done a lot of work that would be time-consuming to repeat if the current design were lost. Let's save the current design and then see how to open a saved report design.

Saving a Report

After creating a report, you should save it so that you can access it easily any time you want to modify or print the report. Let's save the client list report as CLNTLST to identify its contents (that is, a client list report), then exit Crystal Reports to see how to open a saved report.

To save the client list report as CLNTLST:
❶ Click the **Save button** 🖺 on the SpeedBar to display the File Save As dialog box. See Figure 6-13.

Figure 6-13
File Save As
dialog box

❷ Type **CLNTLST** in the File Name text box.
❸ Click **OK**. dBASE adds the extension .RPT to all dBASE reports. The file is saved as CLNTLST.RPT on your Student Disk.
❹ Double-click the **Control menu box** for the Crystal Reports window to close it. You return to the dBASE Desktop and the Navigator window.

When you are designing a report, it is a good practice to save often during the design process. This way you can avoid having to start over if you make a major error in your design that you can't undo. If you make an error, you can close the Report Designer window or the Crystal Reports window without saving the current version of the document. Then you can open a previously saved report file and continue your work.

If you want to take a break and resume the tutorial at a later time, exit from dBASE. When you resume the tutorial, place your Student Disk in the disk drive, start dBASE, make sure the current directory is A:\WM, then continue with the tutorial.

Opening a Saved Report

The CLNTLST report you saved does not look like Figure 6-1 yet. You must still make changes to the Page header and Page footer sections and specify a multi-column layout in the Details section. To make these changes, you must open the report and modify it in the Report Designer window.

You can open a report using the Navigator window, the Open File button on the SpeedBar, or the Open option on the File menu to display the Open File dialog box.

REFERENCE WINDOW

Opening a Saved Report

- Click the Reports icon in the Navigator window, click the report file-name in the current selection panel, then click the Design button on the SpeedBar.

or

- Click the Reports icon in the Navigator window, then click the Open File button on the SpeedBar (or click File then click Open) to display the Open File dialog box.
- In the File Name list box, click the name of the report you want to open.
- Click the Design Report radio button to select it.
- Click OK.

Let's open the CLNTLST report to modify its design.

To open the CLNTLST report:
❶ Click the **Reports icon** in the Navigator window.
❷ Click **Clntlst.rpt** in the current selection panel.
❸ Click the **Design button** 📇 on the SpeedBar to open the report and start Crystal Reports. Notice that Crystal Reports does not automatically open the Insert Database Field dialog box when you open an existing report.
❹ Click the **Maximize button** on the Crystal Reports window to maximize the window.
❺ Click the **Maximize button** on the Report Designer window to display more of the report design. Your screen should look like Figure 6-12.

There are still several changes to be made to the report. Let's start by inserting the W&M logo in the Page header section.

Adding the W&M Logo to the Page Header

The W&M logo is a graphic, or bitmapped, image. A **bitmapped image** is a collection of bits corresponding to a grid of pixels on the screen, created using a scanner or a drawing program, such as Paintbrush. dBASE accepts graphic images from graphics files saved with extensions such as .BMP (for Bitmap), .PCX, .TIF, .GIF, and .TGA.

Inserting a Graphic Image in a Report

- Display the report in the Report Designer window.

- Click the Insert Graphic button on the SpeedBar to display the Choose Graphic File dialog box.

  or

  Click Insert then click Graphic... to display the Choose Graphic File dialog box.

- Click the name of the graphic image file to insert, then click OK.

- Move the pointer to the correct position, then click the mouse button to insert the image.

W&M's logo, which is stored on your Student Disk as WMLOGO.BMP, is a bitmapped image. Let's insert the W&M logo from your Student Disk in the Page header section of the report.

To insert the W&M logo in the Page header section:

❶ Click the **Insert Graphic button** 🖾 on the SpeedBar (or click **Insert** then click **Graphic...**) to display the Choose Graphic File dialog box. See Figure 6-14.

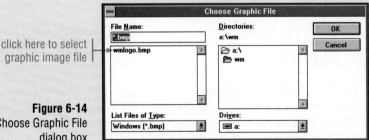

click here to select
graphic image file

Figure 6-14
Choose Graphic File
dialog box

❷ Click **wmlogo.bmp** to select the W&M logo then click **OK** to close the Choose Graphic File dialog box.

Notice that a rectangle, representing the graphic image, appears near the pointer in the Report Designer window. The size of the rectangle indicates the size of the graphic image. As you move the pointer, the rectangle moves with it.

❸ Move the pointer so that the rectangle is approximately centered in the Page header section (with the left edge of the rectangle just to the right of the Client Name data field). The bottom of the rectangle overlaps the Details section a little.

❹ Click the **left mouse button** to insert the graphic image.

Crystal Reports automatically increases the size of the Page header section to make room for the graphic image and inserts the graphic image in the Page header.

Let's add two more blank lines to separate the graphic image from the records in the Details section.

❺ Click to the left of the inserted graphic image, then press **[Enter]** twice to insert two blank lines at the bottom of the Page header section. See Figure 6-15.

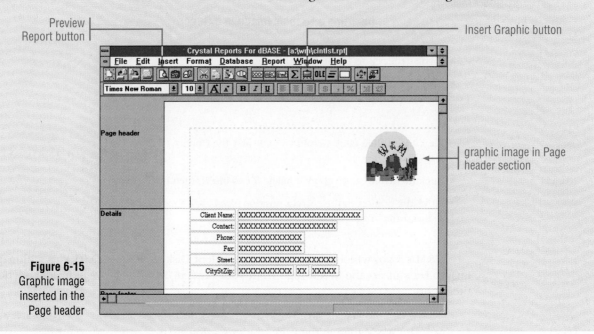

Figure 6-15
Graphic image inserted in the Page header

Nancy stops by to see how the report looks. Although you are not finished making the report look like her sketch in Figure 6-1, let's preview the report so Nancy can view it at this point.

Previewing the Report

As you design your report, you will want to check your progress periodically, just as you did when designing forms in Tutorial 5. You can preview the report on the screen by clicking the Preview Report button on the SpeedBar. Let's preview the report before modifying it further.

To preview the report:
❶ Click the **Preview Report button** 🔍 on the SpeedBar. dBASE opens a new window, called the Preview window, and displays a copy of the first page of your report on the screen. See Figure 6-16.

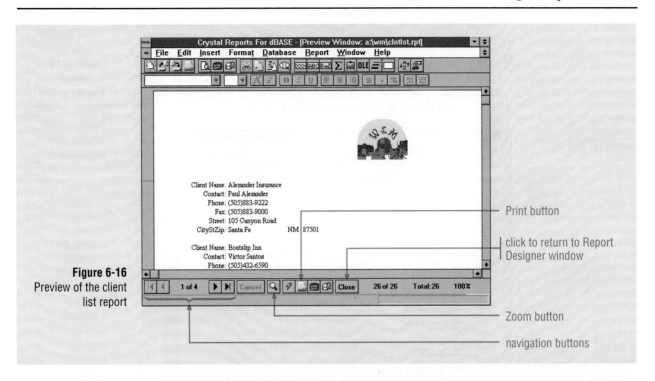

Figure 6-16
Preview of the client
list report

The Preview window displays the report as it will appear printed on paper. Crystal Reports uses the report design to format the records in the CLIENTS table and displays them in the Details section of the report. Crystal Reports uses all available space (after allowing for the margins, page header, and page footer) to fit as many records as possible on a page. The SpeedBar and Format Bar buttons remain at the top of the window. Most of the editing and design functions available in the Report Designer window are available in the Preview window as well. You can format text fields, position fields, insert fields, and so on. The bottom of the Preview window contains navigation buttons for paging through the report and the Zoom button for viewing the report at different levels of magnification.

The Preview window displays the report page magnified so you can see all text and images clearly. At this magnification, a page is too wide to fit on a single screen. You can use the Zoom button to view the report at different magnifications.

Using the Zoom Button

When you first preview a report, the Preview window displays the report in "enhanced page size." Enhanced page size is larger than the actual printed size of the report; it makes it easier to see the text and graphic images in the report. Because most reports are too wide to fit on your screen in enhanced page size, you must use the horizontal scroll bar to view an entire page. Or you can use the Zoom button to decrease the magnification of the report so you can see more of it on the screen. Reducing the magnification eliminates the need to scroll in order to see the entire width of the page.

Let's use the Zoom button to see more of the report.

To fit more of the report on the screen:

❶ Click the **Zoom button** 🔍 at the bottom of the Preview window. (Refer to Figure 6-16.) The Preview window displays the report at the next level of magnification, called "actual page size." Actual page size displays the report at full size, just as it will be printed on your printer. See Figure 6-17.

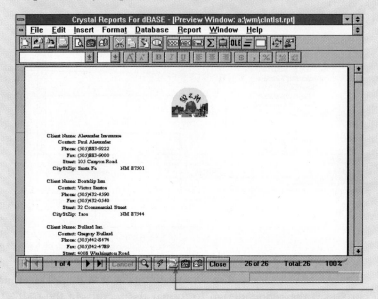

Figure 6-17
Report displayed at
actual page size

full width of page visible

On most screens, actual page size allows you to see the entire width of a page without scrolling horizontally. However, you must still use the vertical scroll bar to see the entire length of a page. The third level of magnification, "full page size," allows you to see the entire page on the screen.

❷ Click 🔍 to zoom to full page size. The Preview window displays the report at the third (and final) level of magnification, full page size. See Figure 6-18.

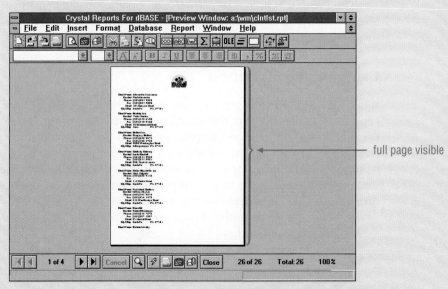

Figure 6-18
Report displayed at
full page size

full page visible

In full page size, it is very difficult to read the actual text in the report. However, it is easy to see the full page layout without scrolling. You will probably find it most convenient to use enhanced page size or actual page size when designing and modifying a report. Use full page size to check the appearance of the entire page. Let's return to enhanced page size.

❸ Click 🔍 to zoom to enhanced page size.

Nancy reviews the report and reminds you that there are still several modifications to make. You must add the date and page number in the Page footer section and display the records in multiple columns instead of a single column. To add the date and page number, you need to insert special fields in the report.

Inserting Special Fields in the Report

In addition to database fields and graphic images, Crystal Reports allows you to insert special fields, such as the current date, the page number, record number, and so on, in the report. Let's insert the current date and page number in the Page footer section.

To insert the current date and page number in the Page footer section:

❶ Click **Close** at the bottom of the Preview window to close the window and return to the Report Designer window.

❷ Use the vertical scroll bar to scroll to the bottom of the report.

❸ Click **Insert**, click **Special Field**, then click **Date** to select the current date field.

❹ Move the pointer (and the rectangle) to the Page footer section and position the pointer in the Page footer section below the text box containing the label "CityStZip:".

❺ Click the **left mouse button** to insert the current date field. See Figure 6-19.

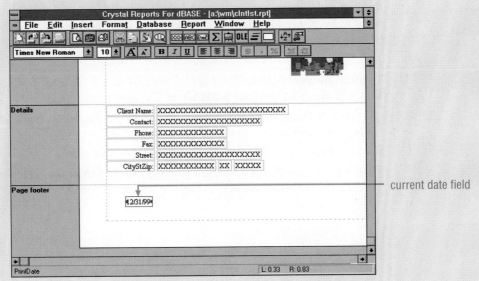

current date field

Figure 6-19
Current date field in
the Page footer

Crystal Reports displays a date field in the Report Designer window as 12/31/99. When the report is printed, the current date will be printed in this field.

❻ Use the horizontal scroll bar to scroll right until the right edge of the page is visible in the Report Designer window.

❼ Click **Insert**, click **Special Field**, then click **Page Number** to select the page number field.

❽ Move the pointer (and the rectangle) to the Page footer section and position the rectangle in the Page footer section so that the rectangle's right edge is approximately one inch from the right margin.

❾ Click the **left mouse button** to insert the page number field. See Figure 6-20.

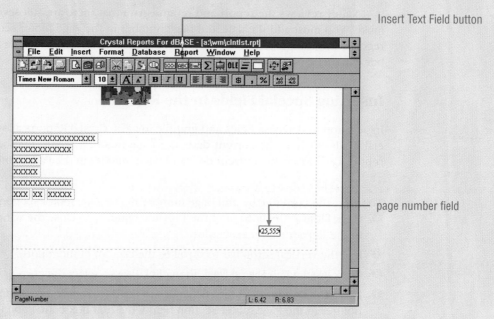

Insert Text Field button

page number field

Figure 6-20
Page number field in
the Page footer

The page number field is a numeric field. Crystal Reports displays a numeric field in the Report Designer window as 25,555. When the report is printed, the actual page number will be printed in the field. To make the page number more meaningful, let's place a label in front of it by inserting a text field in front of the page number field.

To insert the text field for the page number label:

❶ Click the **Insert Text Field button** 🔲 on the SpeedBar.

The Edit Text Field dialog box appears. Crystal Reports is ready for you to enter the text that will appear in the new text field.

❷ Type **Page** then click **Accept** to enter the new text.

❸ Use the pointer to position the rectangle to the left of the page number field, then click the **left mouse button** to insert the text field. See Figure 6-21.

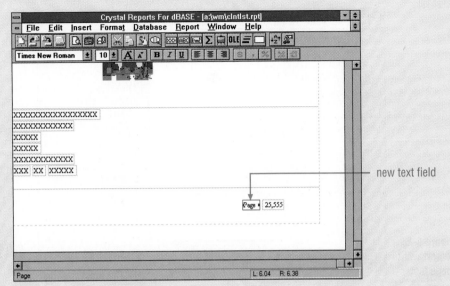

new text field

Figure 6-21
New text field
inserted in
the report

Now preview the results.

❹ Click the **Preview Report button** 🔲 on the SpeedBar. Crystal Reports displays the
Saved Data dialog box. See Figure 6-22. Note that the date and time on your dialog
box might be different.

date and time might be
different

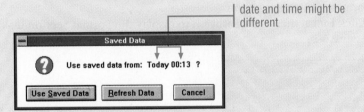

Figure 6-22
Saved Data
dialog box

When you preview a report, Crystal Reports saves the data it uses to create the
report. If you preview the report again, Crystal Reports can use the saved data in
the report or rerun the report using the current data in the table upon which the
report is based. (While you are working with the report, it is possible for a network
user to change the data or for you to change the data yourself by opening another
window.) Using saved data, Crystal Reports can prepare the report quickly.
Preparing the report again from the data table can be time-consuming when the
table is large.

Because you haven't made changes to the table, you can use the saved data.

❺ Click **Use Saved Data** to use the data saved with the report.

❻ Click the **Zoom button** 🔲 *twice* to preview the report in full page size. You can now
see the position of the date and the page number fields in the Page footer section.
See Figure 6-23.

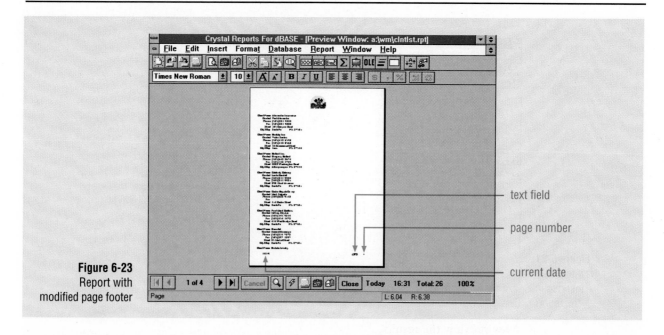

Figure 6-23
Report with modified page footer

The last step in making the report look like Figure 6-1 is to format the Details section so that records are printed in two columns. You can do this from the Preview window.

To format the Details section:

❶ Click **Format** then click **Section...** to display the Format Section dialog box. See Figure 6-24.

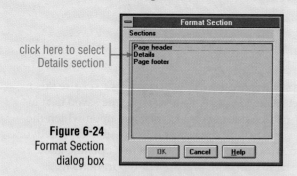

click here to select Details section

Figure 6-24
Format Section dialog box

❷ Click **Details** in the Sections list to select the Details section, then click **OK**. The Format Section dialog box changes to display the options for formatting the Details section. See Figure 6-25.

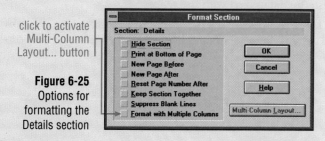

click to activate Multi-Column Layout... button

Figure 6-25
Options for formatting the Details section

This dialog box presents several options that control the formatting of the Details section of the report.

❸ Click the **Format with Multiple Columns check box** to select this option. Clicking this option activates the Multi-Column Layout... button.

❹ Click **Multi-Column Layout...** to display the Multi-Column Layout dialog box. See Figure 6-26.

dimensions of a single record on the page

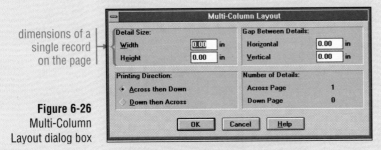

Figure 6-26
Multi-Column
Layout dialog box

The Multi-Column Layout dialog box contains four panels that allow you to customize the layout of the Details section in multiple columns. The options in the Detail Size panel determine the space allowed for a single record. The options in the Gap Between Details panel determine the spacing between records. The options in the Printing Direction panel determine the order in which the records will be placed in the columns, row by row (Across then Down) or column by column (Down then Across). The options in the Number of Details panel display the number of rows and columns that can be printed on a page, based on the size and spacing specifications.

To make the report look like Figure 6-1, you must set the width and height in the Detail Size panel. Setting these measurements is usually a matter of trial and error; first entering estimated settings, then previewing the report to see the resulting layout, then adjusting the settings. The Width text box is already highlighted, ready for you to enter a width setting.

❺ Type **3.75** to set the detail width to 3.75 inches.

❻ Press **[Tab]** to move the highlight to the Height text box, then type **1.5** to set the detail height to 1.5 inches. The Number of Details panel now indicates that the report will contain 2 records across the page and 5 records down the page. See Figure 6-27.

new dimensions

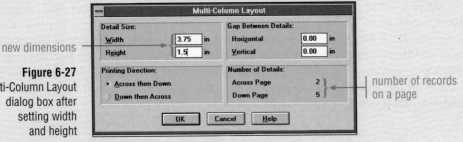

number of records on a page

Figure 6-27
Multi-Column Layout
dialog box after
setting width
and height

❼ Click **OK** to close the Multi-Column Layout dialog box and return to the Format Section dialog box.

The width and height settings might not allow space for a complete record at the bottom of the page. To prevent splitting of a record across pages or columns, you can format the Details section to keep the fields of the record together during printing. Let's do that now.

❽ Click the **Keep Section Together check box** to prevent the splitting of a record across pages or columns.

❾ Click **OK** to close the Format Section dialog box. Crystal Reports returns to the Preview window. See Figure 6-28.

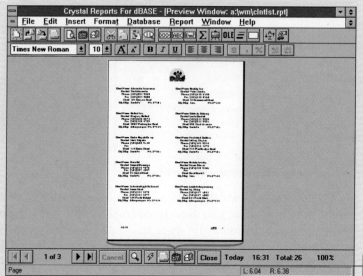

Figure 6-28
Report formatted with multiple columns

two columns of five records each

You have made many changes to the report. Let's return to the Report Designer window and save the report now.

To save the modified client list report:
❶ Click **Close** to return to the Report Designer window.
❷ Use the scroll bars to move to the upper-left corner of the report.
❸ Click the **Save button** 🖫 on the SpeedBar to save the report.

If you want to take a break and resume the tutorial at a later time, double-click the Control menu box for the Crystal Reports window to exit Crystal Reports, then exit from dBASE. When you resume the tutorial, place your Student Disk in the disk drive, start dBASE, and make sure the current directory is A:\WM. Click the Reports icon in the Navigator window, click Clntlst.rpt in the current selection panel, then click the Design button on the SpeedBar. Maximize the Crystal Reports window and the Report Designer window. Then continue with the tutorial.

After previewing the modified report in the Preview window, Nancy decides that she would like you to improve the appearance of the CITY, STATE, and ZIP fields by eliminating the extra spacing and inserting a comma between the CITY and STATE fields. To do this, you will have to replace the individual CITY, STATE, and ZIP fields with a formula field.

Defining a Formula Field

dBASE allows you to place formula fields within your report. A **formula field** is a value that dBASE calculates based on other fields in your table. Formula fields can include field values, summary fields, numeric constants, character strings, and operators.

REFERENCE WINDOW

Defining a Formula Field

- Click the Insert Formula button on the SpeedBar.

  or

  Click Insert then click Formula Field....

- Enter a name for the formula field in the Insert Formula dialog box, then click OK.

- Enter the formula in the Expression Builder, then click OK.

- Use the mouse to place the formula field in the report.

Formula fields are usually based on values in numeric or date fields. For example, you can create a field to calculate gross pay based on hours worked and hourly rate.

You can also use formula fields to combine character strings. dBASE uses the plus sign (+) operator to combine character strings. dBASE does not automatically remove spaces at the end of the character fields before combining them. To remove spaces, you use a string function.

When creating a formula field, you define a name for the formula, then define an expression that performs the calculation. You define an expression using a dBASE tool called the **Expression Builder**, which helps you create the necessary expression.

Before inserting the formula field in the report, you must first delete the CITY, STATE, and ZIP data fields already inserted in the Details section.

To delete the CITY, STATE, and ZIP data fields:
1. Click the **CITY data field** to select it.
2. Hold the **[Shift]** key down, then click the **STATE** and **ZIP data fields** to select them.
3. Press **[Del]** to delete the selected fields.

Let's name the new formula field and open the Expression Builder to begin defining the expression now.

To name the formula field and open the Expression Builder:
1. Click the **Insert Formula button** 🔲 on the SpeedBar. Crystal Reports displays the Insert Formula dialog box. See Figure 6-29.

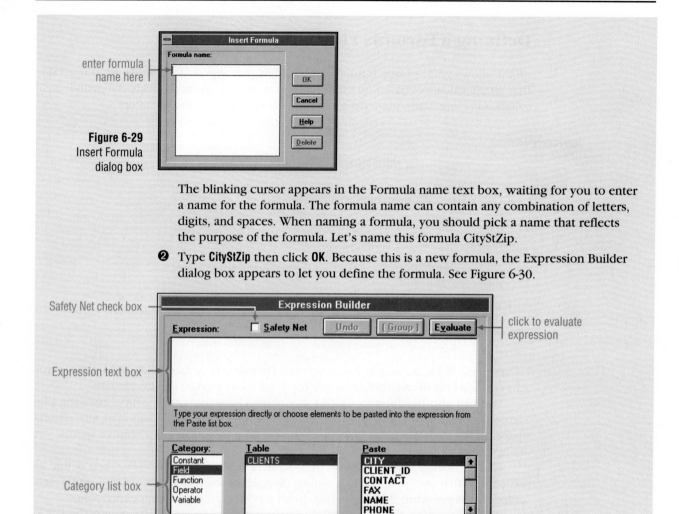

Figure 6-29
Insert Formula
dialog box

enter formula name here

The blinking cursor appears in the Formula name text box, waiting for you to enter a name for the formula. The formula name can contain any combination of letters, digits, and spaces. When naming a formula, you should pick a name that reflects the purpose of the formula. Let's name this formula CityStZip.

❷ Type **CityStZip** then click **OK**. Because this is a new formula, the Expression Builder dialog box appears to let you define the formula. See Figure 6-30.

Safety Net check box

click to evaluate expression

Expression text box

Category list box

Type (Table) list box

Figure 6-30
Expression Builder
dialog box

Paste list box

Defining an Expression Using the Expression Builder

The Expression Builder assists you in creating dBASE expressions. Recall that a dBASE expression is a collection of dBASE elements, such as constants, functions, fields, and operators, that evaluates to a single value. In Tutorial 4, you used the expression QUOTE*1.05 in a calculated field in a query skeleton. This expression evaluates to a numeric value. Other expressions evaluate to values of different types. For example, the expression DUE_DATE>={01/01/96}, which you used in Tutorial 3, evaluates to a logical (True/False) value. For the CityStZip formula, you want to create an expression that evaluates to a character value, the combined CITY, STATE, and ZIP fields.

dBASE expressions can be complicated and difficult to write correctly. There are many operators and functions available. It is not necessary to remember them all; the Expression Builder assists you in selecting them and checks your expression to make sure it is correct.

In the Expression Builder dialog box, the Expression text box is the area where you enter the expression. The Safety Net check box turns the Safety Net on and off. When the Safety Net is off, you can type any characters in the Expression text box. When the Safety Net is on, you can only select and paste elements that appear in the Paste list box. The Safety Net also enables the Undo and Group buttons to assist you in editing the expression. Until you become proficient at creating dBASE expressions, you should have the Safety Net on.

Clicking the Evaluate button causes the Expression Builder to check your expression for correctness. Evaluating the expression will alert you if dBASE cannot understand the expression in the Expression text box.

At the bottom of the Expression Builder dialog box are three list boxes labeled Category, Type (or Table), and Paste. The Category list box displays the categories of expression elements available. When you select a category, the Type list box displays the different types of elements available for that category. (When you select Field in the Category list box, the Type label changes to Table and the list box displays the available tables.) The Paste list box displays the actual elements for the category and type you selected. You can select elements from the Paste list box to insert into the expression you are building.

In the Expression text box, you will enter the following expression to combine, or **concatenate**, the character fields CITY, STATE, and ZIP:

TRIM(CLIENTS->CITY)+", "+CLIENTS->STATE+" "+CLIENTS->ZIP

The field names appear in the format TABLENAME->FIELDNAME. Components of character fields must have a plus sign (+) to connect them. Any character constants in the expression, such as commas and spaces, must be surrounded by quotation marks. Anything within the quotation marks will be displayed in the report.

This expression also contains a function called **TRIM( )**, which removes trailing spaces from the character string named inside the parentheses. Because this function operates only on character strings, it is called a string function.

Let's use the Expression Builder now to insert the first element, the TRIM(CITY->CLIENTS) function, into the expression.

To create the expression using the Expression Builder:

❶ Click the **Safety Net check box** to turn on the Safety Net (if necessary). The Expression text box now becomes gray, indicating that you cannot type directly into it.

❷ Click **Function** in the Category list box. The Type list box now shows the types of functions available. (Only the first few types are visible.) The type All is highlighted, and the Paste list box contains a complete list of all available functions. (Only the first few are visible.) See Figure 6-31.

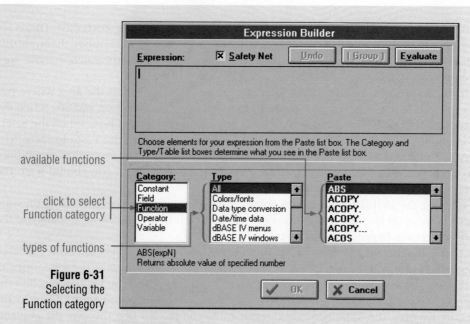

available functions

click to select
Function category

types of functions

Figure 6-31
Selecting the
Function category

❸ Scroll the Type list until the String data type is visible, then click **String data** to display the list of string functions in the Paste list box.

❹ Scroll the Paste list until the TRIM function is visible, then double-click **TRIM** to paste the function in the Expression text box. See Figure 6-32.

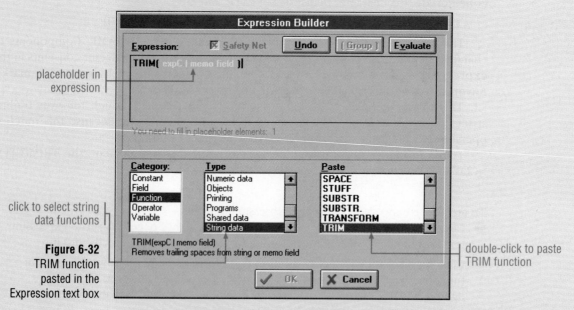

placeholder in
expression

click to select string
data functions

Figure 6-32
TRIM function
pasted in the
Expression text box

double-click to paste
TRIM function

The Expression Builder enters the TRIM function, including the parentheses, in the Expression text box. Inside the parentheses, the highlighted string "expC | memo field" is a *placeholder*, indicating that you must enter a character expression (expC) or a memo field name here. The message at the bottom of the Expression text box indicates that you must replace one placeholder in the expression. You will replace the placeholder with the name of the CITY field from the CLIENTS table.

❺ Double-click the **expC | memo field** placeholder to select it.

❻ Click **Field** in the Category list box. The Table list box displays the list of available tables. Because CLIENTS is the only available table, it is already selected. The Paste list box displays the names of the fields in the CLIENTS table, sorted alphabetically. The first field, CITY, is selected.

❼ Double-click **CITY** to paste it into the expression in place of the placeholder "expC | memo field." See Figure 6-33.

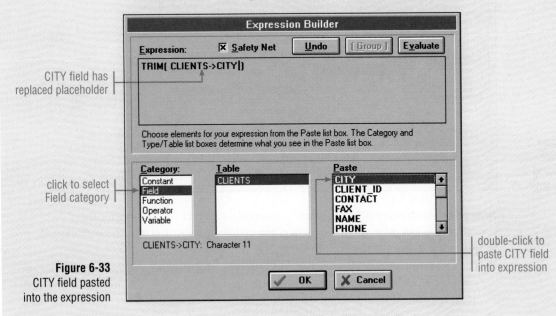

CITY field has replaced placeholder

click to select Field category

double-click to paste CITY field into expression

Figure 6-33
CITY field pasted into the expression

Now let's complete the expression by adding the concatenation operators (+), the string constants, and the STATE and ZIP field names.

To complete the expression:

❶ Click in the Expression text box to the right of the closing parenthesis in the TRIM function. The insertion bar appears to the right of the parenthesis.

❷ Click **Operator** in the Category list box. The Type list box now displays the types of operators available. The type All is highlighted, and the concatenation operator (+ add/concat.) appears in the Paste list box.

❸ Double-click **+ add/concat**. to paste the concatenation operator into the expression. The highlighted placeholder "Value" appears to the right of the concatenation operator, and the message at the bottom of the Expression text box indicates that you must replace one placeholder in the expression. See Figure 6-34.

placeholder

concatenation operator in expression

click to select Operator category

Figure 6-34
Concatenation operator pasted into the expression

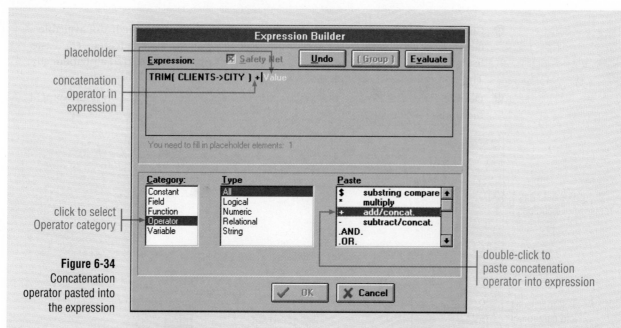

double-click to paste concatenation operator into expression

Now add the character string constant, a comma followed by a space, after the concatenation operator. As noted earlier, any character constants must be surrounded by quotation marks.

❹ Click **Constant** in the Category list box. The Type list box now displays the types of constants available. The type All is highlighted, and the "double quotes" string constant appears in the Paste list box.

❺ Double-click **"double quotes"** to paste a pair of double quotation marks into the expression. Notice that there are no characters between the pair of quotation marks. You must edit this character string constant to insert the comma and the space between the quotation marks. The comma and space will appear after the city name in the report.

❻ Place the pointer on the pair of quotation marks in the Expression text box, then click the **right mouse button** to display a text box below the quotation marks. A cursor appears in the text box, waiting for you to enter the characters that will appear between the quotation marks. See Figure 6-35.

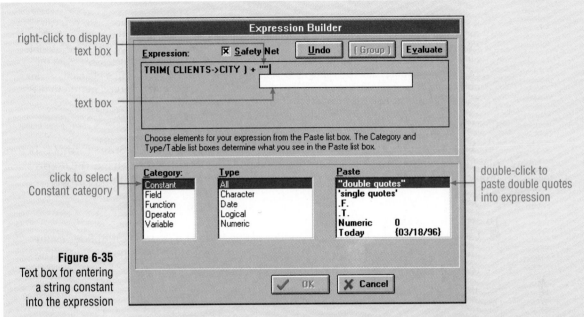

right-click to display text box

text box

click to select Constant category

double-click to paste double quotes into expression

Figure 6-35
Text box for entering a string constant into the expression

❼ Type , (a comma), press the [**Spacebar**], then press [**Enter**] to enter the characters. The text box disappears and the comma and space appear between the quotation marks.

You can use the same method to insert the remaining elements in the expression.

❽ Insert the remaining elements in the expression. When you are finished, your screen should look exactly like Figure 6-36. Note that the character constant following the STATE field is simply a space, which will separate the STATE and ZIP fields in the report.

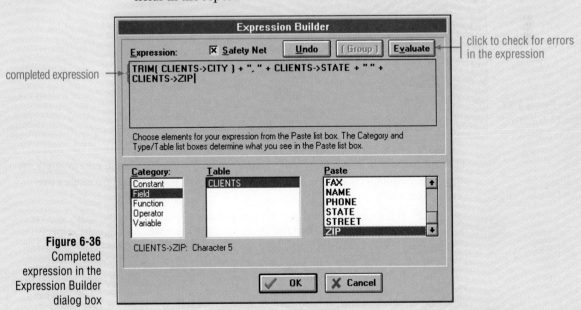

click to check for errors in the expression

completed expression

Figure 6-36
Completed expression in the Expression Builder dialog box

TROUBLE? If your expression does not look like the expression in Figure 6-36, you can make the necessary changes without starting over. Simply double-click the element in the expression you want to change, then, after selecting the correct Category and Type, double-click the correct element in the Paste list box to replace it. To delete an element from the expression, double-click the element to select it, then press [Del]. To edit a character string constant, place the pointer on the character string and click the right mouse button to display the text box. Edit the character string then press [Enter].

You have now completed the formula definition for the CityStZip formula. Before placing the new formula field in the report, it is a good idea to have the Expression Builder evaluate the expression in order to check it for errors. Let's do this now.

To evaluate the expression for errors:

❶ Click **Evaluate** in the Expression Builder dialog box. The Expression Builder evaluates the expression using data from one of the records in the CLIENTS table. The result is displayed below the Expression text box. See Figure 6-37.

expression evaluated for selected record

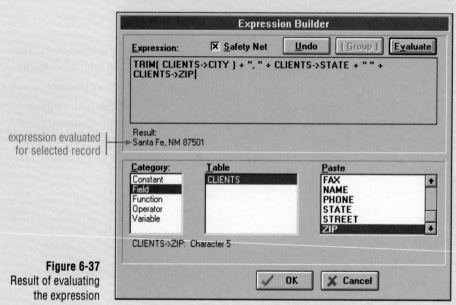

Figure 6-37
Result of evaluating the expression

The result shows exactly how this record's data will appear in the report. By looking at the results, you can verify that the expression you entered produces the results you want.

TROUBLE? If the Expression Builder displays an error message below the Expression text box, read the message to try to determine the nature of the error. Examine the expression closely to see how it differs from the expression in Figure 6-37. Edit the expression to correct it, then repeat Step 1.

TROUBLE? If the Expression Builder displays a result that does not look like the result in Figure 6-37, examine the expression closely to see how it differs from the expression in Figure 6-37. Edit the expression to correct it, then repeat Step 1.

You are now ready to insert the CityStZip formula field in the report.

❷ Click **OK** to close the Expression Builder. The Expression Builder dialog box closes and a rectangle appears with the pointer in the Report Designer window. The rectangle represents the CityStZip formula field.

❸ Move the pointer to position the CityStZip formula field rectangle below the STREET field in the Details section, then click the **left mouse button** to insert the field. See Figure 6-38.

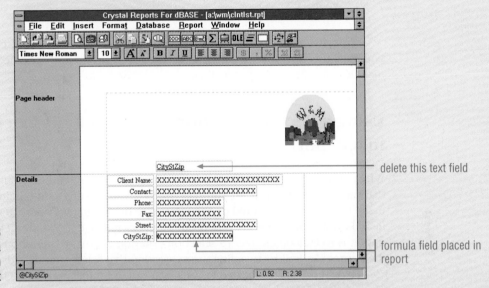

Figure 6-38
CityStZip formula
field inserted in
the report

delete this text field

formula field placed in
report

TROUBLE? If you did not place the CityStZip formula field correctly, click the field rectangle to select it, hold the left mouse button down, and adjust the position. Release the mouse button to place the field in its new position.

Notice that Crystal Reports has placed a label text field for the CityStZip formula field in the Page header section. Because you already have a label in the Details section, this new label is unnecessary. Let's delete it.

❹ Click the **label text field** for the CityStZip formula field in the Page header section to select it, then press **[Del]** to delete the label text field.

Now let's preview the results and save the report.

❺ Click the **Preview Report button** 🔍 on the SpeedBar. The Preview window appears with the first page of the formatted report. See Figure 6-39.

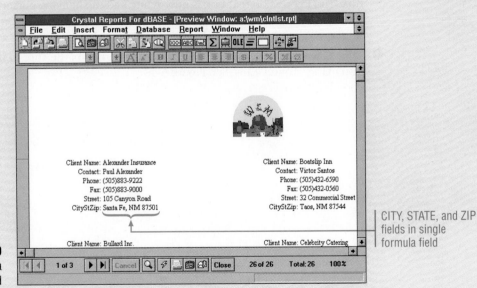

Figure 6-39
Report with formula
field inserted

CITY, STATE, and ZIP
fields in single
formula field

The formula field looks correct. Let's save the report now.

❻ Click **Close** to return to the Report Designer window.

❼ Click the **Save button** 🖫 on the SpeedBar to save the report.

Nancy is satisfied with the appearance of the modified client list report. She reminds you that the prospective client is located in Taos; therefore, the final report should include only clients located in Taos.

Using a Record Selection Criterion to Restrict the Records in a Report

When viewing records in a table, form, or report, you sometimes want to view only those that meet certain criteria. In Tutorials 4 and 5 you did this by designing queries and forms based on queries. You could do the same here by designing a query to select clients located in Taos and then basing the report on the query rather than on the CLIENTS table. Another option is to include the record selection criterion as part of the report design. You can use the Expression Builder to define the expression that selects the records you want.

To select all clients located in Taos, you can use the expression CLIENTS->CITY="Taos." This is a logical expression that evaluates to True when the value of the CITY field for the current record is equal to "Taos." (The expression evaluates to False otherwise.) Only those records for which the expression evaluates to True will appear in the report. Let's set this record selection criterion now.

To set the record selection criterion to CLIENTS->CITY = "Taos":

❶ Click the **Record Selection Criterion button** 🖾 on the SpeedBar. The Expression Builder dialog box appears.

Notice that the Safety Net is still on. Because this is a simple expression, let's enter it without the Safety Net.

❷ Click the **Safety Net check box** (if the box is checked) to remove the "x" from the check box. The Expression text box is now white and the blinking cursor appears in it. You can now enter the expression directly into the Expression text box, or if you prefer, you can use the Paste list box to select and paste elements as you did before.

❸ Type **CLIENTS->CITY="Taos"** in the Expression text box. Be sure to include the quotation marks around Taos. See Figure 6-40.

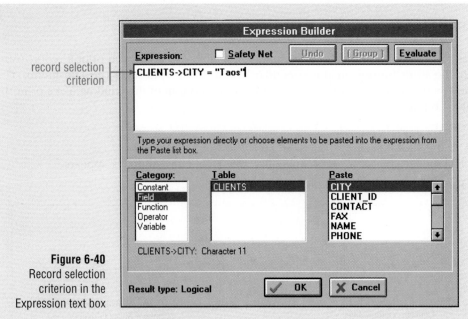

Figure 6-40
Record selection
criterion in the
Expression text box

record selection criterion → CLIENTS->CITY = "Taos"

❹ Click **Evaluate** to have the Expression Builder evaluate the expression for the current record. The result is displayed as .F. (False) because the value in the CITY field for the current record is not "Taos."

❺ Click **OK** to return to the Report Designer window.

❻ Click the **Preview Report button** 🖾 on the SpeedBar. Crystal Reports displays the first page of the report. See Figure 6-41.

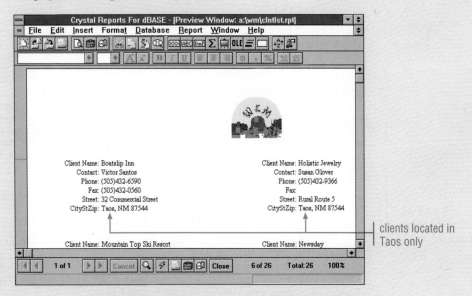

Figure 6-41
Report showing only
clients located in Taos

clients located in Taos only

Notice that only clients located in Taos appear in the report.

After reviewing the report, Nancy asks you to print it so that she can show it to other W&M employees.

Printing a Report

Just as you do when you print the contents of a table or a form, you print a report using either the Print button on the SpeedBar or the Print option on the File menu. The Preview window also contains a Print button at the bottom of the window. Let's print the client list report.

To print the client list report:

❶ Click the **Print button** 📄 on the SpeedBar. The Print File dialog box appears.

❷ Click **OK** to print the report. See Figure 6-42.

Client Name: Boatslip Inn	Client Name: Holistic Jewelry
Contact: Victor Santos	Contact: Susan Glover
Phone: (505)432-6590	Phone: (505)432-9366
Fax: (505)432-0560	Fax:
Street: 32 Commercial Street	Street: Rural Route 5
CityStZip: Taos, NM 87544	CityStZip: Taos, NM 87544
Client Name: Mountain Top Ski Resort	Client Name: Newsday
Contact: Victor Juarez	Contact: Esther Ling
Phone: (505)432-6220	Phone: (505)433-8677
Fax: (505)432-7890	Fax: (505)433-8641
Street: 895 South Wells	Street: 881 Commonwealth
CityStZip: Taos, NM 87544	CityStZip: Taos, NM 87544
Client Name: Shotgun Willy's Lounge	Client Name: Stonewall
Contact: Randy Warren	Contact: Larry Kramer
Phone: (505)439-5327	Phone: (505)432-4534
Fax: (505)439-5573	Fax: (505)432-7812
Street: 320 South Station	Street: 9 Christopher Street
CityStZip: Taos, NM 87544	CityStZip: Taos, NM 87544

4/22/96   Page   1

Figure 6-42
Printout of the
client list report

TROUBLE? If characters or bitmapped images near the edge of the paper are cut off, your margins might be set too narrow for your printer. Click File then click Print Margins and increase the margin size. Then repeat Steps 1 and 2.

Nancy shows the client list report to the other W&M employees, and everyone agrees that the professional look of the report will impress potential clients. You can now save the finished report.

To save the client list report and then exit Crystal Reports:

❶ Click the **Save button** 📄 on the SpeedBar.

❷ Click **Close** to close the Preview window.

❸ Double-click the **Control menu box** for the Crystal Reports window to exit Crystal Reports and return to the dBASE Desktop.

If you want to take a break and resume the tutorial at a later time, exit from dBASE now. When you resume the tutorial, place your Student Disk in the disk drive, start dBASE, make sure the current directory is A:\WM, then continue with the tutorial.

Nancy is interested in analyzing all W&M jobs—completed and in progress—by the different types of media the agency uses to place ads. Figure 6-43 shows the report layout sheet Nancy sketched for the media summary report, which she wants you to produce.

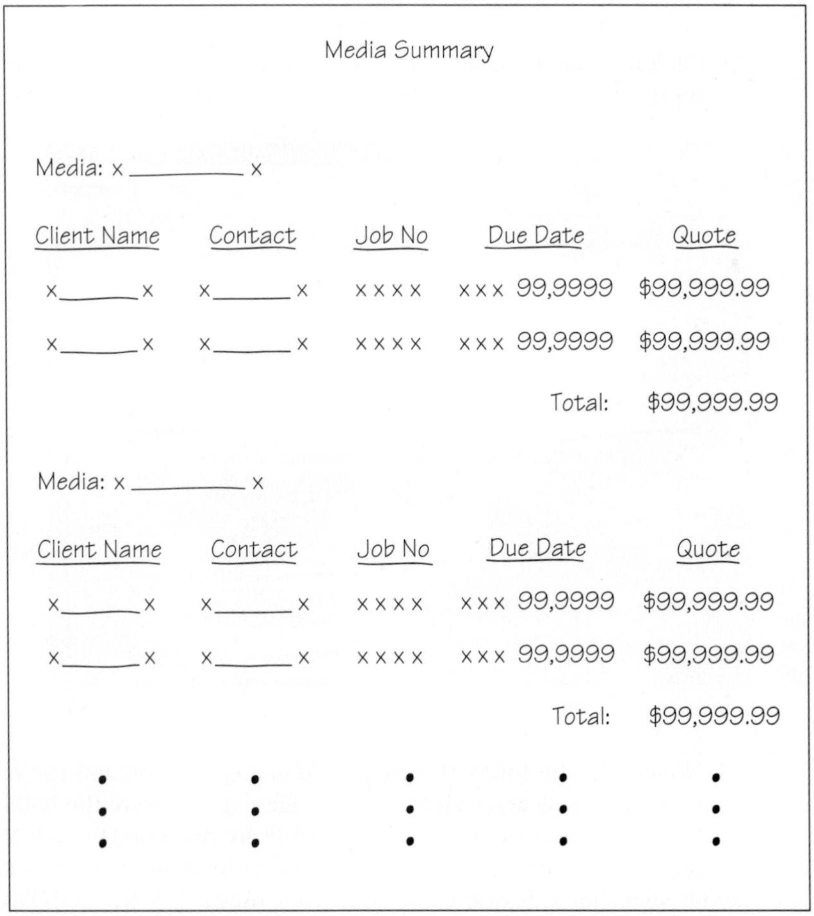

Figure 6-43
Report layout sheet for the media summary report

To create this report, you need to include fields from both the JOBS and CLIENTS tables.

Creating a Report Based on Multiple Tables

The client list report you created was based on just one table. However, you can create reports based on more than one table. To do so, you must base the report on a query that includes the tables you want to include in the report. In this case, you need a query that includes the JOBS and CLIENTS tables, with JOBS as the parent table. The query JOBAUTH.QBE, which you created in Tutorial 5, includes the tables you need. Let's use that query as the basis for this report.

To start a new report based on the JOBAUTH.QBE query:

❶ Click the **Reports icon** in the Navigator window.

❷ Double-click **Untitled** to display the Open Table Required dialog box.

TROUBLE? If you did not exit and restart dBASE, the Open Table Required dialog box will not be displayed. Crystal Reports assumes that you want to use the same table (CLIENTS.DBF) that you used for the last report. Double-click the Control menu box for Crystal Reports to exit Crystal Reports, then exit and restart dBASE. Then repeat Steps 1 and 2.

❸ Click **jobauth.qbe** in the file list to select it, then click **OK**. Crystal Reports begins and displays the Report Designer window.

❹ Click the **Maximize button** on the Crystal Reports window, then click the **Maximize button** on the Report Designer window. See Figure 6-44.

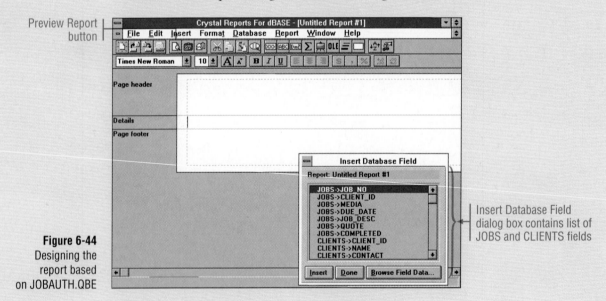

Preview Report button

Insert Database Field dialog box contains list of JOBS and CLIENTS fields

Figure 6-44
Designing the report based on JOBAUTH.QBE

Notice that the Insert Database Field dialog box contains the field names for all fields from both the JOBS and CLIENTS tables. Field names from the JOBS table are preceded by JOBS->. Field names from the CLIENTS table are preceded by CLIENTS->.

Referring to Nancy's sketch of the report in Figure 6-43, you can see that the report layout sheet includes only the following fields: NAME, CONTACT, JOB_NO, MEDIA, DUE_DATE, and QUOTE. The Details section of the report includes the NAME, CONTACT, JOB_NO, DUE_DATE, and QUOTE fields. The MEDIA field is used to group the records. Let's start by setting the page margins and then inserting the required fields in the Details section of the report.

To set the page margins for the report and then insert the fields:

❶ Click **File** then click **Page Margins...** to open the Printer Margins dialog box.

❷ Type **.5** to set the top margin to .5 inches, then press **[Tab]** to move to the Left Margin text box.

❸ Type **.5** to set the left margin to .5 inches, then press **[Tab]** to move to the Bottom Margin text box.

❹ Type **.5** to set the bottom margin to .5 inches, then press **[Tab]** to move to the Right Margin text box.

❺ Type **.5** to set the right margin to .5 inches, then click **OK** to close the Printer Margins dialog box.

Now insert the required fields in the Details section.

❻ Click **CLIENTS->NAME** in the Insert Database Field dialog box, then hold the left mouse button down and drag the NAME field into the Details section of the Edit box. Place the rectangle approximately one inch from the left margin line and release the mouse button.

❼ Repeat Step 6 to place the CONTACT, JOB_NO, DUE_DATE, and QUOTE fields in the Details section. Place the fields horizontally next to each other on a single line in the Details section. Use the horizontal scroll bar to scroll to the right as necessary to place the fields.

❽ Use the horizontal scroll bar to scroll left until the section names are visible, then click the **NAME field** (in the Details section) to select it.

Now check the layout by previewing the report.

❾ Click the **Preview Report button** 🔍 to display the report in the Preview window.

❿ Click the **Zoom button** 🔍 to see the report in actual size. Your screen should look like Figure 6-45. Notice that handles appear around all of the client names, because the NAME field is selected in the Report Designer window.

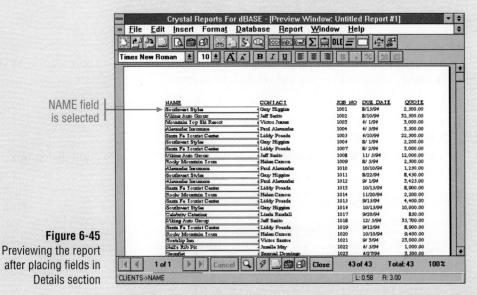

NAME field is selected

Figure 6-45
Previewing the report after placing fields in Details section

TROUBLE? If your report does not look like Figure 6-45, you can adjust the alignment of any object in the report directly in the Preview window. Simply click an object to select it, then drag it to its new position. For example, if you want to move the text label field for the Quote field to the right, click the text label field for Quote (handles appear around the text label field) and drag the field to the right. Release the mouse button when the field is in its correct position.

Looking again at Figure 6-43, you can see that Nancy wants to group the jobs by media type and compute subtotals for the quotes for each type. dBASE lets you group records and provide summary statistics for each group by inserting a Group section.

Group Sections

When you add a **Group section** to a report, dBASE adds two more areas to the Report Designer window: the Group header section and the Group footer section. The Group header section is placed between the Page header and Details sections. Any objects in the **Group header** section appear at the beginning of the group. Typically, information that identifies each group is placed here. The Group footer section is placed between the Details and Page footer sections. Any objects placed in the **Group footer** section appear at the end of the group. Totals for a group, called **subtotals**, are often placed in the Group footer section. When you group on a field value, dBASE places all records with the same value for that field in the same group. When the field value changes, dBASE starts a new group.

REFERENCE WINDOW

Adding a Group Section

- Display the report in the Report Designer window.
- Click Insert then click Group Section... to display the Insert Group Section dialog box.
- Select the field on which you want to group the report.
- Select the sort option you want for groups in the report.
- Click OK to add the Group section to the Report Designer window.

Because Nancy wants to arrange the jobs by media, let's add a Group section to the Report Designer window to group the records by media.

To add a Group section to the media summary report:
1. Click **Close** to return to the Report Designer window.
2. Click **Insert** then click **Group Section...** to display the Insert Group Section dialog box. See Figure 6-46.

Figure 6-46
Insert Group Section
dialog box

The Insert Group Section dialog box contains two drop-down list boxes. The first drop-down list box allows you to select the field to group on. The second drop-down list box allows you to select the sort order for the groups. Let's select the field to group on.

❸ Click the **list arrow** for the first drop-down list box, then click **JOBS->MEDIA** in this list box. The bottom of the panel displays the message: "The section will be printed on any change of JOBS->MEDIA." This signifies that the data will now be grouped on the MEDIA field. The second drop-down list box already shows ascending order for the sort. This means that the groups will be printed in alphabetic order by MEDIA. There is no need to change this sort order.

❹ Click **OK** to close the Insert Group Section dialog box and return to the Report Designer window. dBASE places the two areas of the Group section—the Group header section and the Group footer section—between the Page header section and the Details section, and the Details section and the Page footer section, respectively. See Figure 6-47.

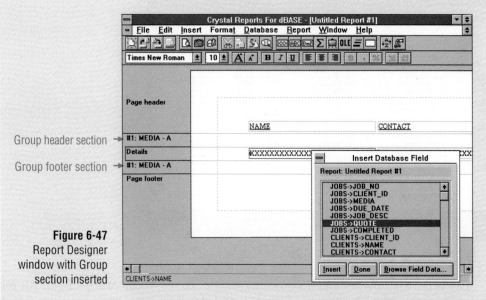

Group header section →

Group footer section →

Figure 6-47
Report Designer
window with Group
section inserted

TROUBLE? If your report is grouped on the wrong field, click Edit then click Delete Section... to display the Delete Section dialog box. In the list box, click the name of the section you want to delete, click OK, then repeat Steps 2 through 4.

The Group header and Group footer sections are labeled "#1: MEDIA - A." If you want to design a report that groups records by major category and within a major category by a secondary category, you can add additional Group sections to a report. When designing a report with multiple Group sections, the outermost Group section determines the primary grouping and is labeled #1 in the Report Designer window. The next Group section is placed inside the outer group to represent a secondary grouping and is labeled #2. For example, to display the jobs by media and within media by client name, you could add the Group section for the MEDIA field first, then add the Group section for the NAME field next.

Notice that the Group header does not contain the MEDIA field or a label for the field. Let's insert those now.

❺ Click **JOBS->MEDIA** in the Insert Database Field dialog box and drag the field to the Group header. Use the pointer to position the rectangle approximately one inch from the left margin.

❻ Click the **Insert Text Field button** 📝 on the SpeedBar to open the Edit Text Field dialog box.

❼ Type **Media:** then click **Accept** to close the Edit Text Field dialog box.

❽ Use the pointer to position the rectangle to the left of the MEDIA field, then click the **left mouse button** to place the text field.

Now preview the report.

❾ Click the **Preview Report button** 🔍 on the SpeedBar to open the Preview window.

❿ Click the **Zoom button** 🔍 to view the report in actual size. See Figure 6-48.

Group header

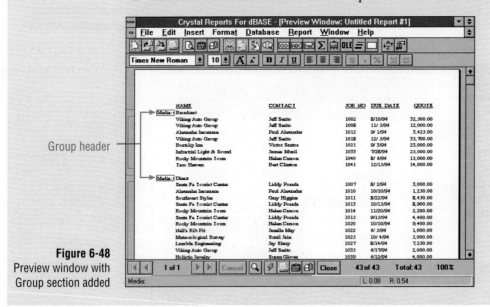

Figure 6-48
Preview window with
Group section added

The report is now arranged according to the values in the MEDIA field. All job records with the value "Broadcast" in the MEDIA field appear in a single group, as do job records with the value "Direct," and so on. The groups are arranged in ascending alphabetical order. The value of the MEDIA field is printed at the beginning of each group, and a blank line separates each group from the following one. Notice that handles appear around the MEDIA field, indicating that it is selected.

Sorting Records Within Group Sections

When you add a Group section to the Report Designer window, dBASE produces a separate group for each distinct value in the field you are grouping on. If you want to sort the records in a report within groups, you could do so by clicking Report, then clicking Record Sort Order to display the Record Sort Order dialog box. The fields listed in the Sort Fields panel determine the sort order for records in the report. The group field (MEDIA) is already listed there and can't be removed unless you remove the Group section from the report. If you wanted to sort the records by client name within each group, you would select CLIENTS->NAME from the Report Fields list and add it to the Sort Fields list. By adding other fields to the Sort Fields list, you could further subsort the records. Clicking OK closes the Record Sort Order dialog box and returns you to the Report Designer window or the Preview window.

Page Breaks

There are times when you want the data for each group to appear on its own page instead of in a continuous stream—perhaps to distribute relevant information to different individuals. To do this, you can place a **page break** before or after each group. To place a page break before a group, click Format then click Section... to display the Format Section dialog box. Select the Group header section and click OK. Click in the check box for New Page Before and then click OK. Crystal Reports automatically reformats the report so that each group is printed on a separate page.

There are several layout and formatting changes to be made before the report looks like Nancy's report layout sheet (Figure 6-43). The column headings (text field labels) should appear in the Group header section (not in the Page header section) and their values must be changed. The Page header section should include a title. Due dates must be reformatted; that is, 11/05/96 should be printed as Nov 5, 1996. And the values for the QUOTE field should appear with dollar signs. These changes are all quite easy to do. Let's do them now.

To move the column headings (text field labels) to the Group header:

❶ Click **Close** to return to the Report Designer window.

❷ Click **Done** in the Insert Database Field dialog box to close the dialog box.

❸ Click in the Group header section between the left margin and the Media text field, then press **[Enter]** twice to add two blank lines to the Group header section.

❹ Click the **NAME text field label**, then drag it into the Group header section immediately above the NAME field. See Figure 6-49.

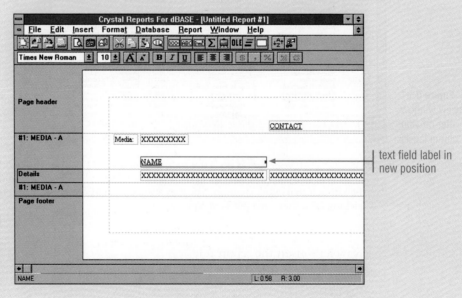

Figure 6-49
Group header section with NAME text field label repositioned

❺ Click **Edit** then click **Text Field...** to display the Edit Text Field dialog box.

❻ Double-click **NAME** to select it, then type **Client Name**. See Figure 6-50.

Figure 6-50
Editing the text
field label

❼ Click **Accept** to close the Edit Text Field dialog box and return to the Report Designer window.

❽ Repeat Steps 4 through 7 to reposition and edit the remaining text field labels to make them look like Figure 6-43. Use the horizontal scroll bar to scroll right as necessary.

Now preview and save the report.

❾ Click the **Preview Report button** 🔍 on the SpeedBar.

❿ Click **Use Saved Data**, then click the **Zoom button** 🔍 on the SpeedBar to preview the report in actual size. The Preview window should look like Figure 6-51.

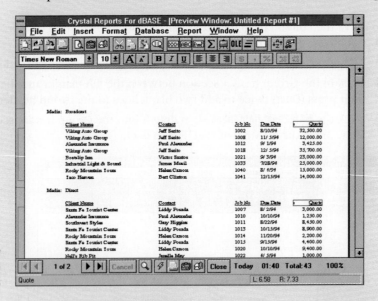

Figure 6-51
Preview window
after moving
column labels

TROUBLE? If your report does not look like Figure 6-51, you can adjust the alignment of any object in the report directly in the Preview window. Simply click an object to select it, then drag it to its new position. You can also edit a text field by clicking the field to select it, clicking Edit, then clicking Text Field....

Now let's insert the report title.

To insert the report title:

❶ Click **Close** to return to the Report Designer window. Use the horizontal scroll bar to scroll left until the section names are visible.

❷ Click in the Page header, then press **[Enter]** three times to insert three blank lines in the Page header section.

❸ Click the **Insert Text Field button** ▦ on the SpeedBar to display the Edit Text Field dialog box.

❹ Type **W&M Job List** then click **Accept** to close the Edit Text Field dialog box. A rectangle, representing the new text field, appears with the pointer in the Preview window.

❺ Move the pointer to position the rectangle in the center of the Page header (above the Contact field), then click the **left mouse button** to place the text field.

Now let's format the due dates that appear in the report so that they look like the dates in Figure 6-43.

To format the due dates:

❶ Use the horizontal scroll bar to scroll to the right until the right edge of the report is visible.

❷ Click the **Due Date field** to select it.

❸ Click **Format** then click **Field** to display the Format Date dialog box. See Figure 6-52.

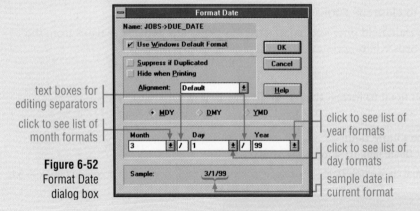

text boxes for editing separators

click to see list of month formats

Figure 6-52
Format Date
dialog box

click to see list of year formats

click to see list of day formats

sample date in current format

The Format Date dialog box allows you to change the way the date is displayed. The panel at the bottom of the dialog box displays a sample date in the current format. The panel immediately above the sample panel allows you to select the format for the month, day, and year and to specify the separator characters.

The sample box shows the date 3/1/99. Nancy wants this to appear as Mar 1, 1999. Let's change the format now.

❹ Click the **Month list arrow**. The drop-down list displays the formatting options for the month.

❺ Click **Mar** to select the three-letter abbreviation option. The sample date changes to reflect your selection.

Now change the separator that will be used between the month and the day. The current separator is a slash. Let's change it to a space.

❻ Double-click the **text box** for the separator between the month and the day to select it, then press **[Spacebar]** to enter a space in the text box.

The format for the day portion of the date does not need to be changed. Let's change the separator between the day and the year to a comma.

❼ Double-click the **text box** for the separator between the day and the year to select it.

❽ Type , (a comma), then press **[Spacebar]** to enter a comma and a space in the text box.

❾ Click the **Year list arrow**, then click **1999** to select the four-digit display of the year. The sample date now displays Mar 3, 1999. See Figure 6-53.

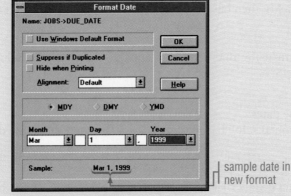

Figure 6-53
The due
date reformatted

sample date in
new format

❿ Click **OK** to close the Format Date dialog box.

The Due Date field now appears as Dec 31, 1999. The actual due dates from the table records will be printed here when the report is printed.

Next you need to format the Quote field with a dollar sign.

To format the Quote field:

❶ Click the **Quote field** to select it.

❷ Click **Format** then click **Field...** to display the Format Number dialog box. See Figure 6-54.

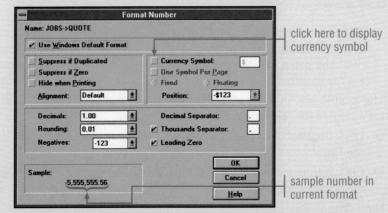

Figure 6-54
Format Number
dialog box

click here to display
currency symbol

sample number in
current format

Like the Format Date dialog box, this dialog box displays the options for formatting a numeric field. The panel at the lower left displays a sample number in the current format. The panel at the upper right allows you to specify that the currency symbol (the dollar sign) be displayed as part of the number.

❸ Click the **Currency Symbol check box**. The sample number now includes a dollar sign.

❹ Click **OK** to close the Format Number dialog box. The Quote field in the Report Designer window is now displayed with a dollar sign. See Figure 6-55.

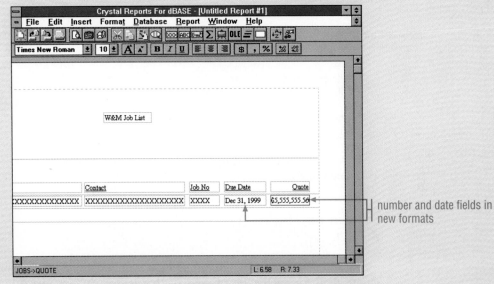

Figure 6-55
Report Designer window with formatted Quote field

You have one more change to make in the report before it looks like Figure 6-43. Nancy's report layout sheet includes totals for the Quote field for each media type. In other words, she wants a total for each group. To display these totals, you need to place a summary field in your report.

Summarizing Data in a Report

Summarizing data in a report means performing arithmetic operations, such as summing, counting, and averaging, on a set of records. There are several types of summarizing operations you can perform in dBASE. Figure 6-56 lists the summary operators available in dBASE.

Summary Operators	Result
sum	sum of values for selected numeric field
average	average of values for selected numeric field
maximum	maximum value for selected character, numeric, or date field
minimum	minimum value for selected character, numeric, or date field
count	count of values for selected field
sample variance	sample variance for selected numeric field
sample standard deviation	sample standard deviation for selected numeric field
population variance	population variance for selected numeric field
population standard deviation	population standard deviation for selected numeric field
distinct count	count of unique values for selected field

Figure 6-56
Report summary operators

dBASE allows you to insert summarizing fields for each group or for the entire report. A summarizing field that summarizes the records for a group is called a **summary field**. A summarizing field that summarizes the records for the entire report is called a **grand total**. A **subtotal** is a special kind of summary field that calculates the sum of numeric values in a group.

Defining a Summary Field

- Click the field you want to summarize.
- Click the Summary Tool button on the SpeedBar.

  or

  Click Insert, click Summary Field..., then select the type of summary field you want.
- Select the summary operator you want.
- Click OK.

In the media summary report, Nancy wants to calculate the sum of the values in the Quote field for each type of media—that is, for each media group. To calculate these sums, you will place a summary field in the Group footer section.

To create a summary field for Quote:

❶ Click in the Group #1:Media-A footer section, then press **[Enter]** three times to insert three blank lines in the Group footer section.

❷ Use the horizontal scroll bar to scroll to the right edge of the report.

❸ Click the **Quote field** to select it.

❹ Click the **Summary Tool button** Σ on the SpeedBar to display the Insert Summary dialog box. See Figure 6-57.

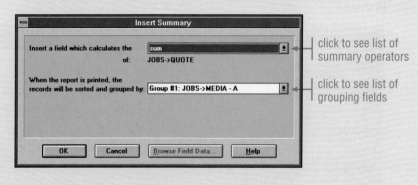

Figure 6-57
Insert Summary
dialog box

The list box in the upper right of the Insert Summary dialog box allows you to select the type of summary operator you want. By default, the sum operator is selected. If you wanted another operator, you could choose it from the drop-down list.

The second list box allows you to specify the groups or subgroups of records to summarize. By default, the summary is calculated for the entire group. In this report, the summary will be calculated for each type of media. If you wished, you could specify that the summary be calculated for subgroups within each media type. For example, if you wanted a summary for each client name in each media type, you would select the CLIENT->NAME field from the drop-down list.

The default choices will create a sum field for each media type, just as Nancy wants.

❺ Click **OK** to close the Insert Summary dialog box. Crystal Reports automatically inserts the summary field in the Group footer section immediately below the Quote field in the Details section.

Let's reposition the summary field and insert a label.

❻ Click and drag the summary field down one line.

❼ Click the **Insert Text Field button** 🔲 on the SpeedBar to display the Edit Text Field dialog box.

❽ Type **Total:** then click **Accept**.

❾ Position the text field just to the left of the new summary field. See Figure 6-58.

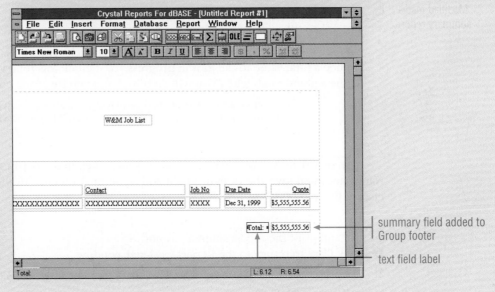

Figure 6-58
Report Designer
window after
defining summary
field and label

Now let's preview the report.

To preview the report:

❶ Click the **Preview Report button** 🔲 on the SpeedBar.

❷ Click **Use Saved Data**.

❸ Click the **Zoom button** 🔍 at the bottom of the Preview window to preview the report in actual size. The Preview window should look like Figure 6-59.

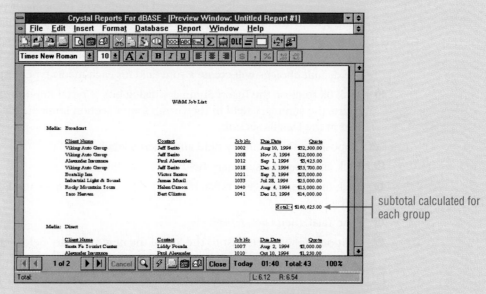

Figure 6-59
Modified media
summary report

subtotal calculated for each group

Note that the report displays Quote subtotals for each type of media but does not include a total value for all jobs in progress. To include this total value, you need to define a grand total field. (You will do this in an exercise at the end of this tutorial.)

TROUBLE? If your summary field is defined incorrectly, return to the Report Designer window, delete the summary field, then repeat Steps 4 through 7 in the previous set of steps.

The report now looks like the design Nancy sketched, so you can print it to show Nancy and then save the design. You'll add some final touches to the report in the exercises at the end of this tutorial.

To save and print the media summary report:

❶ Click **Close** to return to the Report Designer window.

❷ Click the **Save button** 🔲 on the SpeedBar to display the File Save As dialog box.

Name the report MEDIA.

❸ Type **MEDIA** in the File Name text box.

❹ Click **OK**. The file is saved as MEDIA.RPT.

Now print the report.

❺ Click the **Print button** 🔲 on the SpeedBar.

❻ Click **Use Saved Data** to display the Print File dialog box.

❼ Click **OK**. The media summary report prints on two pages. See Figure 6-60.

❽ Close the Crystal Reports window by double-clicking its **Control menu box**.

❾ Exit dBASE by double-clicking its **Control menu box**.

W&M Job List

Media: Broadcast

Client Name	Contact	Job No	Due Date	Quote
Viking Auto Group	Jeff Serito	1002	Aug 10, 1996	$32,500.00
Viking Auto Group	Jeff Serito	1008	Nov 5, 1996	$12,000.00
Alexander Insurance	Paul Alexander	1012	Sep 1, 1996	$3,425.00
Viking Auto Group	Jeff Serito	1018	Dec 5, 1996	$35,700.00
Boatslip Inn	Victor Santos	1021	Sep 3, 1996	$23,000.00
Industrial Light & Sound	James Musil	1033	Jul 28, 1996	$25,000.00
Rocky Mountain Tours	Helen Carson	1040	Aug 6, 1996	$15,000.00
Taco Heaven	Bert Clinton	1041	Dec 15, 1996	$14,000.00

Total: $160,625.00

Media: Direct

Client Name	Contact	Job No	Due Date	Quote
Santa Fe Tourist Center	Liddy Posada	1007	Aug 2, 1996	$3,000.00
Alexander Insurance	Paul Alexander	1010	Oct 10, 1996	$1,250.00
Southwest Styles	Gary Higgins	1011	Aug 22, 1996	$8,450.00
Santa Fe Tourist Center	Liddy Posada	1013	Oct 15, 1996	$8,900.00
Rocky Mountain Tours	Helen Carson	1014	Nov 20, 1996	$2,200.00
Santa Fe Tourist Center	Liddy Posada	1015	Sep 15, 1996	$4,400.00
Rocky Mountain Tours	Helen Carson	1020	Oct 10, 1996	$9,400.00
Nell's Rib Pit	Janelle May	1022	Jun 5, 1996	$1,000.00
Meteorological Survey	Sunil Jain	1025	Oct 4, 1996	$5,000.00
Lambda Engineering	Jay Sharp	1027	Aug 14, 1996	$7,250.00
Viking Auto Group	Jeff Serito	1035	Jun 17, 1996	$2,000.00
Holistic Jewelry	Susan Glover	1039	Jun 12, 1996	$4,000.00

Total: $56,850.00

Media: Other

Client Name	Contact	Job No	Due Date	Quote
Celebrity Catering	Linda Randall	1017	Sep 20, 1996	$850.00
Manana Outfitters	Daniel Gibbs	1030	Aug 10, 1996	$4,000.00
Southwest Styles	Gary Higgins	1042	Dec 3, 1996	$4,200.00

Total: $9,050.00

Media: Print

Client Name	Contact	Job No	Due Date	Quote
Southwest Styles	Gary Higgins	1001	Aug 15, 1996	$2,500.00
Mountain Top Ski Resort	Victor Juarez	1003	Jun 1, 1996	$3,000.00
Alexander Insurance	Paul Alexander	1004	Jun 5, 1996	$3,500.00
Santa Fe Tourist Center	Liddy Posada	1005	Jun 10, 1996	$22,500.00

Figure 6-60 Printout of media summary report (page 1)

W&M Job List

Southwest Styles	Gary Higgins	1006	Aug 1, 1996	$2,200.00
Rocky Mountain Tours	Helen Carson	1009	Aug 5, 1996	$2,500.00
Southwest Styles	Gary Higgins	1016	Oct 15, 1996	$10,000.00
Santa Fe Tourist Center	Liddy Posada	1019	Sep 12, 1996	$8,900.00
Gauntlet	Samuel Domingo	1023	Jun 27, 1996	$3,500.00
Boatslip Inn	Victor Santos	1024	Jul 4, 1996	$10,000.00
Castro Bicycle Co-op	Mark Salgado	1026	Aug 2, 1996	$2,500.00
Viola d'Amore	Julie Edwards	1028	Jul 21, 1996	$2,000.00
Stonewall	Larry Kramer	1029	Jul 16, 1996	$6,400.00
Fire Island Realtors	Jeffrey Stryker	1031	Sep 9, 1996	$7,250.00
Viola d'Amore	Julie Edwards	1032	Sep 26, 1996	$10,000.00
Limelight	Juniaf Montingier	1034	Aug 8, 1996	$3,000.00
Stonewall	Larry Kramer	1036	Dec 25, 1996	$3,500.00
Gauntlet	Samuel Domingo	1037	Nov 11, 1996	$17,000.00
Newsday	Esther Ling	1038	Jun 30, 1996	$38,000.00
Boatslip Inn	Victor Santos	1043	Dec 20, 1996	$5,500.00

Total: $163,750.00

Figure 6-60
Printout of media summary report (page 2)

Nancy and Martin review both the client list report and the media summary report and are satisfied that the reports project a professional, high-quality image for W&M. They are also pleased with how they can use the report features in dBASE to display information in a way that helps them analyze it quickly and easily.

Questions

1. Assume you have a STUDENT table that stores one record for each student. For each of the following situations, indicate what section in the Report Designer window plays the most important role in producing the result.
   a. including today's date at the top of each page
   b. including the name and GPA for each student
   c. including page numbers at the bottom of each page of a report
   d. placing a logo at the top of each page of a report
   e. placing all student records with the same year of graduation together
2. What is the file extension that dBASE uses for saved reports?
3. How does a summary field differ from a formula field?
4. To include subtotals in a report, what section would you use in the Report Designer window?
5. Select the number from Figure 6-61 that best fits the task described.

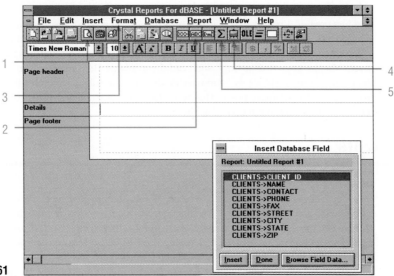

Figure 6-61

 a. Inserting a text field in the report _____
 b. Inserting a graphic image in the report _____
 c. Previewing the report _____
 d. Inserting a summary field in the report _____
 e. Changing the design to a multi-record style ___
6. Select the number from Figure 6-62 that best fits the task described.

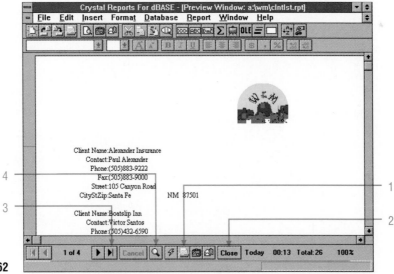

Figure 6-62

 a. Moving to the last page of the report _____
 b. Printing the report _____
 c. Viewing the report at different magnifications _____
 d. Returning to the Report Designer window _____

7. Explain the use of the plus sign (+) operator with character data.

8. You just created a report that displays information on all students at your school. What feature could you use to restrict the output to students majoring in Finance?

9. There are many ways to group data in a report. Explore Crystal Reports Help. Search for the keyword "group" and read the available Help information. Read the topic "Groups (subtotals, summary fields) tips and tricks." Sketch the output from the media summary report that would result if you subsorted the job records within each media type by client name.

Tutorial Assignments

Place your Student Disk in the disk drive, start dBASE, then set the working current to A:\WM.

1. Figure 6-63 indicates some changes that Nancy recommended after seeing a hard copy of the media summary report you created in the tutorial. Do the following:

   a. Open the report file MEDIA.RPT (using the Design button on the SpeedBar).

   b. Make the changes requested by Nancy in Figure 6-63.

   c. Nancy also wants you to sort the records within each media type by the amount of the Quote field. Make this change in the report.

   d. Save the revised report as MEDIAREV using the Save As command on the File menu.

   e. Print the revised report.

place date in
Page header

place page
number in
Page header

sort within Media
by Quote

place dividing line
between groups

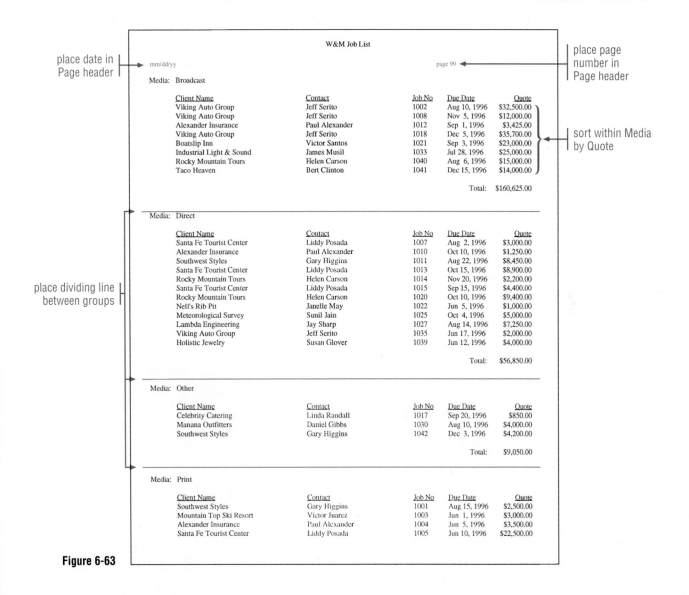

W&M Job List

mm/dd/yy   page 99

Media: Broadcast

Client Name	Contact	Job No	Due Date	Quote
Viking Auto Group	Jeff Serito	1002	Aug 10, 1996	$32,500.00
Viking Auto Group	Jeff Serito	1008	Nov 5, 1996	$12,000.00
Alexander Insurance	Paul Alexander	1012	Sep 1, 1996	$3,425.00
Viking Auto Group	Jeff Serito	1018	Dec 5, 1996	$35,700.00
Boatslip Inn	Victor Santos	1021	Sep 3, 1996	$23,000.00
Industrial Light & Sound	James Musil	1033	Jul 28, 1996	$25,000.00
Rocky Mountain Tours	Helen Carson	1040	Aug 6, 1996	$15,000.00
Taco Heaven	Bert Clinton	1041	Dec 15, 1996	$14,000.00

Total: $160,625.00

Media: Direct

Client Name	Contact	Job No	Due Date	Quote
Santa Fe Tourist Center	Liddy Posada	1007	Aug 2, 1996	$3,000.00
Alexander Insurance	Paul Alexander	1010	Oct 10, 1996	$1,250.00
Southwest Styles	Gary Higgins	1011	Aug 22, 1996	$8,450.00
Santa Fe Tourist Center	Liddy Posada	1013	Oct 15, 1996	$8,900.00
Rocky Mountain Tours	Helen Carson	1014	Nov 20, 1996	$2,200.00
Santa Fe Tourist Center	Liddy Posada	1015	Sep 15, 1996	$4,400.00
Rocky Mountain Tours	Helen Carson	1020	Oct 10, 1996	$9,400.00
Nell's Rib Pit	Janelle May	1022	Jun 5, 1996	$1,000.00
Meteorological Survey	Sunil Jain	1025	Oct 4, 1996	$5,000.00
Lambda Engineering	Jay Sharp	1027	Aug 14, 1996	$7,250.00
Viking Auto Group	Jeff Serito	1035	Jun 17, 1996	$2,000.00
Holistic Jewelry	Susan Glover	1039	Jun 12, 1996	$4,000.00

Total: $56,850.00

Media: Other

Client Name	Contact	Job No	Due Date	Quote
Celebrity Catering	Linda Randall	1017	Sep 20, 1996	$850.00
Manana Outfitters	Daniel Gibbs	1030	Aug 10, 1996	$4,000.00
Southwest Styles	Gary Higgins	1042	Dec 3, 1996	$4,200.00

Total: $9,050.00

Media: Print

Client Name	Contact	Job No	Due Date	Quote
Southwest Styles	Gary Higgins	1001	Aug 15, 1996	$2,500.00
Mountain Top Ski Resort	Victor Juarez	1003	Jun 1, 1996	$3,000.00
Alexander Insurance	Paul Alexander	1004	Jun 5, 1996	$3,500.00
Santa Fe Tourist Center	Liddy Posada	1005	Jun 10, 1996	$22,500.00

Figure 6-63

2. Using the JOBS and CLIENTS tables, create a report that displays only *completed* jobs placed in the Print media. Use the sketch in Figure 6-64 as a guide in creating your report. Save the report using the name PRTMEDIA. Print the report. (*Hint:* Use the JOBAUTH.QBE query as a basis for this report. Use the selection criterion JOBS->COMPLETED=.T.)

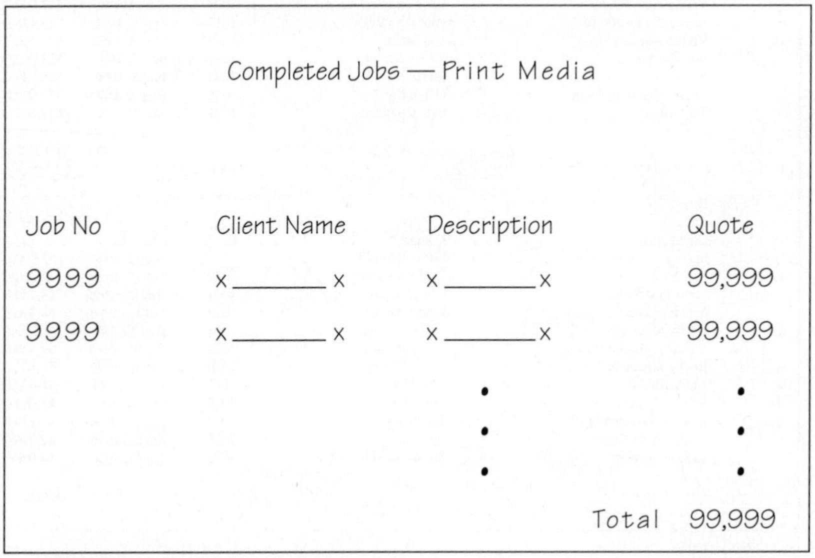

<figure>
Completed Jobs — Print Media

Job No   Client Name   Description   Quote

9999   X _____ X   X _____ X   99,999

9999   X _____ X   X _____ X   99,999
                       .   .   .
                       .   .   .
                       .   .   .
                                                Total   99,999
</figure>

Figure 6-64

3. Create a report that displays completed jobs by client. Use the sketch in Figure 6-65 as a guide in creating your report. Save the report using the name CLNTRPT. Print the report.

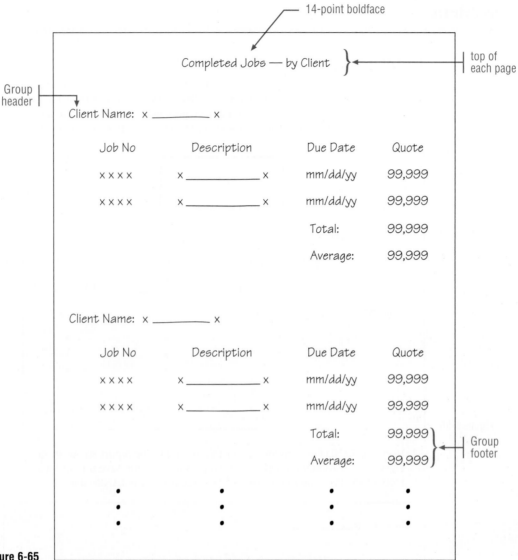

14-point boldface

Completed Jobs — by Client

top of
each page

Group
header

Client Name: x _____ x

Job No	Description	Due Date	Quote
x x x x	x _____ x	mm/dd/yy	99,999
x x x x	x _____ x	mm/dd/yy	99,999
		Total:	99,999
		Average:	99,999

Client Name: x _____ x

Job No	Description	Due Date	Quote
x x x x	x _____ x	mm/dd/yy	99,999
x x x x	x _____ x	mm/dd/yy	99,999
		Total:	99,999
		Average:	99,999

Group
footer

Figure 6-65

E   4. Create a report to produce mailing labels using the CLIENTS table. Change the font of all fields to Arial. Save the labels as MAILLABL. Print the mailing labels.
The label has four lines with the following layout:
Client Name
Contact
Street
City, State Zip

E   5. Customize the MEDIA.RPT file you created in the tutorial. Make the following changes:
   a. Add summary fields for the count and the average quote for each group.
   b. Add grand total fields for the sum, average, and count of the quotes.
   c. Add appropriate labels for all summary fields.
   d. Hide the Details section so that it is not printed. Delete the column heading labels that appear in the Page header section.
   e. Change the title of the report to "Media Summary Report."
   f. Save the report as MEDIASUM.RPT.
   g. Print the report.

Case Problems

1. Inventory of State-owned Land

Place your Student Disk in the disk drive, start dBASE, and set the current directory to A:\LAND.

1. Using the LAND table, create a report according to the report layout sheet in Figure 6-66. Save the report as LNDVALUE. Print the report, using all the records in the LAND table. The State Properties logo is stored as LANDLOGO.BMP on your Student Disk.

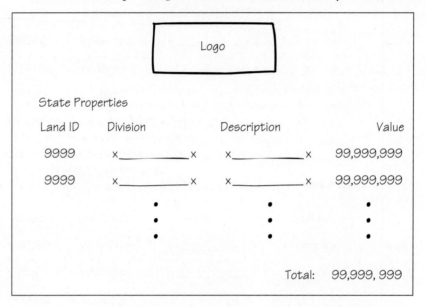

Figure 6-66

2. Using the LAND table, create a report according to the report layout sheet in Figure 6-67. Group the records in the report by Division. Save the report as LNDDIVSN. Print the report, using all the records in the LAND table.

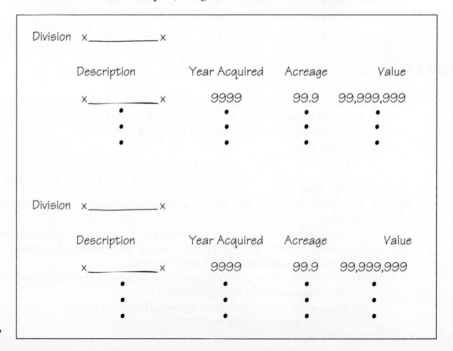

Figure 6-67

3. Create the Land Owned by Year Acquired report shown in Figure 6-68. The report is based on the LAND and LANDUSE tables. Create a query (use a one-to-one relation from LAND to LANDUSE) to use as the basis for the report. Name the query YEARACQ, group the records by year acquired, and use a multi-column layout. Save the report as EXPLLAND. Print the report.

State Properties

Year Acquired: 9999

Land ID:		999	Land ID:	999
Description:	x_____ x		Description:	x_____ x
Division:	x_____ x		Division:	x_____ x
Land Use Description:	x_____ x		Land Use Description:	x_____ x
Acreage:		99.9	Acreage:	99.9
Value:		99,999.99	Value:	99,999.99

Land ID:		999	Land ID:	999
Description:	x_____ x		Description:	x_____ x
Division:	x_____ x		Division:	x_____ x
Land Use Description:	x_____ x		Land Use Description:	x_____ x
Acreage:		99.9	Acreage:	99.9
Value:		99,999.99	Value:	99,999.99

Land ID:		999	Land ID:	999
Description:	x_____ x		Description:	x_____ x
Division:	x_____ x		Division:	x_____ x
Land Use Description:	x_____ x		Land Use Description:	x_____ x
Acreage:		99.9	Acreage:	99.9
Value:		99,999.99	Value:	99,999.99

Year Acquired: 9999

Land ID:		999	Land ID:	999
Description:	x_____ x		Description:	x_____ x
Division:	x_____ x		Division:	x_____ x
Land Use Description:	x_____ x		Land Use Description:	x_____ x
Acreage:		99.9	Acreage:	99.9
Value:		99,999.99	Value:	99,999.99

Figure 6-68

2. FINSTAT Inc.

Place your Student Disk in the disk drive, start dBASE, and set the working directory to A:\FINANCE.

1. Create the Company Profiles 1992 report shown in Figure 6-69. The report is based on the COMP and FIN tables. Use a query to set up a one-to-one relationship between the FIN and COMP tables, with FIN as the parent table. Call the query ANALY1.QBE. The ANALY1.QBE includes the calculated field, "Return." Return is computed as profits ÷ assets. Select all the financial records for the year 1992 with profits greater than 0. Save the report using the name ANALY1.RPT. Print the report.

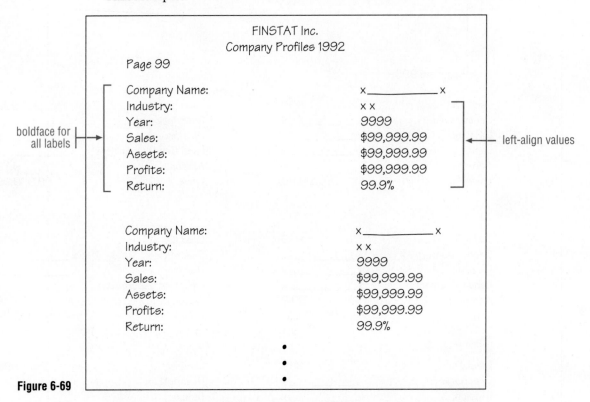

Figure 6-69

2. Create the Financial Analysis - 1992 report shown in Figure 6-70. The report is based on the COMP and FIN tables. Use the ANALY1.QBE query you defined in Question 1. Select all the financial records for the year 1992 with profits greater than 500. Group the data by industry. Save the report using the name ANALY2. Print the report. *Note:* The FINSTAT logo is stored as FINLOGO.BMP on the Student Disk.

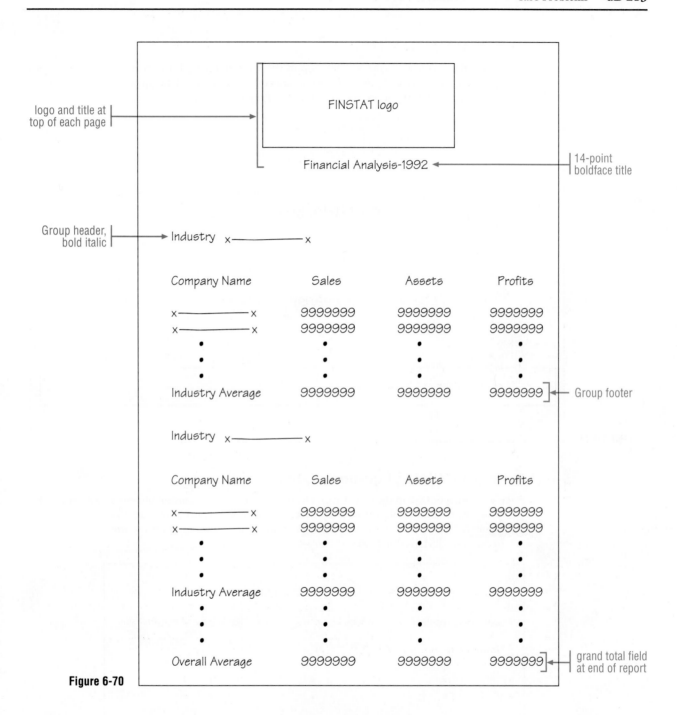

logo and title at top of each page

FINSTAT logo

Financial Analysis-1992

14-point boldface title

Group header, bold italic

Industry   x————x

Company Name	Sales	Assets	Profits
x————x	9999999	9999999	9999999
x————x	9999999	9999999	9999999
•	•	•	•
•	•	•	•
•	•	•	•
Industry Average	9999999	9999999	9999999

Group footer

Industry   x————x

Company Name	Sales	Assets	Profits
x————x	9999999	9999999	9999999
x————x	9999999	9999999	9999999
•	•	•	•
•	•	•	•
•	•	•	•
Industry Average	9999999	9999999	9999999
•	•	•	•
•	•	•	•
•	•	•	•
Overall Average	9999999	9999999	9999999

grand total field at end of report

Figure 6-70

3. Create the Financial Averages—1992 report shown in Figure 6-71. Create a query based on the COMP and FIN tables as the basis for this report. Call the query ANALY2. Save the report design as EXPL1992. Print the report.

FINSTAT logo

Financial Averages -- 1992

Industry	Sales	Assets	Profits
xx	$9,999,999	$9,999,999	$9,999,999
xx	$9,999,999	$9,999,999	$9,999,999
•	•	•	•
•	•	•	•
•	•	•	•

Overall average	•	•	•

Figure 6-71

3. Marine Diving Equipment, Inc.

Place your Student Disk in the disk drive, start dBASE, then set the current directory to A:\MARINE.
1. Using the ORDERS table, create a report according to the report layout sheet in Figure 6-72. Save the report as ORDERS95. Print the report using all the records in the ORDERS table for 1995.

Marine Diving Equipment, Inc.

Order#	Customer#	Sale Date	Total Invoice	Amount Paid
xxxx	xxxx	mm/dd/yy	99,999.99	99,999.99
•	•	•	•	•
•	•	•	•	•
•	•	•	•	•
		Total:	99,999.99	99,999.99

Figure 6-72

2. Create the Orders Above $20,000 by Country report shown in Figure 6-73. The report is based on the ORDERS and CUSTOMER tables. Create a one-to-many relation from CUSTOMER to ORDERS. Save the query as ORDERS2.QBE. Select all the orders with a total invoice above $20,000 and group them by country. Save the report using the name ORDERS2. Print the report.

Figure 6-73

E

3. Using the CUSTOMER and ORDERS tables, create and save a query that computes the balance owed for each order (total invoice – amount paid). Include in the query results the CUST_NAME, COUNTRY, ORD_NO, SALE_DATE, INV_AMT, AMT_PAID, and a calculated field AMT_OWED. Name the saved query BALOWED. Use this query as the basis for creating the report shown in Figure 6-74, which displays orders with an amount owed greater than 0. Save the report using the name BALOWED. Print the report. (*Hint:* When you include a calculated field from a query in a report, you must explicity include the calculated field in the query results by clicking the check box for the field in the query skeleton.)

Figure 6-74

4. Teaching Activity

Place your Student Disk in the disk drive, start dBASE, then set the current directory to A:\TEACH.

1. Using the FAC table, create a report according to the report layout sheet in Figure 6-75. Include only faculty in the Management department (MGT) with a rank of full professor (PROF). Save the report as FACSHEET. Print the report. *Note:* Name is a calculated field (TRIM(Last Name)+", "+First Name). The Teaching logo is stored as TCHLOGO.BMP on your Student Disk.

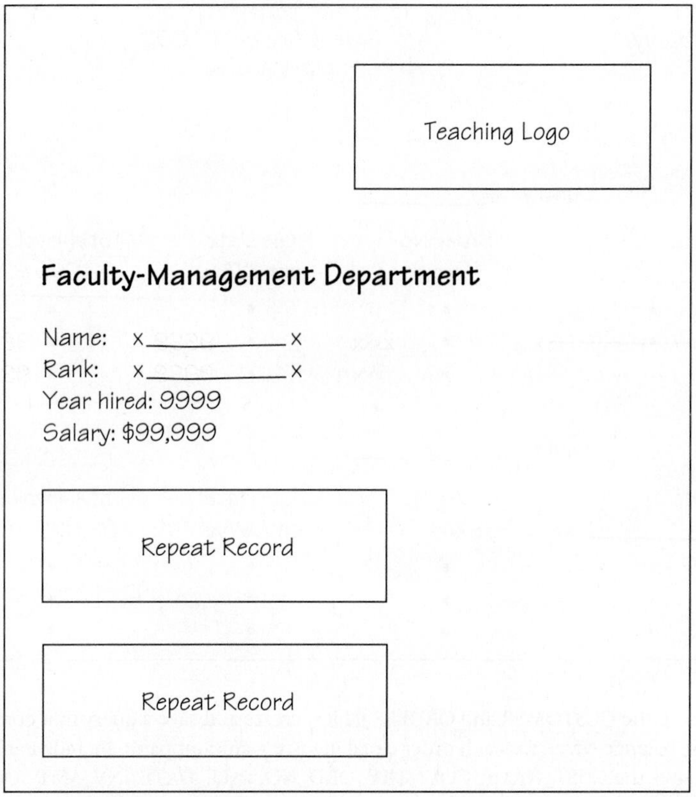

Figure 6-75

2. Using the FAC table, create a report using Figure 6-76 as a guide. Save the report using the name DEPT. Print the report. *Note:* Group the report by department.

Department List

Department: x——————x

Last Name	Rank	Hired	Salary
x—————x	xxxx	9999	99,999
x—————x	xxxx	9999	99,999
•	•	•	•
•	•	•	•
•	•	•	•
		Total:	99,999
		Average:	99,999
		Count:	999

Department: x—————x

Last Name	Rank	Hired	Salary
x—————x	xxxx	9999	99,999
x—————x	xxxx	9999	99,999
•	•	•	•
•	•	•	•
•	•	•	•
		Total:	99,999
		Average:	99,999
		Count:	999
		Grand Total:	99,999

Figure 6-76

3. Create the report in Figure 6-77. First create a query based on the FAC and TCH tables. The relation is one-to-many from FAC to TCH. Save the query as TEACHACT.QBE. Include only faculty in the Accounting department and the courses they have taught in 1993 that had five or more students enrolled. Save the report as TEACHACT. Print the report.

Teaching Activity

Page 99

Last Name: x————x   Rank: xxxx   Dept: xxx

Course No	Section	Year	Term	# of Students
xxx999	99	9999	x	999

Last Name: x————x   Rank: xxxx   Dept: xxx

Course No	Section	Year	Term	# of Students
xxx999	99	9999	x	999

     •   •   •   •
     •   •   •   •
     •   •   •   •

Figure 6-77

E   5. Bank Safe Deposit System

Place your Student Disk in the disk drive, start dBASE, and set the working directory to A:\PRACTICE. Use the Safe Deposit Rent Statement in Figure 6-78 to develop a Safe Deposit Tracking system.

Do the following:
1. Create a table named SAFEDPST based on Figure 6-78.
2. Add three records to the table.
3. Print the contents of the SAFEDPST table.
4. Create the Safe Deposit Rent Statement shown in Figure 6-78. Save the report as RENTSTMT.
5. Print the rent statement for all box holders, one per page.

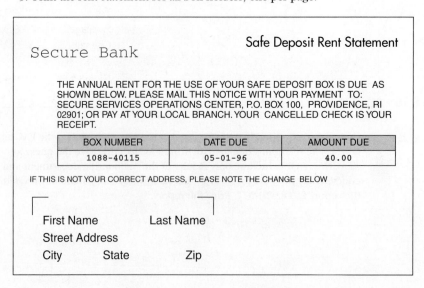

Figure 6-78

Index

TASK REFERENCE
dBASE FOR WINDOWS
Italicized page numbers indicate the first discussion of each task.

TASK	MOUSE	MENU	KEYBOARD
Access context-sensitive Help, *dB 26*	Click Help button in any dialog box	Click Help	`F1` or `Alt` `H`
Add a calculated field to a query, *dB 136*		Click Query, Create Calculated Field	`Alt` `Q` `F`
Add a field to a table, *dB 60*	▣	Click Structure, Add Field	`Ctrl` `A` or `Alt` `S`, `A`
Add a record to a table, *dB 56*	▣	Click Table, Add Records	`Ctrl` `A` or `Alt` `T`, `A`
Add a table to the Query window, *dB 143*	▣	Click Query, Add Table	`Ctrl` `A` or `Alt` `Q`, `A`
Back up a table	see Backing up a Database File, *dB 105*		
Calculate a summary statistic for a query	see Using Summary Operators, *dB 139*		
Change colors on a form	see Changing Colors, *dB 178*		
Change column width in Table Records window	see Changing Column Width, *dB 23*		
Change the current directory	see Changing the Current Directory, *dB 18*		
Change object properties in a form	see Using the Object Inspector, *dB 175*		
Change a property of the Table Records window	see Changing the Properties of the Table Records Window, *dB 25*		
Close a table, *dB 33*	Double-click the Table Records window Control menu box	Click File, Close	`Alt` `F`, `C`
Copy a table	see Backing Up a Database File, *dB 105*		
Correct errors in field definition	see Correcting Errors in the Field Definitions, *dB 52*		
Create a form using the Form Expert	see Using the Form Expert to Design a Single-Table Form, *dB 161*		
Create an index	see Defining Fields, *dB 47*		
Create a key field	see Defining Fields, *dB 47*		
Create a multi-table form	see Multi-Table Forms, *dB 194*		
Create a query	see Creating a Query to View All the Records in a Table, *dB 121*		
Create a report	see Creating a Report Using Crystal Reports, *dB 226*		
Create a table	see Creating a Table, *dB 46*		
Define an expression using the Expression Builder	see Defining an Expression Using the Expression Builder, *dB 248*		
Define fields in a table	see Defining Fields, *dB 47*		
Define validity checks for a form	see Entering Validity Checks, *dB 186*		
Define validity checks for the Table Records window	see Defining Validity Checks, *dB 85*		

TASK	MOUSE	MENU	KEYBOARD
Delete a field in a table, *dB 53*	[icon]	Click Structure, Delete Selected Field	`Ctrl` `U` or `Alt` `S`, `D`
Delete a record, *dB 100*	Click Del check box	Click Table, Delete Selected Record	`Ctrl` `U` or `Alt` `T`, `D`
Delete a selected object from a report or form, *dB 197*		Click Edit, Delete	`Del`
Deselect an object, *dB 174*	Click anywhere outside the object		
Edit record values	see Making Changes to Records, *dB 95*		
Edit a text object in a report, *dB 232*		Click Edit, Text Field	`Alt` `E`, `X`
Enter filter conditions in a query	see Filter Conditions in a Query, *dB 127*		
Examine a table's structure	see Modifying the Structure of a Table, *dB 59*		
Exit dBASE, *dB 34*	Double-click dBASE for Windows Control menu box	Click File, Exit	`Alt` `F`, `X` or `Alt` `F4`
Find a record, *dB 96*	[icon]	Click Table, Find Records...	`Ctrl` `F` or `Alt` `T`, `F`
Insert a field in a table, *dB 54*	[icon]	Click Structure, Add Field	`Ctrl` `N` or `Alt` `S`, `I`
Insert a group section in a report	see Group Sections, *dB 262*		
Link tables in a query	see Introduction to Linking Tables, *dB 141*		
Mark a record for deletion, *dB 100*	Click Del check box	Click Table, Delete Selected Record	`Ctrl` `U` or `Alt` `T`, `D`
Modify the structure of a table	see Modifying the Structure of a Table, *dB 59*		
Move a column in the Table Records window	see Moving Columns, *dB 24*		
Move down one page in report, *dB 239*	[icon]		`PgDn`
Move down one screen, *dB 21*	[icon]	Click Table, Next Page	`PgDn` or `Alt` `T`, `X`
Move to bottom record, *dB 21*	[icon]	Click Table, Bottom Record	`Ctrl` `PgDn` or `Alt` `T`, `M`
Move to first page in report, *dB 239*	[icon]		`Ctrl` `PgUp`
Move to last page in report, *dB 239*	[icon]		`Ctrl` `PgDn`
Move to next record, *dB 21*	[icon]	Click Table, Next Record	`↓` or `Alt` `T`, `N`
Move to previous record, *21*	[icon]	Click Table, Previous Record	`↑` or `Alt` `T`, `P`
Move to top record, *dB 21*	[icon]	Click Table, Top Record	`Ctrl` `PgUp` or `Alt` `T`, `O`